Fifty Years after *The Big Sky*

New Perspectives on the Fiction and Films of A. B. Guthrie, Jr.

A. B. Guthrie, Jr., *ink portrait by Frances O'Brien, ca.* 1940s

Fifty Years after *The Big Sky*

New Perspectives on the Fiction and Films of A. B. Guthrie, Jr.

~

EDITED BY WILLIAM E. FARR AND WILLIAM W. BEVIS

Published by
Montana Historical Society Press
Helena

in cooperation with
O'Connor Center for the Rocky Mountain West
The University of Montana
Missoula

2001

Fifty Years after *The Big Sky:*
New Perspectives on the Fiction and Films of A. B. Guthrie, Jr.

Produced by Zadig, L.L.C., Helena, MT
Book design by DD Dowden, Helena; cover design by Kathyrn Fehlig, Helena
Typeset in Adobe Minion and Phaistos
Printed by Thomson-Shore, Dexter, MI

Cover: *Free Trapper,* 1911, by Charles M. Russell, oil on canvas, 33" x 24", Montana Historical Society, Mackay Collection
Frontispiece: Courtesy of Yale Collection of American Literature, Beinecke Library

For more copies of this book, contact the Montana Historical Society Press, P.O. Box 201201, Helena, MT 59620-1201

01 02 03 04 05 06 07 08 10 9 8 7 6 5 4 3 2 1

Library of Congress Cataloging-in-Publication Data
Fifty years after The big sky : new perspectives on the fiction and films of A. B. Guthrie, Jr. / edited by William E. Farr and William W. Bevis.

p. cm.

Includes bibliographical references and index.

ISBN 0-917298-72-1 (cloth : alk. paper)—ISBN 0-917298-73-X (pbk : alk. paper)

1. Guthrie, A. B. (Alfred Bertram), 1901——Criticism and interpretation. 2. Western stories—History and criticism. 3. Western films—History and Criticism. 4. Montana—In literature. 5. Indians in literature. 6. Nature in literature. I. Farr, William E., 1938– II. Bevis, William W., 1941–

PS3513.U855 Z64 2001
813'.52—dc21 2001018031

To the memory of A. B. Guthrie, Jr.

~

Contents

Illustrations

Acknowledgments

This project began as a conference, and the conference began as an idea in the fertile imagination of Mark Sherouse, executive director of the Montana Committee for the Humanities. Mark not only had the seminal idea of a conference dedicated to A. B. Guthrie, he also urged the O'Connor Center for the Rocky Mountain West to apply for funding from the Montana Committee for the Humanities. When joined with the enthusiasm and assistance of Bill Bevis of The University of Montana's English Department, these two gave the rest of us the determination and the confidence to move forward.

Besides Mark Sherouse and Bill Bevis, this volume has benefited from the help of the Guthrie family: Carol Guthrie and Helen "Gus" Guthrie Miller provided photographs and reference materials. Ripley Hugo, a long-time family friend from Choteau, also helped with advice along the way as we scoured the West for people who Guthrie had counted among his oldest friends.

While the presentations of the 1997 conference, "A. B. Guthrie's *The Big Sky*—After Fifty Years," were provocative enough to entertain the idea of a book, it took a good deal of editorial assistance. Rick Newby of Zadig, L.L.C. of Helena provided this and is deserving of our thanks. He was insightful, constant, clarifying, and above all, patient. Thanks as well to Charles Rankin, former editor of *Montana The Magazine of Western History* and director of the Montana Historical Society Press, and to the editor of the Montana Historical Society Press, Martha Kohl, likewise supportive, judicious, and patient.

Finally, thanks are due Jeannie Thompson, administrative assistant at the O'Connor Center for the Rocky Mountain West. At my insistence, Jeannie became the designated and managing "nag"—always helpful, frequently reminding, and determined that this project would be done with humor—on time and on budget.

Thanks, one and all.

—WILLIAM E. FARR

William E. Farr and William W. Bevis

Introduction

As westerners in the new millennium, we all know that change, tremendous change, has come to the Rocky Mountain West in all of its manifestations in the past fifteen years. And while we embrace many of its features, there remains the nagging feeling that somehow the "glory days" are behind us and that we "ain't seen the end of it yet." The pace is too fast. The numbers of immigrants are too great. And while we reluctantly admit to ourselves that we were never the first to arrive and we too have initiated alterations, we also believe that, as we did so, those changes were largely beneficial. Besides, they were imposed slowly and upon a cultural landscape that remained remarkably integrated and resilient.

There was never the sense that westerners were too many or that we were doing too much. Quite the contrary. There existed the belief that for things to get better there would need to be more of us to counteract the distances, the weather, the isolation, the inherent conservatism, the features of our world. New numbers and ideas would bless the old and the new, the earlier and the later arrivals, initiating alterations desperately needed.

In fact, the new numbers have brought changes to the Mountain West, abrupt changes, and now features so common elsewhere in the United States bless us with their transformative power, visiting us in our backwardness and innocence with future possibilities both exhilarating and threatening.

This change is so overwhelming that many fear we are about to lose the world we had grown intimate and comfortable with. Although this threat has become a regional preoccupation, it is particularly pronounced among the new arrivals, especially those with education and aspiration, those who were certain they were moving to a better place, one with more amenities and greater identity. It was not surprising, then, that in 1995 the new director of the Montana Committee for the Humanities, Mark Sherouse, set out to learn something of the distinctive history and features of the "Big Sky" state. In doing so Professor Sherouse turned to narratives and novels, not histories and chronicles, for guidance, and while Montana is the subject of a large number of novels, after some consideration Sherouse turned to—what else?—Montana's fictional center, A. B. Guthrie's *The Big Sky,* as the particularly apt story for all arrivals.

As Sherouse read the novel, he discovered to his amazement that the fiftieth anniversary of its publication was coming up and that, for others as for him, the message of *The Big Sky* remained both powerful and cautionary. Somehow though, Guthrie's seminal work of 1947 was remembered but seldom read or discussed. In 1998 people were concerned with trophy homes on blue-ribbon trout streams, Lycra running outfits, the reintroduction of wolves to Yellowstone National Park, and urban sprawl in the mountain valleys. Perhaps what was needed to relocate the centrality of Guthrie's message was a conference. Sherouse suggested such a Guthrie conference on *The Big Sky* to Bill Bevis, MCH member and author of *Ten Tough Trips: Montana Writers and the West.* Bevis concurred.

For over twenty years, the students in Bevis's Montana Writers class voted *The Big Sky* as the one book that could not be dropped from the course. It was the indispensable book, even though it was never the favorite book—compared to James Welch and D'Arcy McNickle and Ivan Doig and Richard Hugo and Norman Maclean and others. Why? Because some of the best discussions were on *The Big Sky;* because *The Big Sky* forced them to examine and re-examine their core western mythologies.

Sherouse and Bevis took the idea of "*The Big Sky* after Fifty Years" to the Montana Committee for the Humanities for their general support. The Montana Committee for the Humanities in turn, because of their busy schedule, decided to ask the O'Connor Center for the Rocky Mountain West at The University of Montana for assistance in organizing what would become a joint enterprise.

At the O'Connor Center for the Rocky Mountain West, we thought the Guthrie *The Big Sky* project would fit very nicely with our goals to describe the changing regional West and the contrary responses it evoked. Change has been a commanding theme in the Mountain West and the very focus of what we are about. We may have been settled last in Montana, but the task now was, given additional time, to settle it best. The transformations registered and implied in Guthrie's work, the ambivalent emotions it raised, are still with us, challenging us to embrace change positively and not to reject it out of hand. We are not looking back at something finished. Making the Rocky Mountain West something we can be proud of is a work in progress. "You ain't seen the end of it yet" represents a moving pageant, and that was the motive force in putting together the conference in Missoula in September of 1997.

The conference on "A. B. Guthrie's *The Big Sky*—After Fifty Years" proved more productive precisely because, like the book, its presentations were fractured—half in and half out of old romantic notions of the West, half in and out of contemporary revisions. When the verbal smoke cleared, a consensus emerged: Guthrie was pretty cynical about Boone, but pretty romantic about Boone's dream of living happy and free in a wild West. It was easy to see our paradoxically progressive and reactionary selves prefigured in the book, cynical revisionist yet communitarian professors with new fly rods and a secret spot on the Blackfoot, students who have fled to Montana to escape Pap and New Jersey ("I don't hanker to live in no anthill"), Aryan nations retreating from modernity to homestead compounds, stockbrokers pioneering fiber optic connections in trophy cabins on the Missouri.

For the past twenty years, western revisionists have been saying that we in the region must "rewrite our narrative," tell a different story, change our values. We have written, since Dee Brown, a better Native American history, we have written better women's history and the stories of western communities to offset the myths of the lone rogue male; by the time of Patricia Limerick and Richard White, we have indeed told different tales. Yet the myth of escaping the evils of society to live in a broad, free West, of rejecting civilization in favor of nature—a myth both cowardly and dangerous—remains a determining myth in our popular arts, in the environmental movement, in the new economy of Montana. The heart of Guthrie's book and dream still beats in our culture. Around the world, when people ask Montanans where they are from—in Borneo, India, northern Italy—a quick "Marlboro Country" describes our home. The billboards are everywhere, sharing the dream of escape.

The Big Sky provides an excellent occasion to discuss just what our western stories have been, how they have been revised, and how they may still need revision.

When we began discussing the idea of a conference on "*The Big Sky* at Fifty," we reviewed the scholarship and were surprised at how little had been written on Guthrie in the past fifteen years, since Thomas Ford's book, *A. B. Guthrie, Jr.*, in 1981. We realized that for an entire generation—our own—Guthrie had become "retro," a part of the story we were determined to rewrite. However, at the same time—1995—scholarship on Wallace Stegner was increasing again, and the entire circle of 1947 revisionists—DeVoto, Stegner, Guthrie—was claiming new respect. After fifty years, it seemed clear that Guthrie's revisionism and romanticism were worth a new look, and it also seemed clear that the overlooking of Guthrie was itself now a part of history: When we revisionists cleared the decks, what went overboard? Those of us who still taught *The Big Sky* knew the continuing vitality of the text, and of the questions it raised.

From the very beginning, then, we thought of Guthrie as the occasion for a discussion of our intellectual history, and the present volume reflects that concern. The literary criticism here largely serves to excite debate about the last fifty years of western thought. What was Guthrie's moment, what is ours? Guthrie, of course, not only became overnight a well-known author (Bill Bevis was assigned *The Big Sky* in eighth grade in Connecticut in 1954), but he also entered popular culture through his work on films, especially the screenplay of *Shane*.

The authors and editors have reworked the conference papers for this more permanent venue, and the editors have rearranged the material—at a conference, people sometimes answer each other a day apart—so that harmonies and discords are juxtaposed. Section One offers an introduction to the literature in question, from *The Big Sky* in 1947 to Guthrie's extended series of historical "westerns" over the course of his career (he even returned to the characters of *The Big Sky* in 1990, in *Fair Land, Fair Land*). This section should acquaint readers with the range of Guthrie's work and with some interesting new appraisals of it.

Section Two, "Guthrie, in Context," begins with very original investigations of Guthrie in Hollywood, and *Shane* as a cold war film, then moves to comments on the women in *The Big Sky* and to more personal reflections on the man and his work by authors Sue Hart, James Welch, and Mary Clearman Blew.

Section Three, "Moving beyond Guthrie's View of Nature," addresses major issues of intellectual history raised by Guthrie's work, from environmental history (viewed by an environmental historian, and then by a rancher), to economic history, to a reconsideration of our mythology of nature.

In Section Four, three local and politically "engaged" observers (a state NEH director, a former radical mayor, and a retired, long-term congressman) address the present. This is where we wanted to come out: here and now, in Montana and the West, fifty years after *The Big Sky.*

Reading Guthrie

A. B. Guthrie, Jr., at his desk, n.d.

COURTESY OF HELEN GUTHRIE MILLER

Ken Egan, Jr.

The Big Sky and the Siren Song of Apocalypse

I write as a perverse Jeremiah, preaching against the temptation of apocalypse. I take as my text A. B. Guthrie's canonical *The Big Sky,* or, to be more exact, Zeb Calloway's words to his nefarious nephew: "She's gone, goddamn it! Gone! . . . The whole shitaree. Gone, by God, and naught to care savin' some of us who seen'er new."[1] Zeb's dire words, his unassuageable sense of loss, form the emotional and ideological center of the novel. Indeed, Zeb's vernacular description of paradise lost drives the entire plot of Boone's failure. This tragedy in five acts renarrates the American fall from innocence. But the novel leaves us no exit, no sense of what to do about the collapse of another great dream. The novel's apocalyptic structure, destroying Boone's (and our) dream world, reveals no alternative, no means of redress, no goal for amelioration. In this way, the seminal Montana book generates a curious resignation, even fatalism, that has an enduring currency in this state and the West. As we will see, Guthrie's apocalypse represents a resurgent urge in this region's self-reflection that is defeating and destructive. I take as my doctrine, then, the need to critique and even oppose the mythology of failure embedded in Guthrie's most important novel.

To restate my thesis in medical terms, the novel infects the reader with the disease of self-pity originating in an irreparable break from past greatness. Zeb carries the germ of our loss in his bitter self, transmits it to Boone, who in turn transmits it to the reader. By the novel's end, Jim is dead, Teal Eye abandoned and disgraced, Dick Summers puzzled and passive, and Boone a misanthropic drunk. The Big Sky country has been abandoned by the key white players, left to lick its wounds perhaps, but never to be the same. This germ of self-pity is carried more precisely in a mythology of the lost Eden analyzed by William Bevis.[2] As the literary critic observes, Guthrie's novel has a curious romance quality to it, one founded on the myth of the American Adam celebrated in a male tradition of writing. The success of the narrative, then, depends upon Guthrie's giving that Adamic dream heft and credibility, and so he does. For this reader, returning to *The Big Sky* many times out of personal and pedagogical necessity, what endures are the haunting landscape descriptions, the sense of absolute space, of Nature untouched by Eurocentric greed. In these descriptive moments, the gap between the narrator and the main character collapses, revealing the writer's full commitment to the awestruck quality of Boone. There can be no mistaking the novelist's investment in the vision of Montana as pre-fall Eden. And given the dominant Judeo-Christian theology of American culture, what other outcome can we imagine than the destruction of the Garden and the casting out of the protagonists?

As contemporary readers invariably detect, this is an intensely male fantasy. Annette Kolodny has critiqued the male archetype by showing how literary Adamism translates into visions of deflowering the natural world.[3] *The Big Sky* is a case study in such wish fulfillment, though I must be sure to acknowledge Guthrie's partial consciousness of what he's about here. In the erotic subtext of the novel, Teal Eye becomes the embodiment of Nature (or more specifically, Montana), and so Boone's quest to "have" the Indian female becomes his quest to "have" the Big Sky. The antisocial male character penetrates feminized Nature on the Missouri River, merging imperial and sexual possession. Narrative logic dictates, then, that once Boone has deflowered Montana/Teal Eye, the game's up. The plot has reached its necessary but self-defeating climax, for the conquest of paradise means you can never have it over again. By definition, to penetrate the place is to lose what you value most. As Zeb puts it, "She's gone."

My readers (or to extend the metaphor, my congregation) might at this point object that Guthrie was far more circumspect about this mythology than I have allowed. Boone's decision to help Peabody find a path through the mountains, for example, appears pigheaded and morally suspect. As though to reiterate and criticize Caudill's male violence, Guthrie also has him sexually abuse a young white woman on his return trip to Kentucky. These actions suggest a character deeply flawed, made violent and destructive by his horrific upbringing. For these reasons Boone may be interpreted as the counterexample, the instance of the failed westerner, the warning to us all about our possible depredations. But if the writer has skillfully undermined his main character, he has left intact the mythology of possession that powers his plot. As with the landscape descriptions, the narrator's presentation of Teal Eye seems fully in sync with the character's. I do not detect irony in those longing gazes toward the female. Guthrie in fact reinforces the image of Teal Eye as Nature embodied through the sympathetic character of Jim Deakins. There can be no doubting the sexual and ideological appeal of this Indian maiden.

Furthermore, if Guthrie desired to censure Boone and Boone alone, why must he destroy Jim and drive Summers out of paradise? In a literal sense of overkill, Guthrie has his character murder everything. The only outcome must be a total apocalypse. As Boone tells us, echoing his uncle, "It's like it's all sp'iled for me now, Dick—Teal Eye and the Teton and all. Don't know as I ever can go back, Dick. Goddamn it! Goddamn it!"[4] Invoking a near-Biblical judgment in those final two exclamations, Boone emphasizes his utter alienation from the place he loved. In the end, we, like Dick Summers (surely meant to be the male reader's surrogate), scratch our heads, wondering how it all went wrong, and sink into our easy chairs, resigned to the attenuated bitterness of living after the fall.

My readers might still object that Guthrie relies upon a sense of history that takes us beyond Boone's disaster. After all, the novelist went on to compose five more novels in his narrative cycle. Surely this rich texture of stories fills out Guthrie's vision of settlement, his sense of Montana's destiny. These six novels collectively narrate the historical process of settling the High Plains, a process that moves beyond Boone's juvenile misconduct to the mature actions of Ben Tate in *The Last Valley*. We may further speculate that Guthrie later saw the danger of Boone, the latent appeal of his story, for he has Hig shoot down Caudill like a rabid dog in *Fair Land, Fair Land*. While I agree that Guthrie aspired to this revision of the apocalyptic story, his tactic does not work for two obvious reasons. First, as the conference on "*The Big Sky* at Fifty" eloquently testified, his lead novel in the hexalogy so completely dominates our sense of Guthrie's achievement (and our teaching of western literature) that the other texts have receded into obscurity. For most readers, Guthrie's accomplishment is summed up in his first and most famous novel. If we consider his cultural presence, then, his influence on the wider society, *The Big Sky* carries his charge.

Secondly, Guthrie's novels reinforce cataclysm by replicating the argument of James Fenimore Cooper's *Leatherstocking Tales.* Cooper's historical vision was profoundly cyclical, that is to say, apocalyptic. Writing as a conservative suspicious of American claims to a special destiny, the New York novelist demonstrated repeatedly the venality of humans and the failure of human institutions. His hero Natty Bumppo ironically advances the cause of settlement, acts that only assure Eden's demise. Summers echoes Bumppo's complicity, explaining to Boone that "There was beaver for us and free country and a big way of livin', and everything we done it looks like we done against ourselves and couldn't do different if we'd knowed."[5] Guthrie has thus carried over into the late twentieth century a grimly pessimistic vision of historical change.

Guthrie of course was not alone among the canonized Montana writers to embrace apocalyptic tragedy as the predominant mode of western discourse. The very title of *The Last Best Place* anthology hints at this sensibility. Two of the most prominent writers of contemporary Montana, Norman Maclean and Richard Hugo, repeat Guthrie's narrative tactics. The novella "A River Runs Through It" is a formally accomplished account of the narrator's break with his Montana wonderworld. In part because of age, in part because of his occupation, in part because of his brother's death, the storyteller can only gaze back in astonishment at the lost time of youthful Montana. It is true that Maclean's Biblical subtext teaches that a Logos endures beyond the loss, beyond the tragedy, but those words point back to the father's instruction and forward to the writer's death. In other words, the language beneath the water provides cold comfort for the here and now, the living and the present, supplying solace through the voice of the father, both familial and spiritual, that inhabits the sealed-off past and the unknowable afterlife. Hugo's best-known poems tell over and over again of absolute, pure loss. His confessional voice carries the woe of the misbegotten, the estranged, the misplaced, the lonely. His personae enunciate with uncommon clarity and frankness the loneliness of the long-distance poet. Montana's wind-scarred landscape carries the metaphorical weight of his woe, the pain writ large. Similar to Guthrie, Hugo endured beyond these poignant cries of the heart, composing more balanced and kinder "letter" poems, for instance. But as with Guthrie, the posthumous Hugo remains a victim of his own genius, his harshest, most daring, most existentially terrifying poems calling to us, enthralling us.

It is most appropriate that we revisit these tragic texts as we approach the end of the factitious "millennium." Apocalyptic dreaming is once again in vogue, especially in this part of the world. Given the recent construction of "Montana" in the national media, it is not difficult to list instances of end-of-the-world visions: the Militia of Montana, the Freemen, the Unabomber, Earth First!, and the Church Universal and Triumphant. These groups share an attraction to a Manichean sensibility that teaches the conflict between the light and the dark, the virtuous and the sinful, the saved and the damned. In this way these groups consistently reaffirm the apocalyptic story of paradise lost. It is true that the disparate movements propose alternative responses to that loss, ranging from the violently millennialist to the defeatist. But their official narratives reinforce the intensely nostalgic sense that the world was once better, we've lost Eden, "it's all sp'led."[6]

We can speculate briefly why Montana, and the West in general, inspire such a multitude of madnesses. A psycho-social interpretation might argue that the isolation of place and the toughness of climate encourage inward-turning, a fantasizing made all the more extreme because there are few social checks. A historical account might note the tradition of frontier violence, the willingness to use excessive force to assure that one's desires triumph. An economist might hold that given the boom-and-bust cycles of the colonized West, participants in the culture develop a brooding despair that translates into lurid conspiracy stories. Finally, we should observe that these are often transplanted dreams, carried into Montana by individuals who develop their beliefs elsewhere, then seek out the protection of a sparsely populated state. This fact reminds us once again that Montana culture participates in the defining dreams of Eurocentric culture.

But what, ultimately, is at stake here? What difference does it make that Montanans seem drawn to visions of the apocalypse? Apocalyptic dreaming breeds a desperation and resentment that harms us all. Most obviously, these fanciful narratives are masculinist through and through. The story of deflowering, of virginal innocence found and lost, runs through these seemingly diverse agendas like a fever in the blood. In this sense (as in others), the culture of apocalypse is immature, demanding simplistic answers to complex dilemmas. Perversely, this way of figuring the world feels good, for it allows us obvious answers and thrilling resolutions. The apocalyptic imagination also imposes an abstract schema, a vision of history, upon this particular place. Much as the Puritans transplanted the jeremiad tradition to New England, Montanans have a tendency to metaphorize this region as the site of battle between good and evil. In the process we lose that very place.

I have now arrived at my application of the doctrine. We must grant *The Big Sky* less canonical priority. We must, quite literally, put this text in its place. We must embrace an alternative tradition of Montana culture. I urge a turn away from apocalyptic tragedy toward what I call "pragmatic comedy." The term "pragmatic" suggests an engagement with immediate issues, concrete dilemmas, practical needs. Here "comedy" is not meant to suggest humor.

(It's difficult to imagine a less overtly humorous tradition of writing than that practiced in Montana. Set Guthrie, Doig, and Blew beside O'Connor, Welty, and Toole, representatives of the contemporary southern tradition.) Instead, "comedy" names a narrative structure that pulls toward the resolution of tension, of difficulty, of despair. Here I run the risk of substituting one naive "emplotment" for another.[7] It may appear that we are asked to accept uncritically a "progressive" reading of regional destiny that is at least as destructive as the apocalyptic view. By modifying "comedy" with "pragmatic," I intend to cut against the danger—ingenuous optimism. Conjoining the two terms suggests the difficulty of the process, the inherent struggle toward a resolution. We must hopefully seek answers but not naively expect their easy arrival. In contrast to the arrogant certainty of Enlightenment progress, this narrative type demonstrates humility and perspective, a knowledge that our solutions are often provisional and incomplete.

Our cultural self-analysis has recently been aided by eloquent accounts of how we might just achieve pragmatic comedy in this region. Daniel Kemmis's *Community and the Politics of Place* and David Strong's *Crazy Mountains* articulate the need for engagement with the concrete dilemmas facing the contemporary westerner. Building upon a poetic commitment to this region's landforms, people, and history, both writers suggest that communities find consensus through shared love for the real "things" of land and society. Guthrie's own environmental essays, concrete and specific as they are, provide a pretext for this source of possibility, this space for action.

But literature too can play its role in displacing Guthrie's paternal narrative with pragmatic comedy. Let's counterbalance the seductive call of its male fantasy with profound rethinking of masculinity in the West. Two narratives with special claim on our attention, then, are *This House of Sky* and *Hole in the Sky,* thoughtful, detailed, exacting first-person narratives about growing up male. These titles reflect their writers' revisionary goals. Doig would take us inside a house of sky, showing us domestic relations, strained and loving, within the Big Sky. Kittredge explains early in his fractured, postmodern autobiography that his title plays upon two senses of the image: existentialist despair and a Native American sense of belonging to a sacred order. Doig and Kittredge substitute facticity and a strong sense of place for the violent melodrama of Guthrie's novel. They also self-consciously challenge the apocalyptic myth of the West, showing the horrors of domination, yes, the foolish and destructive habits of the imperial heart, but also life beyond the debacle, life not "after the fall" but as a compassionate response to failure.

We should further counterbalance Guthrie's male dreaming with women's stories that implicitly and explicitly critique that fantasy. Mary Clearman Blew's gritty, anti-romantic, darkly humorous essays in *All But the Waltz* reorient the reader away from male narcissism, evoking the intelligent, resilient females who endure after the male characters' dreams die. Mildred Walker's *Winter Wheat* narrates a growing-up story about a young woman who balances love of the place with a realistic assessment of its limitations. Though deeply hurt by a failed relationship and the absurd death of a student, Ellen Webb does not lapse into complacency or bitterness. Instead, she gathers up her parents' love and the lessons of the farm into an agenda for action, for a life.

Even more importantly, we must decenter Guthrie's canonical voice with the texts of our major contemporary Indian writer: James Welch. *Winter in the Blood* reminds us of the naiveté and arrogance of white preoccupation with American failure. That novel's narrator struggles toward an identity erased by his culture's deracination. More tellingly still, *Fools Crow* narrates apocalypse from the Native American perspective, showing the virtual destruction of a way of life as the whitehorns replace the blackhorns, as the U.S. cavalry decimates innocent people. But again Welch doesn't allow the reader to wallow in pleasurable guilt or helplessness. Instead, the title character, an important revision of the hapless Boone, sees beyond apocalypse to what his people must do to endure: The stories must be handed down. Fools Crow cannot afford the luxury of despairing passivity, for he must share his visions.

What lessons can we draw from these pragmatic comedies? In contrast to immersion in a solipsistic mirror world, we observe a strong sense of the concrete history of this place, including human depredation. In contrast to the violence and melodrama of the male stories, we witness thinking-through, dialogue, and provisional solutions. These alternative stories are not for the faint of heart, but they can sustain us emotionally, spiritually, and politically long after the cataclysmic story has merged into the background noise of late-twentieth-century dread.

I do not call for the abandonment of *The Big Sky*, then, but its re-placement. To ignore or bury the novel would be to deny a powerful current in our culture and to maim our historical memories. But we are often seduced, unconsciously, by the siren song of apocalypse. We have struggles enough to engage, from balancing ecology and ranching to protecting air quality in expanding cities to thoughtfully using coal-tax monies. We must set against the comfortable despair of Boone's failure the courage and resilience written into alternative western narratives, those pragmatic comedies. Rather than settling for Dick Summers' befuddlement, let's go to school with Ellen Webb.

Notes

1. A. B. Guthrie, Jr., *The Big Sky* (New York: William Sloane Associates, 1947; New York: Bantam, 1952), 142.

2. See Chapter One, "Guthrie's Big Sky," in *Ten Tough Trips: Montana Writers and the West* by William W. Bevis (Seattle: University of Washington Press, 1990), 3–19. For a helpful overview of the mythology of Edenic wilderness and the pitfalls of that ideology, see William Cronon, "The Trouble with Wilderness; or Getting Back to the Wrong Nature," in *Uncommon Ground: Toward Reinventing Nature,* ed. William Cronon (New York: W. W. Norton, 1995), 69–90.

3. Annette Kolodny, *The Lay of the Land: Metaphor as Experience and History in American Life and Letters* (Chapel Hill: University of North Carolina Press, 1975).

4. Guthrie, *The Big Sky,* 366.

5. Ibid.

6. An excerpt from the Unabomber's "Manifesto," "Industrial Society and its Future" (repr. from *The Washington Post,* 19 September 1995, at fts://ftp.ai.mit.edu/pub/users/misc/unabomber) summarizes the apocalyptic tenor of these movements: "We hope we have convinced the reader that the system cannot be reformed in such a way as to reconcile freedom with technology. The only way out is to dispense with the industrial technological [sic] system altogether. . . . A revolutionary movement offers to solve all problems at one stroke and create a whole new world. . . ." (paragraphs 140–41). Earth First! founder Dave Foreman calls for embrace of the "Big Outside" and so tellingly echoes Guthrie's haunting title. He seems to demand a return to a Caudill-like relationship with wilderness: "We believe we must return to being animal, to glorying in our sweat, hormones, tears, and blood" (quoted in Cronon, *Uncommon Ground,* 84).

7. I am invoking Hayden White's useful terminology in *Metahistory: The Historical Imagination in Nineteenth-Century Europe* (Baltimore: Johns Hopkins University Press, 1973), especially 7–11.

Celeste River

Lige Mounts: Free Trapper and *Beyond Law*: Antecedents to *The Big Sky*?

Before A. B. Guthrie's *The Big Sky,* other, earlier stories were told about fur hunters and free trappers on the upper Missouri River. In fact, twenty-five years before Guthrie's amoral mountain man, Boone Caudill, came to life in 1947 through the pages of *The Big Sky,* another Kentucky-born runaway was introduced to Americans in *Lige Mounts: Free Trapper.* Written by one of Montana's first literary figures, Frank Bird Linderman, this historical novel was published by Charles Scribner's Sons in 1922; republished by The John Day Company in 1930, under the title *Morning Light;* and followed by a second Linderman novel about Lige Mounts, titled *Beyond Law,* in 1933.

In this essay, I explore connections between Linderman's stories of Lige (Elijah) Mounts, who was nineteen when he first traveled up the Missouri in 1822, and Guthrie's tale of Boone Caudill, who was seventeen when his story began in 1830. It is first necessary, however, to provide background on Guthrie (1901–1991), Linderman (1869–1938), and H. G. Merriam (1883–1980), a prominent teacher and direct intermediary between the two Montana authors of different generations.

In his 1965 autobiography, *The Blue Hen's Chick,* Guthrie wrote of his first inspiration to craft a novel that would "tell of the fur-hunters who followed hard on the heels of Lewis and Clark." His would be an "honest" story, revealing "that dark strain so often found in the [Kentucky] hill folk who could claim more than one mountain man," including his protagonist, Boone Caudill:

> With the exception of a couple of antique and artless attempts only one novel was tied to the fur trade insofar as I knew. That was one in a series whose protagonist was Stewart Edward White's Andy Burnett. I had followed Andy's adventures with pleasure and inactive consideration. White told a good and clean and therefore short-of-truth story. Not for me a Sunday-school representation of men mostly amoral, I thought with growing conviction. No bowdlerizing of documented behavior. No heroes, or villains for that matter, who never unbuttoned whether to make water or squaws. Be wholly honest! Get to the whole truth! Live and make live again that unfettered life! Don't heroize, keeping in mind that all heroes are errant and that the mountains counted cowardice the first sin and seldom listed a second.[1]

In a 1969 interview with biographer Charles E. Hood, a future dean of The University of Montana's school of journalism, Guthrie, who graduated from UM with a journalism degree in 1923, again talked about his impulse to write an honest version of the mountain man's story:

> The idea occurred to me early in 1940. It occurred to me because, so far as I knew, no honest story about the fur trade had been written, and—you say I am a romanticist—well, read the earlier stories about the fur trade if you want to run into some romanticists. They really idealized, heroized everything and everybody.[2]

Nearly a decade later, Montana literature professor William Bevis also interviewed Guthrie, who said the idea for *The Big Sky* really came to him with urgency around 1944. "I was motivated," he said, "by the thought, the almost certainty, that no one had written honestly about the days of the fur hunters. Other books had been written," he told Bevis, "but most of them were 'romantic'—the hero-type books, and they glossed over all the brutality, the amorality, and all, of the mountain man."

When Bevis asked Guthrie, in this audiotaped interview, if there were some books he was thinking of that were romantic, or any particular works that seemed false to the mountain man notion, Guthrie answered:

> Well, Stewart Edward White, for one. And the rest are very hard to find. Harvey Ferguson wrote a book, the title of which I forget, too, about the mountain man. And then, um, who's the man in the Flathead country? Frank Linderman—wrote a book called *Lige Mounts: Free Trapper.* But none of them dealt with the honest, day-by-day, the real guts of that life. And so I decided to do it, if I could.[3]

In researching his subject, Guthrie read more than one hundred primary sources—mainly journals of trappers. His friend Tom Clark, in Lexington, Kentucky, recalled that during his research and writing of *The Big Sky,* in the mid-1940s, Guthrie "came to think like the mountain men, and at times I thought he felt that he was, in a way, vicariously at least, a reincarnation of Boone Caudill."[4]

Guthrie wanted to understand with his senses the landscape of his stories. After the publication of *The Big Sky* (1947), and his follow-up, Pulitzer Prize–winning novel, *The Way West* (1949), he and his friend Bernard DeVoto took a trip with the Army Corps of Engineers, from the headwaters to the mouth of the Missouri River. Again, he vicariously lived in the past of the West:

> Just as of old. Just as if the old were now. And Benny and I were Lewis and Clark, seeing as they saw, running aground as they did, getting sun-burned and calloused and developing that look of wonder that stares at you from old reports. We looked at each other. He called me Deacon. I called him Pope or Brigham Young. But we were Lewis and Clark.[5]

When Hood interviewed Professor Harold G. Merriam for his biography on Guthrie, Merriam, who founded The University of Montana's well-known creative writing program in 1920, was direct in his assessment of his former student's novel, *The Big Sky:*

> It will be hard for anyone to write a better novel about the mountain man than *The Big Sky.* It is the definitive book. Do you know what I mean by that? I mean that nobody's going to write a better one. . . . There's love in *The Big Sky.* I got the feeling that Guthrie was having a grand time when he wrote that book.[6]

Merriam, who came to the university as chair of the English department in 1919, was a personal connection between Guthrie and the seasoned Montana pioneer and author, Frank Bird Linderman. Linderman had come to Montana Territory from the Midwest in 1885, when he was sixteen years old, going directly to the Flathead and Swan Valley wilderness, where he lived the life of a hunter and trapper until 1892. After working at various careers—as a prospector; a newspaper owner in Sheridan, Montana; a state legislator from Madison County in 1903 and 1905; assistant secretary of state from 1905 to 1907; and an assayer in Helena, to name a few—Linderman was, by 1917, living with his family in a secluded log home at Goose Bay, on the western shore of Flathead Lake. His daughters were enrolled at the university in the early 1920s, during the same years Guthrie was in school at UM and Merriam was starting the creative writing program.

Linderman had retired to Goose Bay in pursuit of his dedication "to preserve the old West" as he knew it "in printers' ink."[7] His first book, *Indian Why Stories,* illustrated by Charles M. Russell, was published by Charles Scribner's Sons in 1915; a second book of legends, *Indian Old-man Stories,* and a book of short stories called *On a Passing Frontier* came out in 1920; a book of poems, *Bunch Grass and Blue Joint,* and a book of stories about animal traits called *How It Came About Stories* were published in 1921.

A colorful feature of Linderman's life was his thirty-year friendship with Montana's cowboy artist, Charley Russell. Whereas Guthrie and DeVoto, flying over and motoring down the Missouri River in 1950, vicariously felt they were explorers of old, imagining themselves as Lewis and Clark, Linderman and Russell had actually canoed together through the White Cliffs area of the Missouri nearly forty years earlier, in 1913. They took along a copy of the journals of Lewis and Clark, which they read aloud at intervals, and they, too, imagined themselves in another time and were inspired in their creative works by this journey.

In 1927 Linderman received an honorary doctorate from The University of Montana for his literary work and research in the field of Indian customs, beliefs, and traditions. In the 1920s and 1930s he contributed stories to the Northwest literary magazine, *Frontier,* published by Merriam, and in the 1930s there was even a writing club at UM called the Linderman Club.

A skilled raconteur who, it was said, could hold large audiences "spellbound" for hours or get them "roaring" with laughter,

Linderman frequently was asked to speak at the university. Of his standard lectures, titled "The Indian" and "Men of the Old Northwest," he said: "In one, I talk of the Indian's life, beliefs, customs, etc.—and from my own observations after an acquaintance of forty-three years. In the other, I tell of early days on the plains of the northwest, give dialect readings, stories of cowboys, trappers, and French voyageurs."[8]

In a letter to a friend dated April 26, 1922, Linderman gave a synopsis of his first novel, *Lige Mounts: Free Trapper,* that was soon to be published, and he mentioned a lecture he would give in May at the university:

> "Lige Mounts: Free Trapper" . . . is the story of the boy, Lige Mounts, who at the age of 19 came up the Missouri River into Montana with Wash Lamkin, whom he called Dad. The story is laid in 1822 and the only trading post then on the upper Missouri was the Ashley Henry Fort at the mouth of the Yellowstone. The party had several battles with Indians before it finally reached the fort where the boy Lige, first saw the young Cree woman with whom he fell in love.
>
> After a short time spent at the post for a rest Lige and his party moved to the mouth of the Marias where they built a small stockade of their own. Here the Hudson Bay people, tampering with the Blackfeet, caused a raid on the little fort which was beat off with the help of the Crees who had fortunately moved up to the Marias from the Yellowstone country. Both Dad and Bill, the other older partner of Lige's, were killed in the battle at the post and Lige is left alone among the Crees with a fair stock of trade goods which he disposed of with a profit by spring. Believing that he disliked the plains and grieving sorely for Dad whom he loved the boy determined to leave the plains and even the Cree woman, Blue Bird, and go back to his home at Coon Creek Crossing about one hundred miles from St. Louis.

> Accordingly when he could get away, he did go back where soon the sordid conditions and narrowness of the people he had known turned him again toward the plains which after many difficulties he reached and found the Crees and Blue Bird again. The story leaves him here happy with the Cree woman.

In this letter, Linderman affirms the validity of Lige Mounts' story and says it is "true to life":

> The boy tells his own story . . . and I am sure the book will find many appreciative readers because it is true to life and I am competent to tell of that life. For instance in the book is a description of the buffalo pound and the methods used in corraling the wild herd of buffalo on the plains, a thing I have never seen in print. The book abounds in scenes of Indian village life of the early days and the sound logic of the plainsmen both white and red.
>
> I am to speak for the fourth time at the State University [in Missoula] on the 22nd of May, and this time I am to speak on my books and work.[9]

In that same month a new associate editor named "Bert" Guthrie signed on with the university's student newspaper, *The Kaimin.* During Linderman's talk, Guthrie may have heard some of the following words from *Lige Mounts,* about the influence of the plains on a man's character:

> I could see far out over the plains in the clear night and across the Missouri, from where I stopped. Such nights fetched me what I wanted of the plains. And always my love for them got stronger. I couldn't never see how any man could be small or ornery and live on the plains. It seemed to me that men ought to measure up to their country, someway, and be big like it was.[10]

In another place Lige told about the "fun and frolic" in the village, and the antics of a young Cree named Big Sky, who turned around on his "hoss" and rode backwards, "but the hoss didn't like it and before he could get straightened out he was on the ground." The young women laughed, and Big Sky got up and danced while his friends caught the horse. On the facing page, Lige talked about "the way of the plains" where "there's no time but the present":

> Directly, like it was planned to surprise the young women, we dashed away up the Marias, looking for a herd of buffalo. I could hear the young women singing for more'n a mile, till the sound finally died away. I felt right good; and the plains looked so far-spread and free. . . .
>
> We talked and cut up and rode pretty fast till we saw a herd of buffalo away off on the plains towards the east. It was might pretty to see. The plains, lit up by the morning sun, yellowish-brown, with the dry grass striped with long narrow snow-drifts crusted hard as ice, seemed to be without end. And as far as I could see the Missouri's course was clean-marked by leafless cottonwoods. I thought of the morning I first saw it, from the hill-top nigh St. Louis, and tried to imagine leaves on the trees, and flowers. But I couldn't. That's the way of the plains. They hold you to theirse'fs. There's no time but the present on the plains, and the hour itse'f is so plumb full of wonder or fun or beauty or misery, or something that no other place offers the same way, that you can't mope in the past or dream about the future.[11]

The story of *Lige Mounts: Free Trapper* could easily have impressed the young student, Guthrie, just as it did Hollywood actor and producer William S. Hart, who wrote to Linderman in 1925: "The most striking thing which stands out in my mind about the story is the atmosphere which it creates. It seems to be absolute truth and not fiction at all."[12]

In a similar vein, when *Lige Mounts: Free Trapper* was reprinted as *Morning Light* in 1930, the *Saturday Review* reported that the story throughout is "sincere and convincing in its picture of the interaction between human life and the land in which it is lived. We do not know that any other, better way of life or any better way of relating it, could be wished for, than one which makes this interpenetration of the man and his natural environment seem both soul satisfying and secure."[13]

In 1933 Linderman wrote to fellow author Frederic van de Water, "I've often held that no man can possibly know the idiom of this land unless he has lived the life he portrays here."[14] When his second novel, *Beyond Law,* was published later that year, a *New York Times* book reviewer acknowledged Linderman's faithful rendering of the western frontier:

> As an interpreter of the Western plains, Mr. Linderman is second to none. . . . With a dry fidelity to the scenes and characters of the American frontier, Mr. Linderman combines a narrative skill which sweeps the reader on irresistibly to the climax of his tale.[15]

Reviewer C. L. Skinner's remarks about Angus Cameron, the antagonist in *Beyond Law*, remind us of Boone Caudill in the deleterious effect he had on the world around him:

> "Beyond Law" brings back the guide, Lige Mounts, the hero of Frank Linderman's earlier book, "Morning Light," and offers us a slice of life as it was when the American Fur Company was the big business and gang-leader in the Far West. . . . Indians and their ways, the trade, life at a trading post and on the trail, are

> blended easily with the story of [Angus] Cameron who made any wilderness too small for other men, so long as he was in it.[16]

We hear the "idiom" of the land in the opening lines of *Beyond Law,* and imagine life on the plains in 1833 as Linderman portrayed it through Lige Mounts' narrative. In his words, the story begins:

> A thing can lay hold of a person, and hang on, without him knowing it. When I come to the plains I reckoned on going back to Coon Creek Crossing, or mebby St. Louis. And I did, but I didn't stay long, because the plains had layed hold of me. They have never let go; not for a minute.
>
> . . . Till right lately I have been living mostly at Fort Union on the Missouri, six and a half miles above the mouth of the Yellowstone, where white men, some of them ornery as Mike Fink, are plentiful enough. The reason I compare the low-down whites to Mike Fink is that Mike was the orneriest white man I ever knowed. I saw him kill his own pardner on the Yellowstone in 1822.[17]

In his day, Linderman was considered a master of the idiom of the land of the inland Northwest and the plains of the 1800s. He had lived a version of the life he portrayed in the two novels about Lige Mounts. In a letter written in 1937, in answer to a reader's query from London about the books, he clearly states that his characters are based on the lives of real people, including himself:

> Fifty-three years ago I was a trapper and hunter here in Montana. Most of my associates, or partners, were men who had grown old on the plains and in the mountains. Lige Mounts and "Dad" Lampkin were two of these men; but in telling their story I did not confine myself entirely to their own experiences.

> Instead I used a few of the experiences of others, including some of my own. Nevertheless I cannot declare that Lige Mounts and "Wash" or "Dad" Lampkin are fictitious characters.[18]

In the 1960s, while editing two unpublished manuscripts written by Linderman in the early 1930s—his *Recollections of Charley Russell* (1962) and Linderman's own memoirs, *Montana Adventure* (1968)—H. G. Merriam found, among Linderman's papers, the letter written in 1922 describing the story of Lige Mounts. Merriam wrote at the top of the letter, "Did Guthrie draw on *Lige Mounts* for his *The Big Sky?*" He later wrote, in a finer pen: "It would seem so, HGM."[19]

While Guthrie in the 1960s and 1970s said the earlier books he had read about trappers were romanticized, in the 1960s Merriam, who had known Linderman as a friend and literary advisor for eighteen years, said of *Lige Mounts: Free Trapper,* "With his knowledge of the plains and mountains, of the trapper's life and of Indians, and with his extreme care for accuracy, the novel certainly is as authentic as any book about early days in Montana." In fact, he said both *Lige Mounts* and *Beyond Law* "have unmistakable feeling for the country and the wise ways of living in and with it and its people."[20]

In the introduction to *Recollections of Charley Russell,* Merriam made a strong statement about the worth of Linderman's writings:

> Frank Bird Linderman was one of Montana's most accomplished writers. He possessed a fine conscience in his effort to interpret the red man, an almost fanatically painstaking regard for accuracy, a sense of form, and an ear for language. His writing has lasting value and should be more widely known than it is.[21]

Merriam wrote that both Linderman and Russell "had a passion for preserving Western life as it was twenty years and more before the turn of the century." They also "greatly respected the old-time Indian, his way of life, his love of fun, his beliefs, and perhaps, most of all, his co-operation with nature, his adjustment to it." But, according to Merriam, who knew both men, Russell "did not see as deeply into the Indians' inner life as Linderman did; he knew their outward life." Linderman, on the other hand, "knew Plains Indians as friends whom he admired. He also, being curious about their inner life as well as the outer, before white contamination, treasured their legends and beliefs and their relationship to all that is in heaven and on earth."[22]

This authenticity is what sets Linderman's *Lige Mounts* and *Beyond Law* apart from Guthrie's *The Big Sky*. Linderman's sensitivity to the Indian people he wrote about was developed through his own personal experience and knowledge. In fact, he had worked constantly, for more than ten years (from at least as early as 1906), to get a home for Montana's landless Chippewa and Cree Indians, whom he had come to know personally in 1885 when they were living in the Flathead area as refugees from the Riel Rebellion in Canada. Many people in Montana objected to giving these homeless Indians a place to settle down, saying they were aliens or "Canadian" Indians. Finally, in 1916, the Rocky Boy Indian Reservation was created by federal law for the Montana Chippewa and Cree.[23]

In *Lige Mounts: Free Trapper,* the Indians that the young man ends up living with are Crees. In fact, their chief's name is Big Bear, the name of the father of the Cree chief, Iamsees, or Little Bear, who Linderman knew so well from his early days in the Flathead and through the years to the founding of the reservation. In Lige's story these people, the Crees, are living during the winter beside the Missouri River across from the mouth of the Marias. In this way, Linderman wrote down for the record that certain bands of Cree Indians, accused in Montana in the early 1900s of being aliens from across "the medicine line," were living and trading in Montana Territory even in the early 1800s. The landscape and ecology of the place was a rhythmic part of their semi-nomadic cycle.

Through Lige's observant eyes, Linderman takes the reader within the lodges of the people and amidst the everyday activities of the village. Through questions Lige asks of Bluebird, her father Red Robe, and his other friends in the village, we learn much about the inner world and family life of the Indian people. For example, through a conversation Lige has with Bluebird beside the fire in her father's lodge, we learn about her people's relationship with the spirit of the land:

> "Tell me of Manitou," I said. . . .
>
> "We do not speak His name often," she began softly. "The sun, the earth, and everything that lives is Manitou, even the ants and the tiny things that live under the leaves that lie on the ground beneath the forest trees. . . . Greater and more wonderful than the moon and stars is the sun, but All is Manitou. The Sun, the father, makes the grass and the flowers to grow upon the Earth, the mother, of all things. And through the great Sun we thank Manitou with the Sun-dance each year."[24]

This faithful attention to the native peoples' relationship with nature arose from Linderman's own beliefs about the environment. For instance, in another letter written in 1922 (soon after *Lige Mounts* was published), when invited to speak at a banquet for the Montana Department of Fish and Game, he responded in part:

> I am interested in all things out-of-doors, especially in the wild inhabitants of our forests and streams.
>
> I want to see them adequately protected for I realize that, plan as we may, we shall leave but little of the wilderness to our sons and daughters. There is a broad streak of vandalism in our race which defies competition. No savage people have ever possessed it in the same manner as does the self-exalted whiteman. And instead of taming with the times he is growing more and more efficiently fierce with his high-powered guns of automatic mechanism, his automobiles, and his flying machines. Where, now, in the Almighty's footstool may a wild creature hide?
>
> I would protect the bear. I'd stop men from killing "just because it's a bear". I'd teach people that the bear is not dangerous to man or brute.[25]

Linderman had a strong bond with the Indian people through their mutual appreciation for nature and the spirit of the land in Montana Territory. He was, in fact, an early advocate of religious freedom for the Indians, whom he considered to be the real—the first—Americans. Because of his unflinching efforts to help the homeless Chippewa and Cree, critics in Montana newspapers derisively labeled him a "sympathetic white." Yet still, in the foreword to his final work, *Wolf and the Winds,* he spoke out boldly, once more, for the humanity of the Indian:

> The average oldtimer in the Northwest who too often judged the Indian wholly by his depredations may easily believe that I have idealized him. If I have, then it is idealization by omission, . . . I have known the red man of the Northwest for half a century. He is not a saint. . . . here I do not defend him further than to declare that for every atrocity perpetrated by him against the white race I will undertake to name two equally revolting crimes which have been committed against him by white men.[26]

In his writings, Linderman sought to educate readers about the humanity of the Indian people, record details of their way of life, and reflect upon the soundness of their spiritual beliefs. One method he used to transmit respect for Indians was linguistic:

> In order to give the reader an idea of the dignity with which the old-time Indian conversed, I have assumed that in speaking the Cree language, which he had learned perfectly, or in translating conversations from the Cree, Lige Mounts used nearly perfect English.[27]

In *Montana Adventure,* Linderman reveals the impetus that drove his writing, while defending the style and direction of his literary voice:

> By now the reader may believe that I see the old Indian in too warm a light. I do not. I know his shortcomings well enough. . . . Ever since our advent in North America, the red man's misdeeds have had willing heralds. Few have spoken of his finer qualities. And yet, it is only the discovered good in man that builds humanity.[28]

In writing his two novels about free trapper Lige Mounts, Linderman's purpose was different than Guthrie's in writing *The Big Sky.* The books represented different functions for the authors, both political and personal. "Whatever *The Big Sky* is," Guthrie said, "it owes much to nostalgia." He had grown up in Montana, and living in the East while he wrote the book, he suffered loneliness and an "almost physical hunger for the West." He found company in his characters, and at times felt he "was alive in unpeopled space and at home with it, counting buttes and streams and mountain peaks as friends." Guthrie told us why he wrote the story—to give an honest account of the days of the fur trade. In his portrayal of the errant fur hunters, he focused on "men mostly amoral," from 1830 through 1843, to the time of their "self-wrought ruin." He wrote, "I had a theme, not original, that each man kills the thing he loves. If it had any originality at all, it was that a band of men, the fur-hunters, killed the life they loved and killed it with a thoughtless prodigality perhaps unmatched."[29]

The fact that earlier publications about fur hunters on the upper Missouri, in the 1820s and 1830s, featured protagonists of strong moral character does not preclude the validity or worth of their stories. Amoral men existed in Lige Mounts' world: from the infamous Mike Fink, who killed one of his rowdy partners in 1822, to the treacherous goings-on of Angus Cameron in 1833, to unscrupulous traders and trading companies that were present throughout the times. In both *Lige Mounts* and *Beyond Law,* Linderman exposed some of the misdeeds of the fur companies and traders in their dealings with the free trappers and the Indians.

In contrasting the differing functions of the two authors' books, it is worthwhile to note that when Scribner's editor Maxwell Perkins wrote to Linderman in 1927, "it would be hard to write a better story than 'Lige Mounts,'" he also said Linderman's literary works had "an intrinsic value far beyond their mere fictional value, which in itself is considerable . . . throwing great light on the quality of the Indian mind, and imagination, and on his ways of living."[30]

While Linderman's motivation might have been, in part, nostalgic, it was more a nostalgia for "the scenes of Indian village life of the early days and the sound logic of the plainsmen both white and red," than for the West of Boone Caudill and his ilk. In the foreword to *Lige Mounts: Free Trapper,* Linderman wrote, "In this book I have sought to tell of life in the very early days of the fur trade on the upper Missouri River, and to show something of the real customs of both the white and red men who lived on the plains."[31]

Together, the lead characters in the stories of Lige Mounts and Boone Caudill give us a more complete picture of the fur hunters during their heyday on the Missouri. For his generation, Guthrie introduced a new level of reality to the mountain man's story, or as he said, "the real guts of that life." But Linderman's was a different, earlier generation. Through the character and voice of Lige Mounts, and informed by his own experiential knowledge, he wrote from a cross-cultural perspective with the hope of fostering greater understanding toward the Indian people. Twenty-five years later, through the consciousness of Boone Caudill and his partners, Guthrie resurrected the psychological tension and impulse toward destruction—that "dark strain" of the mountain man—that haunts the pages of *The Big Sky*.

Notes

1. A. B. Guthrie, Jr., *The Blue Hen's Chick: An Autobiography* (New York: McGraw-Hill, 1965), 148–49.

2. Charles E. Hood, Jr., "Hard Work and Tough Dreaming: A Biography of A. B. Guthrie" (M.A. thesis, University of Montana, Missoula, 1969), 33.

3. William Bevis interview with A. B. Guthrie, Jr., 1978, "Montana Writers" audiotape series, Instructional Media Services, Maureen and Mike Mansfield Library, University of Montana, Missoula.

4. Hood, "Hard Work," 36.

5. A. B. Guthrie, Jr., "DeVoto—A Memoir," *Nieman Reports* (January 1958): 6.

6. Hood, "Hard Work," 62–63.

7. Letter, Frank Bird Linderman to Harry Cunningham, 28 June 1922, quoted in *Frontier and Midland* (Spring 1939): 146.

8. Letter, Frank Bird Linderman to Blanche N. Toohey, 23 November 1928, Frank Bird Linderman Papers, Collection 7, K. Ross Toole Archives, Maureen and Mike Mansfield Library, University of Montana, Missoula, Box 4: File 6 [hereafter referred to as FBL Box #: File#].

9. Letter, Linderman to E. Ralph Edgerton, 26 April 1922, FBL 1:46.

10. Frank Bird Linderman, *Morning Light* (New York: John Day Company, 1930), 148. *Morning Light* is a 1930 reprint of *Lige Mounts: Free Trapper* (New York: Charles Scribner's Sons, 1922).

11. Ibid., 242, 243.

12. Letter, William S. Hart to Frank Bird Linderman, 12 January 1925, FBL 2:18.

13. Review, *Saturday Review,* 27 September 1930, 168.

14. Letter, Linderman to Frederic van de Water, 4 March 1933, FBL 4:9.

15. Review, *New York Times* , 22 October 1933, 22.

16. Review, *Books*, 1 October 1933, 10.

17. Frank Bird Linderman, *Beyond Law* (New York: John Day Company, 1933), 3, 4.

18. Letter, Linderman to Mr. G. Thompson, 16 June 1937, FBL 4:6.

19. Letter, Linderman to E. Ralph Edgerton, 26 April 1922, FBL 1:46.

20. Harold G. Merriam, "Sign Talker with Straight Tongue: Frank Bird Linderman," *Montana The Magazine of Western History* 12 (July 1962): 17–18.

21. H. G. Merriam, introduction to Frank Bird Linderman, *Recollections of Charley Russell,* ed. H. G. Merriam (Norman: University of Oklahoma Press, 1963), xxi.

22. Ibid., xii, x, xxiii, xx.

23. Background information on Linderman is drawn from (a) Celeste River, "A Mountain in His Memory: Frank Bird Linderman's Role in Acquiring the Rocky Boy's Indian Reservation for the Montana Chippewa and Cree" (M.I.S. thesis, University of Montana, Missoula, 1990); and (b) Celeste River, "The Great Stillness: Visions and Native Wisdom in the Writings of Frank Bird Linderman" in *New Voices in Native American Literary Criticism* (Washington, D.C.: Smithsonian Institution Press, 1993), 291–316.

24. Linderman, *Morning Light,* 270.

25. Letter, Linderman to Thomas N. Marlowe, 13 December 1922, FBL 3:2.

26. Frank Bird Linderman, *Wolf and the Winds* (Norman: University of Oklahoma Press, 1986), 4–5.

27. Linderman, *Morning Light,* viii.

28. Frank Bird Linderman, *Montana Adventure,* ed. H. G. Merriam (Lincoln: University of Nebraska Press, 1968, 1985), 162–63.

29. Guthrie, *The Blue Hen's Chick*, 186, 171, 148, 200.

30. Maxwell Perkins quote is in Merriam's Appendix A in Linderman, *Montana Adventure,* 211.

31. Letter, Linderman to E. Ralph Edgerton, 26 April 1922, FBL 1:46; Linderman, *Morning Light,* vii–viii.

Louie W. Attebery

"Companion to the Wide Horizons": Exploring the Guthrie Hexad

Although A. B. Guthrie had earlier written a "virgin" novel (*Murders at Moon Dance,* 1943), his first major work was *The Big Sky,* published in 1947. *The Big Sky* launched Guthrie's series of six related novels, his "hexad," made up of *The Big Sky; The Way West; These Thousand Hills; Arfive; The Last Valley;* and *Fair Land, Fair Land.* Occurring from 1836 to 1843, mostly in or near the Rocky Mountains, *The Big Sky* was clearly viewed by its author from three perspectives: historical, obviously; geographical, equally clearly; and mythical, perhaps not quite so transparently. But to infer from this that Guthrie was writing about old-timey-placey things would be a rank injustice to that superb intellect. Something like the following would be closer to the mark: At that time in the nation's continuing story, Euro-American civilization was moving west, but settlement that had started along the Atlantic coast had not yet established union with that other great body of salt water to mark both the end of struggle and continental and national limits. It is the familiar Turner hypothesis in which geography and history fuse into a dynamic template for the study of American national destiny. At the same time, Guthrie saw the Rocky Mountain part of the world as an Edenic wilderness, and at least four important characters are archetypal. Two of them are orphans (Boone Caudill and Jim Deakins), one is the genius or spirit of the place (Teal Eye), and one is a Wise Old Man (Dick Summers). This is the stuff of myth.

The book begins in Kentucky, and we follow the progress of Boone Caudill, who doesn't mesh with civilization, and Jim Deakins, who does but hankers after excitement, to the Rocky Mountains, and their association with Dick Summers, their father surrogate. The reader will note that this book is divided into five sections—classical tragedy developed through five acts. And surely there are grounds for considering the book as Sophoclean, in some respects. Indeed, one of the great claims the book advances—call it a theme—is that man lacks vision. He cannot see ahead. In mythic terms he is Epimethean; in dramatic terms he is like Oedipus. Old Zeb Calloway casts his eyes back to the country he knew and compares it to this of 1830. Give five more years, says Zeb, and there will be only coarse fur and that going fast. The gray-eyed Dick Summers is wrong when he says it will be fifty years at the least. Time proves Zeb closer to the mark. Near the end of the book, Dick expresses his realization of the lack of vision in language that is affecting and idiomatic, American English that Mark Twain would sanction.

But there is another aspect to the metaphor of sight. Boone and Teal Eye's son is born blind, a consequence of a venereal infection Boone carried with him from civilization. So there is physical blindness and intellectual blindness, blindness literal and blindness metaphorical.

For yet another classical and Sophoclean allusion, refer to Chapter 20 in which Jim Deakins reflects upon ambition in language that defines *hubris*, establishes the nature of *hamartia*, and posits the necessary (*ananke*) consequence of *nemesis*. To the classical

Greek mind, there was a moral order to the universe. When that order was violated, it was necessary that the perpetrator of the violation be punished. A serviceable synonym for necessity is *ananke*. *Hubris*, an inaccurate transliteration of *hybris*, describes human behavior that is proud, arrogant, and excessive. Perfection in beauty, wisdom, and accomplishment is the preserve of the gods; a human who is superbly beautiful, wise, or accomplished encroaches on that divine presence and therefore fails to conform to what the universe has determined is appropriate for mortals. *Hubris* thus causes the mortal to commit *hamartia*, a term borrowed from archery to indicate that an arrow has overshot or otherwise missed its target. And the target, of course, is human behavior that is appropriate. *Hamartia* necessarily brings punishment—*nemesis*—in its wake.

Jim Deakins encapsulates all this when he says:

> I reckon God don't like a man to set his sights too high. Time he overaims, God sics something on him. Reckon he thinks nobody's got a right to feel big savin' himself. Ain't room in the puddle but for one big frog. . . . Maybe that's why we're still kickin'; we ain't aimin' at nothin' except keepin' our hair on and our bellies full, and havin' a time at rendezvous or maybe Taos. Ain't nothin' in that to git God's dander up. . . . Like Jourdonnais now. . . . He thought to be a mighty big nabob. He did, now, till God cut him down.[1]

To connect this book with another great piece of literature, draw parallels between Boone and Huck Finn, for both are orphans separated from brutal fathers and both find spiritual fatherhood in other men. Further, both books deal superbly with the motif of solitariness. In *Huckleberry Finn* (1884), the feeling of aloneness can be modified or terminated by nature; it is the society-engendered feelings of loneliness that depress Huck. To put the matter slightly differently, solitude and solitariness do not necessarily create depression. In several places in *The Big Sky* the reader witnesses characters confronting solitude, and how they react to it shows Guthrie's superb control of their emotional attachment to or estrangement from their environments. Call it a sense of place.

We are taken, for instance, into the mind of Jourdonnais as he reflects on solitude: "A raw, vast, lonesome land, too big, too empty. It made the mind small and the heart tight and the belly drawn, lying wild and lost under such a reach of sky as put a man in fear of heaven." How different from Boone, who by day "could get himself on a hill and see forever, until the sky came down and shut off his eye. There was the sky above, blue as paint, and the brown earth rolling underneath, and himself between them with a free, wild feeling in his chest, as if they were the ceiling and floor of a home that was all his own."[2]

A final examination of this motif through the understanding of Jim Deakins, the philosophical, speculative, social member of this family, is insightful against the background of Huck and loneliness and the sound of a spinning wheel. Are there sounds that make us feel lonesome, abandoned? Jim "hunched his shoulders inside his shirt as he felt the evening chill coming on. Overhead, from somewhere or everywhere, there was a high, fine singing. Only when a man was quiet did he hear it, but there it was then, thin and coming on and fading and coming on again, and it might have been the high pines talking, or the mountains, or time humming, far off and old, so that a body felt little and short-lived, so that he felt lonesome and hungry for people so's to forget how big the world was, so's not to be thinking how long a mountain lived."[3]

A query for the reader finishing this book is who, or what, is the protagonist? Boone? Dick? Something greater?

Guthrie turned to the next stage of the Turnerian analysis of the westward movement: the hunters-trappers-fur traders replaced or displaced by settlers. The second book he called *The Way West*, Pulitzer Prize winner for 1949, and it is the greater for the constraints under which the subject placed him. Not, for heaven's sakes, another heroic and dusty journey by ox team from Independence, Missouri, to the Willamette Valley of the Oregon country with wagons circled up and flaming Sioux arrows and buffalo . . . and. . . . You know the familiar ingredients.

But none of that, and instead of raids it has a carefully and convincingly done analysis of how democracy works and how a new nation may be formed; its people are real, and the problems they face are not just the problems of coping with a new and hostile environment; some of their gravest problems are those they carry with them, Walt Whitman's old delicious burdens: "Still here I carry my old delicious burdens/ I carry them, men and women, I carry them with me/ Wherever I go/ I swear it is impossible for me to get rid of them."[4]

Dick Summers, the wise old gray-eyed archetypal father is the guide to the Promised Land. The perspectives are geo-historic and mythic. If the prevailing tone of the first novel is elegiac, in the second it is lyrically hopeful; if, in the first, a primitive paradise is lost, in the second a new entity is born, and optimism prevails. After all, these were the years of manifest destiny!

Of all the books in the saga, if I may so designate the hexad, this one asks a religious interpretation. Moses and successor Joshua seem prefigured in Dick and Lije Evans, for Dick leads the wanderers but does not settle in the promised land. Further, there are the two traditional views of the nature of God. To Dick, God is transcendent, above, apart from His creation, not indifferent to it, perhaps, but so far beyond it that one can infer nothing of the creator's nature from His creation: "Preachers and medicine men—they were cut from the same cloth. They made out to know what nobody could. Companyeros to the Great Spirit." The other view is Brother Wetherby's, a Methodist from "Indianny": "I feel the Lord has guided me here, to this house of grief"; "I feel the Lord is calling me to the new land," and "The Lord will provide." For Wetherby, God is immanent; He is near at hand, He intervenes in His creation, He is not apart from His works.[5]

Not only do we find these two views of God, not only do we watch sojourners in the wilderness moving toward the promised land of the Willamette Valley, but we find people committing the sin of lust—the lust of the flesh, the lust for power—and we find a saving gospel of the need for, and the power of, forgiveness.

Some other accomplishments of this novel beg for attention. In shaping the adolescent Brownie Evans, Guthrie shows that he remembers what it was like to be a boy, with adolescent self-consciousness, dreams, desires, fears, and potential. Brownie is yet another who finds a spiritual father in Dick Summers. Finally (not because there are not other accomplishments to talk about but because we must get on), Guthrie makes the passage of time an important motif. Summers reflects on the differences between the settlers and the mountain men:

> These [settlers] couldn't enjoy life as it rolled by; they wanted to make something out of it, as if they could take it and shape it to their way if only they worked and figured hard enough. They didn't talk beaver and whisky . . . they talked crops and water power and business and maybe didn't even notice the sun or the pale green of new leaves except as something along the way to whatever it was they wanted to be and have. Later they might look back . . . and wonder how it happened that things had slid by them. . . . They would hanker back for the day and wish they

> had got the good out of it. But, hell, a man looking back felt the same, regardless. There wasn't any way to whip time.[6]

The details of the crossing—its agony, labor, and sacrifices that humanize the great historical process that began in the early 1840s and was not ended even by the time the Oregon Short Line railroad came along the Snake River in 1883 and 1884—make the book a superb way of learning history. My brief comments on it end by calling attention to the verb specifying Dick's disappearance along the Columbia while the train was sleeping: Dick had slipped away. What slips away, cannot be held: Dreams? Desires? Fame? Youth?

The third book deals with an aspect of the western migration and settlement often called the backwash, as people moved eastward from the Willamette Valley to settle within the vast areas of Wyoming, Idaho, eastern Oregon, and western Montana, some of which they had passed over in the initial surges of the 1840s, 1850s, and 1860s. It also takes up the refinement of the cattle industry on the plains east of the Rockies. Titled *These Thousand Hills* (1956), the book offers as protagonist the grandson of Lije Evans (who became leader Joshua of *The Way West*). He is Albert Gallatin Evans.

Here Guthrie closes the lens of myth and looks at his subject the way we must—geo-historically. It is difficult to talk about the novel in regional terms because it is hard to answer the question, "Where is the West—which means the frontier—in the 1880s?" It cannot be located statically because it—the frontier—is moving west. The Bureau of the Census would continue to recognize a diffuse line of settlement for about another decade. Although statehood cannot be used in any absolute sense to show that a geo-historical process has been completed, the end of territorial status may be an indicator of the approaching conclusion. And until the backwash movement of population ended and there was some kind of cultural if not demographic stability, it would be difficult to be very specific about a region, a place in America we can all agree to call the American West. If that thought is troublesome, remember that George Washington would have thought Kentucky and Ohio the West. Recall the Old Northwest and its hero George Rogers Clark.

Lat Evans, the son of Mercy McBee and Brownie, the lad who so admired Dick Summers, is a skilled horseman and has many other admirable qualities. Even so, he does not measure up to the hero of the tradition. He is merely himself, an Oregon rider who sins and suffers and eventually succeeds in a way in Montana in the 1880s. With no financial security but with a rich inheritance of integrity, he advances by stages from an Oregon "buccaroo" helping drive a herd of good beef cattle from the eastern Oregon cattle hearth to the plains of Montana, through wolfing, until via a combination of luck and skill and a loan from one of Aunt Fran's girls, he becomes a rancher. He marries a girl from Indiana who had school teaching on her mind—I want to return to the eastern schoolmarm in a moment—and as Lat finds success he also finds himself caught in a superbly conceived and executed conflict of loyalties. From this careful and imaginative plotting, much of the structural excellence of the novel emerges. It is from the nature of the conflicting loyalties that the ethical or thematic value derives.

These can be identified if not developed. First, there is the conflict of Lat's loyalty to his parents, their Methodist reticence and moral values, as Lat meets the raw naturalness of a Montana frontier town, including liquor (which he does not abuse) and a prostitute, with whom he will not allow himself to fall in love. There is also conflict in his loyalty to his partner, Tom Ping, who does marry a prostitute, steals cattle, and has to be rejected by Lat in a moment of superb self-control. There is the conflict of loyalty to Callie, the prostitute who, in the absence of a "good" woman, supplies some graciousness, some quality of gentle sensibility, as well as money to the struggling rancher-to-be. Another test of Lat's integrity involves his willingness to testify for Callie in an act of moral courage that conflicts with his loyalty to Joyce, the Indiana girl whom he married. There is, finally, the conflict with Lat's call to civic duty. He could have championed Callie when she needed him. These conflicts of loyalties make Lat a richly human figure caught up in the ambiguities of life that we learned to appreciate in the great nineteenth-century writers Melville and Hawthorne.

Back to Lat's wife, Joyce, for a moment. Just as Guthrie was able to get beyond the triteness of the covered wagons crossing the plains by paying careful attention to the realities and filtering them through his imagination (the craft of writing may be that simple and that difficult), so in this book he gets beyond the cliché of the cowboy and the schoolmom. Let me share my interview with Victoria Schweitzer in the summer of 1958, near Nyssa, Oregon:

> I began teaching in Barren Valley in 1909. I was nineteen and just out of Indiana. There was a shortage of women in that community and a lot of cowboys. They nearly danced our legs off. One Friday noon a cowboy I knew rode up in a buggy to the little schoolhouse and dismissed the children. He told me we were going to the Diamond Ranch for a dance, and we'd have to leave early to make it. We drove the fifty miles in a good time and danced all night. When daylight came we had breakfast, then drove out to Bud Smith's for a turkey feed. After dinner the whole crowd went on up to Brown's Ranch on the mountain (Steens Mountain) and danced all Saturday night. We finally got back home late Sunday night. We must have covered close to two hundred miles.[7]

There are many connections between *These Thousand Hills* and the two earlier books in Guthrie's hexad. I've mentioned the obvious one of the Evans family. Let me cite one more, an image of the landscape, that richness of sense of place, in Guthrie's lyric prose: "This was even better, though, this country now around, this giant spread of land, this plain on which the herd had spilled out from the hills. Everywhere but to the mountains west it flowed forever. Farther than a man could think, beyond buttes blued by distance, floating in it, the earth line lipped the sky. . . . Air like tonic, days like unclaimed gold."[8]

Setting (sense of place) and historic diachronism (chronology) establish continuity between *These Thousand Hills* and the next (fourth) book of the saga, a painful novel titled *Arfive.* Set in Choteau-like country just about the time of World War I, it brings the cattle industry and the cowtown up to the threshold of contemporary times, and the winds of change blow steadily. Simpler responses to nature will no longer serve. For instance, hay is cut and stacked by the more progressive ranchers. It will not do to let cattle run out all winter. Natural or no-religion is being displaced by Methodism. And the house of prostitution is on the way out. The town of Arfive is on its way: Witness the decision to build a high school.

This process of change, bringing all manner of unforeseen consequences, is at the center of the book. The high school principal is staunchly Victorian, and when it is discovered that his best teacher is an aggressive lesbian, the teacher kills herself, creating enormous shock waves for the community: ah, yes, the winds of change, Victorian morality, the advance of civilization. The old order changes reluctantly, but change it must.

The next book, number five in the saga that began with the mountain men, is *The Last Valley* (1975). Certain characters from

Arfive re-appear here, and the setting is again Arfive, Montana, where Ben Tate buys the local newspaper just after World War I. In so doing he casts his lot, sink or swim, with the town and community served. This book is regional, it seems to me. The transformations wrought by the world war have occurred, those dramatic and pervasive changes Frederick Lewis Allen talks about: "Since 1919 the circumstances of American life have been transformed. . . ."[9] H. G. Merriam's regional publications *Frontier* and *Frontier and Midland* (1920–1939) have appeared and testify to a growing consciousness of self, worth, and identity. By self-consciousness I mean an awareness of regional resources, human and other natural richness, and an awareness that history has conferred a certain distinction upon the settlement and growth of the area. If there are those confused by the attempt to establish a region by a dating process, thinking that surely there were Rocky Mountains and Great Plains and the Great Basin before World War I—so why wouldn't books set there be regional?—I lean upon Terry Jordan, cultural geographer at the University of Texas, who questions the whole notion of there being regions at all. They exist not in nature but in human consciousness. Perhaps. I do see "sense of place" used more frequently than the "R" word.

But for my purposes here I call *The Last Valley* a regional novel. In it Ben Tate learns, along with the reader, that wherever man goes, he takes his problems with him. They change individually from age to age, but there is rarely a moment when a personal or social crisis does not face an individual or society. Indeed, this is one of the unifying themes of the saga from first to last. There is the problem of personal integrity when Ben is subjected to the power of domineering corporations. There is the problem of the building of the dam, not one but a host of problems. The reader and Ben are reminded of the first law of ecology: Nothing is ever done alone. In the end, what can mitigate the distress of such problems? These: personal integrity, friendships, the ability to learn wisdom from those who have been this way before, love in its most selfless sense, and the presence of an external nature in whose variety and numinous beauty humankind can learn perspective and endurance and silent awe.

The sixth book of the saga, a book that came out in 1982 titled *Fair Land, Fair Land,* returns us to *The Big Sky* and *The Way West*, for this novel is an answer to the question of what happened to Boone Caudill, Teal Eye, and their blind child, and to Dick Summers after he slipped away from the "On to Oregon" party. As Guthrie says in an introductory note, the book fills in the gap between, roughly, 1845–1870.

I'll talk about the book, concentrating upon its strengths as I see them, and about a serious under-emphasis in our national literature as it appears to my provisional understanding. Certainly Dick and Boone and Teal Eye are too compellingly real to have been abandoned; of course something happened to them in that imagined American setting, so we adjust our eyepieces and rediscover them through the lenses of geo-history and myth. That, I think, is what A. B. Guthrie did.

When Dick slips away from the wagon train to head back to the country he had known as a trapper, he discovers three things: the pristine loveliness, peacefulness, and sustaining power of the Teton-Maria country; Teal Eye and her blind red-haired boy living as outcasts; and Boone Caudill. Dick and Teal Eye marry, but from that state of bliss, Dick is compelled to search for Boone, not to punish him, but to bring him knowledge, to enlighten him. Dick becomes the instrument through which *hubris* and *hamartia* can be neutralized; that is, he is Boone's *nemesis.*

Their meeting is one of the points of high drama in the book. Boone, bigger and broader now than when young, is likewise moodier and more drawn into himself. It is Dick's intention to convince Boone that Teal Eye had been faithful, that red-haired Jim Deakins was not the father of the blind son. So Dick, the mythic spiritual father of this orphan, faces the task that has been given him. Dick doesn't know, but the reader remembers that, in *The Big Sky,* Boone himself discovers red hair in his family upon his return to Kentucky. In *Fair Land, Fair Land,* Boone and Dick meet in three pages, and Boone is unreflective, quick-tempered but tormented all the same by years of doubt and perhaps something akin to remorse. He attacks Dick, who refuses to use his knife to defend himself. Higgins, Summers' sidekick, shoots Boone, saving Dick's life.

There is more drama; there is a re-statement of the theme of change with the accompanying sense of loss; there is re-establishment of the tone of regret. *Fair Land, Fair Land* is an engaging story, taken as a novel unattached to anything else. Read following *The Big Sky* and *The Way West,* it proves a fine extension of, and variation upon, themes found in them: time and change, a land ethic, the vulnerability of things that stand for or symbolize natural freedom (I refer to the marvelous evocation of the West in the form of the wounded grizzly, named, of course, Old Ephraim). We must, I think, ask with Guthrie, "In whose keeping do the legacy and memory of the West lie?" Other themes are the stabilizing force of landscape amid change and the sounds of silence—"There was the voice of silence, the far thrum that sounded deep in the ear."[10] And there are new matters as well, evocative, well-handled, challenging. Among them I would list greed for gold and the consequential subversion of nobler human impulses, the difficulty faced by people of mixed blood who must somehow find a place in a changed world, military arrogance and stupidity, and the ameliorating potential of enlightened Christianity.

The book ends painfully. Myths are abandoned in just such pain as the facts of geo-history displace dreams, however true. If that seems ambiguous, it is so deliberately. The reader is challenged to work through the book's ending again and to try to see what it was that has brought us to where we are.

For some time, I have considered the Guthrie saga as our American Hexateuch, our Genesis, Exodus, Leviticus, Numbers, Deuteronomy, and Joshua. Certainly there is a correspondence in such themes as beginnings; trans-settlement; justice, first expressed as *lex talionus,* then as articles of governance for a wagon train, and then as a growing sense that ethics and justice include far more than these and must include the land as well. Such a scheme can be explored. But other considerations have claimed my attention.

The first of these is the conviction that finally there has been produced an American saga, a worthy parallel to those great saga-inspired European novels that treat related characters and places over time so that the reader feels a sense of history and sees in the fourth generation the consequences of the actions of the first. Too few American writers have given us this long and studied look, so beautifully demonstrated in works like *Kristin Lavransdatter* (1920–22), Gulbranssen's Bjorndahl cycle beginning with *Beyond Sing the Woods* (1936); Hamsun's *Growth of the Soil* (1917); Rolvaag's trilogy starting with *Giants in the Earth* (1927); and I would include *The Forsyte Saga* (1922). With Guthrie's hexad, we do have a saga, an extensive and detailed novelistic account of the generations of humankind over space and time as a way of telling us who we are, how we got that way, and what the delicious burdens of that experience are. Earlier I said, "Too few American writers have given us that long and studied look." I do not mean absence; I mean paucity. In fairness I recognize with praise Ruth Suckow's *The Folks* (1934); Faulkner's output; the fine work of another Montanan, Ivan Doig; and the passionate, lovely, wrenching novel by Ross Lockridge, Jr., *Raintree County* (1948). Helen Santmeyer's *And the Ladies of the Club* (1982) belongs here.

As I draw these remarks to a close, if there is anyone even beginning to think that parochialism or narrow-mindedness is associated with that long and studied look, I say listen to what a respected recent thinker has to say. John A. Kouwenhoven declares, "Humanity is not an abstraction but a set of particulars. There is no way to be universal, as Huck Finn, for instance, is, without being idiosyncratic, or to be international without being untranslatably localized." Kouwenhoven also notes: "Our primary allegiance, as sentient creatures, is surely not to the creations of our verbal ingenuity but to the particular sights, tastes, feels, sounds, and smells that constitute the American world we are trying to discover."[11]

In view of that and in view of this western hexad, one can only wonder why John Barth in a 1985 article in the *New York Times Book Review* gave the West such short shrift, for here in the legacy I've been talking about is one of the twentieth century's finest contributions to American, to world, literature.[12]

Notes

1. A. B. Guthrie, Jr., *The Big Sky* (Boston: William Sloane Associates, 1947; Boston: Houghton Mifflin, 1992), 169–70.

2. Ibid., 156, 123.

3. Ibid., 220.

4. Walt Whitman, "The Song of the Open Road," in *Leaves of Grass: The Inner Sanctum of the Poetry and Prose of Walt Whitman,* ed. Louis Untermeyer (New York: Simon and Schuster, 1949), 185.

5. A. B. Guthrie, Jr., *The Way West* (New York: William Sloane Associates, 1949; Boston: Houghton Mifflin, 1993), 44, 43, 76.

6. Ibid., 65.

7. Louie W. Attebery, "The Fiddle Tune: An American Artifact," in *Readings in American Folklore,* ed. Jan Harold Brunvand (New York: W. W. Norton, 1979), 325–26.

8. A. B. Guthrie, Jr., *These Thousand Hills* (Boston: Houghton Mifflin, 1956, 1995), 34.

9. Frederick Lewis Allen, *Only Yesterday* (New York: Bantam, 1931), 1.

10. A. B. Guthrie, Jr., *Fair Land, Fair Land* (Boston: Houghton Mifflin, 1982), 123.

11. John A. Kouwenhoven, "The Trouble with Translation," in *Half a Truth Is Better than None: Some Unsystematic Conjectures about Art, Disorder, and American Experience* (Chicago: University of Chicago Press, 1982), 49, 29.

12. John Barth, "Writing: Can It Be Taught?," *New York Times Book Review,* 16 June 1985, 1, 36–37.

Fred Erisman

Murders at Moon Dance and the Evolution of A. B. Guthrie's Fiction

Murders at Moon Dance, A. B. Guthrie, Jr.'s first novel, is in many ways the forgotten book of the Guthrie canon.[1] No short study of the author's writings makes more than passing mention of it, while Thomas W. Ford's *A. B. Guthrie* (1981) gives it barely four sharply critical pages, principally calling attention to the author's use of Choteau names and settings and other local materials.[2] Begun in 1936 but not published until 1943, it has drifted in and out of print over the years, while Guthrie himself made little effort to push its cause; though he never wholly disavowed the work, he calls it "a contender" for the label of "the worst book ever written" and confesses to buying up the last hardcover copies in the local bookstore, just to remove them from public view.[3]

On further examination, however, the book's near-invisibility seems largely undeserved. Though it without question has all the weaknesses of an apprentice effort, *Murders at Moon Dance* when read in the present becomes a revealing yardstick against which the magnitude of Guthrie's later achievements can better be measured. It is, as he later points out, his first try at anything but journalism, but in it one finds, in embryonic, even primitive, form, the central concerns and over-arching themes that come to the fore in the later novels.[4] Thus, when one places Guthrie's earliest fictional comments about the natural world, the personal world, and the socio-political world alongside his later remarks, the degree to which his thinking and his expression retain their internal consistency and integrity becomes strikingly clear, even as the qualities develop in maturity and insight.

The natural world is at the heart of Guthrie's major works, as such titles as *The Big Sky* (1947), *The Last Valley* (1975), and *Fair Land, Fair Land* (1982) imply. This eye for nature appears as well in *Murders at Moon Dance*. The Moon Dance locale is not a charitable one: "During most of the summer, the sun keeps it burned to a panther tan, and in winter the bitter winds whip great drifts along the bases of its low buttes."[5] Yet there is compensation; when spring comes, it yields beauty:

> Red willow and black birch were tipped with green. In the swales, violets and johnny-jump-ups lifted their shrinking beauty in the shielding grass. Meadow-larks, yellow-vested and black-lapelled, showered the silence with their songs. . . . Above, the sky hung close and cloudless, blue as lupine.[6]

Harsh or beautiful, the natural world is an explicit part of the larger setting.

But, in *Murders at Moon Dance*, that is all the world is—a stage prop before which the action of the story unfolds. The book holds none of the engagement with place that characterizes the later works, none of the sensitivity to environmental concerns, none of the sense that human life and the natural world are inseparably linked. Guthrie tells us what we are to see, a technique he later says will "damn a story," and makes no effort to develop the emotional intensity that comes when later characters reflect on their whereabouts.[7] Nature in *The Big Sky*, in contrast, takes on profound resonance when the characters speak of it, so that, for example, Zeb Calloway sets the elegiac tone for the entire book when he drunkenly grumbles, "This was man's country onc't. Every water full of beaver and a galore of buffler any ways a man looked, and no crampin' and crowdin'. Christ sake!"[8]

Guthrie, moreover, in his later books presents the natural world's human effects upon the characters who move through it. Some are made reflective; New England-born Elisha Peabody, who seeks to capitalize upon the mountain West, muses at first sight of the land, "It was an enormous world, a world of heights and depths and distances that numbed the imagination. . . . The great sprawling magnitude of the west made the hills and parks of home seem small and artificial, like a yard with a picket fence around it."[9] Others are overwhelmed, and some find identity. May Collingsworth, of *Arfive* (1970), finds the country "too big for the heart, too vast to contain, too wild for love, too empty for home," yet her husband, schoolmaster Benton Collingsworth, comes to see it as a part of his being:

> Who would choose to abandon this land? Here was his homestead, his point of outlook on heaven and earth, on the world and America. And it was part of his America, part of her riches, part of her essential rightness, part of her stamina and invulnerability.[10]

None of the three is untouched by the land, and their varied responses supply a far greater sense of the land and its nature than one finds in *Murders,* though they grow directly from the same close observation of the land and its traits apparent in the earlier book.[11]

Into the natural setting of his works Guthrie introduces the social setting and its concomitant people, and in *Murders at Moon Dance* he offers two character types who recur in the later novels: the person who does not know, or understand, himself, and the person who, through experience of the world and in-born self-knowledge, comes to see the complexity of the world in all its darkness and all its richness. As they appear in *Murders at Moon Dance,* these characters are little more than cardboard types. But, as starting points for the complex characters who increasingly populate his later works, they demand attention.

The unknowing, imperceptive person appears in the amiably bumbling Tandy Deck, restaurant-keeper in Moon Dance and father of Tana Deck, the virginal young woman who provides the story's love interest. Deck's life, Guthrie writes, is

> a record of polished ineffectuality, of graceful mistake, of beautiful incompetence. . . . As a student he was obedient, eager, ingratiating, and wrong. . . . By turns grocer, hotel clerk, salesman, make-shift teacher and small-time promoter, he had wandered from locality to locality, everywhere elegantly incapable, in all pursuits exquisitely inept. . . . Gentle, well-meaning, hopeful, handsome, gracious and utterly incompetent, he had been a constant promise, with never a fulfillment.[12]

He is a near-comic figure in *Murders at Moon Dance*, even in his death (he is shot by mistake when an overexcited blacksmith fires at the wrong shadow), but his blithe indifference to his limits and incapabilities makes his life tragic. He blunders thoughtlessly through the story, and only circumstances destroy him before he destroys someone else.

Contrasting with Deck in every respect is the book's protagonist, West Cawinne, whose face reveals his character: It "had the look about it of youth that had seasoned early. It was lean and strong and narrowed at the lids as if for laughter, but the eyes that looked out of it were unsmiling and deliberate."[13] Returning Shane-like to Moon Dance after a career as a lawman in the Southwest, he wants only to run cattle and be left alone, living the life he has deliberately chosen.[14] Circumstances dictate otherwise, however, and he reluctantly but deliberately accepts involvement in the town's troubles. He is, as the aged Judge LaFrance points out to Tana Deck, a vestige of the essential western man, with all the virtues the label implies:

> First of all about the western man was that he wasn't waiting for anyone else to do what he could do himself, or expecting him to either. . . . He saw a job had to be done, and he done it. Direct action, that's what he was, and no waiting around for some bolder, stronger, saltier man to come along and tend to his knittin' for him. He was the man, that genu-ine [sic] western man, who made things safe. . . . He was the man that settled the country.[15]

Familiar though Cawinne's character is in outline, Guthrie hints at developments to come. Such a person, the judge continues, must know himself, if he is to retain the balance and the stability that he represents. And that knowledge, in turn, comes at a cost, as Cawinne's appearance and actions reveal. "Sad and tired and old before his time," the judge remarks. "This gun business does that to you if you got any feelings. . . . But whatever his feelings . . . , a man's got to answer if the case calls for a man."[16] Even for the A. B. Guthrie who writes *Murders at Moon Dance*, the defining qualities of an admirable person are clear: He knows when not to act, he knows when to act, and he knows that, when action is called for, it must be confronted unflinchingly until the task is complete.

Cawinne's contrast with Tandy Deck is too vivid to overlook, and the simple self-knowledge that underlies his lethal competence makes him an ideal vehicle for Guthrie's purposes.

The easy contrasts of *Murders at Moon Dance* take on new dimensions as Guthrie matures. He retains his admiration for the self-knowing person, but comes to see that knowledge (like its absence) carries its own problems. The later counterpart of Tandy Deck becomes, ironically, Boone Caudill, the epitome of the mountain man. Boone is, to be sure, a far cry from Tandy Deck in skills, courage, and self-sufficiency, but he suffers the same destructive flaw: He lives in an eternal present with the happily ignorant belief that things will work out. "This was the way to live," he thinks complacently to himself,

> free and easy, with time all a man's own and none to say no to him. . . . Here a man lived natural. Some day, maybe, it would all end, as Summers said it would, but not any ways soon—not so soon a body had to look ahead and figure out what to do with the beaver gone.[17]

Whereas Deck's uninformed optimism damages only himself, Caudill's contributes to the destruction of a region and of a way of life. Guthrie's recognition of this consequence reflects his own considerable artistic growth.[18]

Balancing Caudill is Dick Summers; yet, whereas West Cawinne is a diametric opposite of Tandy Deck, Summers shares many of Caudill's traits, suggesting the older Guthrie's recognition of the complexities of life. He differs, however, in one telling way. More experienced, more reflective, and more knowing of himself and the world, Summers understands that life and change go hand in hand. "A place didn't stand alone after a man had been there once," he muses:

> It stood along with the times he had had, with the thoughts he had thought, with the men he had played and fought and drunk with. . . . There was the first time and the place alone, and afterwards there was the place and the time and the man he used to be, all mixed up, one with the other.[19]

Indeed, he comes to understand, "a man didn't give up the life but . . . it was the other way about."[20] Life will move on, and can pass one by, if one is unaware; if the responsible, effective person is to survive, he must know himself and his times.

The blurring of the confident assurance of *Murders at Moon Dance* continues as Guthrie perfects his art. He continues to extol the merits possessed by the self-knowing person, as the steady balance of Lije Evans, eventual leader of the wagon train in *The Way West* (1949), makes clear.[21] But with such balance comes a still greater uncertainty, as increased knowledge of self and circumstance makes agonizingly vivid the conflicts of an ever more complex world. Ben Tate, newspaper editor in the town of Arfive, comes to this realization while on a hunting trip in the 1930s.

Drowsing by a campfire with his companions, he thinks of others, like themselves,

> talking about leaders and policies, about money wasted as against the saving of lives, about wilderness exploited or left pristine, about dreams versus practicality, and each would make a good case and leave judgement shaky. . . . Where [he thinks] are the clean choices?[22]

And with his characters' realization that choices are never clear or clean (a recognition voiced first in his 1954 essay, "The Historical Novel"), Guthrie offers the final, most richly complex statement of the importance and frustrations of self-knowledge.

Ben Tate returns to the theme in post-war Arfive, telling young Mike Murchison, "That's the trouble with choices. They're never clean, almost never. Take sides, and you'll come to know regret or misgiving. That's the hell of it." And Chick Charleston, sheriff of Midbury, Montana, states the issue explicitly for young Jason Beard: "Choices, Jase. Choices. They come so damn hard, but a man has to make them, knowing or not knowing they'll be trailed by regrets." Life is not certain, but one does what one must.[23]

As the theme of "no clear choices" becomes clearer in Guthrie's work, his treatment of it documents his movement from the simplistic characterizations and conventional elements of *Murders at Moon Dance* to the more reflective vision that characterizes his later works. He is, in *Arfive* and *No Second Wind* (1980), no less concerned with what establishes "a man" than he is in *Murders at Moon Dance*, but he now understands that "manhood" is more complex and more ambiguous than the traditional definitions imply. Moreover, by equating self-knowledge, ambiguity, and the inescapable need to act, he brings his human characters into the natural world and prepares the way for his third concern, the complex interaction of society, civilization, and change.

Change, whether personal, social, or environmental, is the theme most consistent throughout Guthrie's work. Only as that work matures, however, does the author fully realize that change cannot unthinkingly be called progress, and that progress itself may not be entirely desirable. The realization comes slowly, but as it grows, it gains ever-increasing prominence. Early on, for example, Guthrie hints at change, in his portrait of West Cawinne, returning to his old home town and taking comfort in the apparent lack of change: "It hasn't changed," he says to himself. "It hasn't changed, and maybe the people haven't." He is, however, to be disappointed. A decrepit Model T chugs through the early pages of the book, and Moon Dance itself sports a combination restaurant and filling station: "Patterned after roadside resorts on busier thoroughfares, alien to a class of people who still traveled largely by horse, it was as out of place as a Chinese pagoda in this old cow town of frame stores, hitching racks and cottonwoods."[24] The "Motorists' Mecca" is out of place among the western rusticity of Moon Dance, but it is a harbinger of changes to come.

Change in a more abstract sense pervades the novel. Moon Dance is increasingly a community of the old: "We don't have any young men anymore," says Judge LaFrance. "The sons of cattlemen are hopping counters and peddling gas and pecking typewriters in the cities. . . . There's no youth in the cattle business these days. Just us old duffers. No young men any more." With the change in population, moreover, comes a change in ways, as modern values and attitudes replace the old. "Old times, old ways, they're important, too," the judge continues. "And when the old ways go, it ain't always to make room for progress."[25] Even in this novel, a work of his artistic youth, Guthrie has an inkling of the tension between change and progress; although quickly overshadowed by the melodrama of the rest of the story, the tension lays the foundation for his later views.

For many, change is progress. Elisha Peabody, the entrepreneur of *The Big Sky*, waxes lyrical in his defense of settlement: "We are growing. The nation is pushing out. New opportunities are sure to arise, bigger opportunities than ever existed in the fur trade. Transport, merchandising, agriculture, lumbering, fisheries, land! I can't imagine them all." Lije Evans, in *The Way West,* echoes Peabody's excitement at a more personal level: "Yonder it was, yonder was home, yonder the rich soil waiting for the plow, waiting for the work of hands, for the happy cries of children."[26] Here is the West of convention, the West waiting for commerce and cultivation. It is man's to do with as he will.

Or is it? Dick Summers offers an alternative view. Preparing to leave the mountains himself, he reflects on circumstances: "New times are a-coming now, and new people, a heap of them, and wheels rolling over the passes, carrying greenhorns and women and maybe children, too, and plows. The old days are gone and beaver's through." And, at the book's end, he frames his realization in grimly prophetic terms:

> "We went to get away and to enj'y ourselves free and easy, but folks was bound to foller and beaver to get scarce and Injuns to be killed or tamed, and all the time the country gettin' safer and better known. We ain't seen the end of it yet, Boone, not to what the mountain man does against hisself."[27]

Progress does, indeed, have its consequences, and they are not always desirable.

Early in his career, Guthrie takes temporary comfort in the belief that, while populations and values move on, the land stays constant. This view appears in *The Way West,* as Dick Summers observes:

> It was only the earth that didn't change. It was just the mountains, watching others flower and seed, watching men come and go, the Indian first and after him the trapper, pushing up the unspoiled rivers, pleased with risk and loneliness, and now the wanters of new homes, the hunters of fortune, the would-be makers of a bigger nation.[28]

It reappears in *These Thousand Hills* (1956), with Lat Evans's equating of civic progress (schools, courts, impending statehood for the territory) with the contributions of persons "who, if they were worthy, wanted to feel that something of themselves, some strength and hope and work and vision, went permanently to public benefit."[29] Increasingly, though, Guthrie bows to the evidence of his own eyes and his own awareness of the problems created by irresponsible change.[30]

This is the view that dominates the books of Guthrie's maturity. *Arfive* sets the stage, as the aged Sterling McLaine makes explicit early in the book: Change, he says, is inevitable. "It is in the nature of things as camps grow older. First lawlessness, then loose law and order, then churches and schools and social sanctions and, finally, a town, not a camp. The preacher and the schoolmaster are harbingers." But that change can now affect the physical worlds. Growth, Benton Collingsworth at last concedes, takes its toll on the environment. Where many see progress in homesteaders' cabins and plowed fields, he sees "impertinences . . . , violations of the first and true purpose, no matter the Christian ethic that the earth was created for man. Man would put it to his use, never fear. Let fellow creatures go hang. The land was there to tear up."[31] Tear it up mankind will, with no thought for the future.

In this realization is Guthrie's most considered position on change. Change is inevitable, but it can, and must, be guided by principled, contemplative persons whose vision extends beyond the crassly material and the invincibly parochial. The rancher Mort Ewing and schoolmaster Benton Collingsworth speak for Guthrie in advancing this view. Talking with Ben Tate, soon to take over the Arfive newspaper, they offer two bits of gnomic advice. From Collingsworth: "Be chary that you don't assume the coloration of the community [which is] only provincial, only parochial, as are other communities, little or big, in their way." And, from Mort Ewing: "Watch out for progress because you can't backtrack." The views seem whimsical to Ben, who has a young man's optimism, but, as time and circumstance age him, he realizes the profound truth between the simple caveats. The earth, he comes to see, "is all we have. Her riches are limited. When she goes, we go. That's plain to see, or should be. But in the name of progress we keep drawing on an account that can be overdrawn."[32] The events of the century that separates Dick Summers from Ben Tate make clear that man can, indeed, change the earth.

Yet, as is only appropriate, Guthrie acknowledges that the dilemma is not a simple one; the choices are not clean. This is the gist of a long passage in *No Second Wind,* as a corporate representative sings the praises of economic development in the Midbury region: What, he asks, is the secret of America's "once and continuing greatness? What has made us the greatest nation on God's green earth? The answer lies plain before us. It is growth. It is onward development. It is the plain fact of bigger and better." He is countered by Midbury's Judge Church, who challenges the myth of physical growth as progress ("The dinosaurs tried that.") and calls for the longer view: "Granted an immediate growth in business and jobs if mining is permitted . . . we must ask how long will this blush of prosperity last. An honest answer is thirty years."[33]

Both persons have legitimate points; Guthrie's executive is a reasonable person, not a villain, and the economic boom he predicts is probable. But the consequences that Judge Church points to are equally legitimate and must be considered. Almost four decades separate *Murders at Moon Dance* and *No Second Wind,* and the complexly intertwined questions Guthrie poses for his characters make clear the distance that he himself has come.

The origins of *Murders at Moon Dance* lie in the whodunits and "gun-and-gallop" stories that Guthrie used to drug himself during his mother's last illness; prompted by their thinness and conscious of the need for money, he set out to shape his own blend of the conventional materials.[34] He manipulates the formulas well, yet despite its well-worn plot and familiar characters, the book suggests his openness to new views and new visions and, still more significantly, offers a first, tentative statement of the themes and issues about which he feels so passionately. Like its models, the book makes blatant use of stock situations and formulaic patterns, but it also starts Guthrie on the path that produces the honored novelist of fifty years later.

When Macalester Cleveland turns the *Arfive Advocate* over to Ben Tate early in *The Last Valley*, his final words resonate throughout the book: "Stand for something," he tells the puzzled younger man, and it takes Ben thirty years to realize the wisdom of what he hears.[35] But the growth of that fictional wisdom over thirty years is paralleled by the growth of genuine wisdom in the forty years of Guthrie's career. Utterly consistent in his sense of his materials, his judgment of their worth, and the integrity of his own development, Guthrie goes on to grow as much as, if not more than, Ben Tate. He consciously studies the craft of writing, he absorbs the lessons of experience and age, and he speaks more and more of the complexity of the world, the implications of change, and the ambiguity of informed existence.

He folds these insights into his developing work, letting his characters and their actions speak where once he would have spoken for them. And as he does, he himself evolves, growing from reporter to analyst, from critic to advocate, from journalist to novelist. He leaves behind ten novels, a host of memorable characters, and a body of hauntingly persistent ideas; it is no small achievement for any writer, and it demonstrates the part that *Murders at Moon Dance* plays in Guthrie's artistic and intellectual evolution. The movement of his writing and thinking from simplistic to sophisticated, from indifferent to perceptive, has to begin somewhere. *Murders at Moon Dance* is that beginning, and, for all its flaws, it adds provocative insights to the record of Guthrie's long and illustrious career.

Notes

1. An earlier and modified version of this essay was published as "A. B. Guthrie's Literary Maturing" in *Studies in the Western* [Münster, Germany] 6 (1998).

2. Thomas W. Ford, *A. B. Guthrie, Jr.* (Boston: Twayne Publishers, 1981), 58–61.

3. A. B. Guthrie, Jr., *The Blue Hen's Chick: An Autobiography* (New York: McGraw-Hill, 1965; Lincoln: University of Nebraska Press, 1993), 128, 133.

4. Ibid., 129.

5. A. B. Guthrie, Jr., *Murders at Moon Dance* (New York: E. P. Dutton, 1943; Lincoln: University of Nebraska Press, 1993), 73–74.

6. Ibid., 213.

7. Guthrie, *The Blue Hen's Chick*, 174.

8. A. B. Guthrie, Jr., *The Big Sky* (New York: William Sloane Associates, 1947; Boston: Houghton Mifflin, 1992), 68, 150.

9. Ibid., 284.

10. A. B. Guthrie, Jr., *Arfive* (Boston: Houghton Mifflin, 1971), 81, 179.

11. Guthrie's later use of nature and matters environmental has drawn substantial attention. See, for example, William W. Bevis, *Ten Tough Trips: Montana Writers and the West* (Seattle: University of Washington Press, 1990); or Fred Erisman, "Western Fiction as an Ecological Parable," *Environmental Review* 2 (Spring 1978): 15–23.

12. Guthrie, *Murders at Moon Dance*, 141–42.

13. Ibid., 34.

14. *Murders at Moon Dance* appeared six years before Jack Schaefer's *Shane* (1949). As is well known, however, Guthrie wrote the screenplay for George Stevens's film treatment of Schaefer's novel and was nominated for an Academy Award as writer; his affinity for the book may be closer than previously thought. See Guthrie, *The Blue Hen's Chick*, 216–22; and Thomas W. Ford, "A. B. Guthrie's Additions to *Shane*," *Western American Literature* 29 (Winter 1995): 299–304, for details of Guthrie's time in Hollywood and his work on *Shane*.

15. Guthrie, *Murders at Moon Dance,* 235–36.

16. Ibid., 237.

17. Guthrie, *The Big Sky,* 201.

18. A valuable consideration of Boone Caudill as the failure of a type is Michael K. Simmons, "Boone Caudill: The Failure of an American Primitive," *South Dakota Review* 22 (Autumn 1984): 38–43.

19. Guthrie, *The Big Sky,* 194.

20. Ibid., 212.

21. A. B. Guthrie, *The Way West* (New York: William Sloane Associates, 1949; Boston: Houghton Mifflin, 1993), 299.

22. A. B. Guthrie, *The Last Valley* (Boston: Houghton Mifflin, 1975), 166.

23. Ibid., 281; A. B. Guthrie, *No Second Wind* (Boston: Houghton Mifflin, 1980), 214. The importance of self-knowledge and the theme of "no clean choices" are explored more fully in Fred Erisman, "The Education of Jason Beard: A. B. Guthrie's Western Suspense Stories," *Clues: A Journal of Detection* 1 (Fall/Winter 1980): 126–31.

24. Guthrie, *Murders at Moon Dance,* 23, 51.

25. Ibid., 36–37, 42.

26. Guthrie, *The Big Sky,* 278; Guthrie, *The Way West,* 340.

27. Guthrie, *The Big Sky,* 211, 385.

28. Guthrie, *The Way West,* 217.

29. Guthrie, *These Thousand Hills,* 253–54.

30. Guthrie's use of, and views on, social, personal, and environmental change have been extensively examined. See, for example, David C. Stineback, "On History and Its Consequences," *Western American Literature* 6 (Fall 1971): 177–89; Donald C. Stewart, "A. B. Guthrie's Vanishing Paradise: An Essay on Historical Fiction," *Journal of the West* 15 (July 1976): 83–96; Thomas W. Ford, "A. B. Guthrie's *Fair Land, Fair Land:* A Requiem," *Western American Literature* 23 (May 1988): 17–30; and Fred Erisman, "Coming of Age in Montana: The Legacy of A. B. Guthrie," *Montana The Magazine of Western History* 43 (Summer 1993): 69–74.

31. Guthrie, *Arfive,* 28–29, 236.

32. Guthrie, *The Last Valley,* 31, 284.

33. Guthrie, *No Second Wind,* 51–52, 55–56.

34. Guthrie, *The Blue Hen's Chick,* 130.

35. Guthrie, *The Last Valley,* 25.

A. B. Guthrie, Jr., in front of Ear Mountain, 1970s
Photograph by Jay L. Fowler.
Used for the promotion of Fair Land, Fair Land, *published in 1982.*
COURTESY OF CAROL GUTHRIE

Guthrie, in Context

Publicity poster for national release of The Big Sky *motion picture, depicting Kirk Douglas (as Jim Deakins) and Elizabeth Threatt (as Teal Eye), 1951*

COURTESY OF JAMES D'ARC COLLECTION

James V. D'Arc

A. B. Guthrie, Jr., in Hollywood: Variations on the Writing Experience

In his autobiography, *The Blue Hen's Chick* published in 1965, Pulitzer Prize-winning novelist A. B. Guthrie, Jr., conflated the ten years of his life in the movie industry, beginning in 1950, into just 7 pages.[1] What those 7 pages (out of a total of 261) do not detail, among other things, is the essentially agreeable experience Guthrie enjoyed in Hollywood. Guthrie's juggling act as novelist and screenwriter enlarged his capacity as well as clarified his limitations. He wrote two scripts for films adapted from novels by other writers and saw three of his own novels adapted into films that he would subsequently refer to in shades of despair. Guthrie's first screenplay, for the 1953 classic *Shane,* brought him an Academy Award nomination. In this essay, I strive to present this decade-long aspect of Guthrie's writing career by frequently invoking not only his words, but those of other principal players—agents mainly—who worked closely with him.

The Big Sky (1952)

Guthrie's Hollywood career began virtually at the same time as his career as a major novelist in the late 1940s with *The Big Sky.* What appealed to him most about Hollywood and the movies was the enormous amount of money it had to shower on its favored authors. What he liked least was the lack of control over what Hollywood ultimately did to his cherished literary properties. Guthrie was also painfully surprised at what he did to his own works in order to see them on the big screen. As far as the money was concerned, its impact on the journalist-cum-novelist can be appreciated with this comparison. The prodding that Guthrie needed to complete *The Big Sky* as a novel occurred in 1944 when publisher William Sloane gave Guthrie an advance of $5,000. Contrast that with the $30,000 for the screen rights Guthrie received from noted director-producer Howard Hawks three years after the publication of *The Big Sky*. To Guthrie, as well as to other writers on the Hollywood payroll, this was a writer's financial heaven. A tidy nest egg could be had without writing an additional page of prose; better still, movie companies paid thousands just for an option on a literary property—that is, for the privilege of keeping the prized work from any other producer for a specified period of time. Little wonder that since the late 1920s so many journalists and novelists had rushed to the West Coast in search of such California gold.[2]

It is clear that, even before Guthrie had completed the manuscript initially called "Boone Caudill," "Mountain Man," and "Hunter's Moon" (and what finally would be known as *The Big Sky*), he and his first New York literary agent Maxwell Aley were discussing the aspects of a possible sale of the novel to the movies. With barely nine chapters completed by November 1945, Aley wrote to Guthrie that "I want to work on the motion picture side."[3] Five years of effort trying to sell *The Big Sky* proved futile. Contracts were almost drawn up with Twentieth Century–Fox, Paramount, and independent producers Walter Wanger (producer of the classic western *Stagecoach*) and Mark Hellinger, but high production costs and diminishing audiences for movies in the late 1940s thwarted a sale.

Matters became complicated after the publication of Guthrie's *The Way West* in 1949 because of concerns by his agents about Guthrie's second book eclipsing the possibility of a movie sale of *The Big Sky*. This was a strange circumstance indeed where an author's work canceled out the marketability of his own previous work. In the fall of 1948, Aley explained to Guthrie that the active pursuit of the Hollywood sale was halted because "if *The Big Sky* screenplay was sold and was in production at the time the new novel comes out next fall, it would kill the chances of a sale of the new novel for at least three years."[4] More than a year later, Aley was concerned about *The Way West* eclipsing *The Big Sky*: "We have got to protect the independent property status of *The Big Sky* in any sale of *The Way West*."[5] Money matters further plagued studios at the end of the 1940s due to the end of an anti-trust suit lodged by the government against the "Big Eight" motion picture studios. The resulting break-up of the studios from ownership of theater chains resulted in a sharp decline in the number of features produced and a trend towards greater economy by the studios.[6]

By 1950, producer-director Howard Hawks was known for a number of popular films that included *His Girl Friday, Sergeant York,* and *The Big Sleep.* His most recent film was the enormously successful Western *Red River,* starring John Wayne and Montgomery Clift, released a year after the publication of *The Big Sky* and a little over one year before *The Way West* appeared in bookstores. Hawks was attracted to Guthrie's self-described device of "internal monologue" in *The Big Sky*. The purchase of the novel by Hawks in March 1950 for his Winchester Pictures production company for release by RKO Radio Pictures was a welcome relief to Guthrie and his agents although it was, by this time, well deserved. Wrote a pleased Aley to Guthrie: "I felt very confident that the deal would go through from the first, but we have had so many disappointments on this book that I didn't want to overstress that with you."[7]

Veteran screenwriter and Hawks collaborator Dudley Nichols prepared a screenplay of Guthrie's novel.[8] The sale of rights to *The Big Sky* was a clean one: Guthrie was given no script approval rights and was not involved in the story conferences, although he was consulted from time to time by Hawks and his associate producer and financial backer Edward Lasker. Hawks and Nichols took Guthrie's admittedly episodic, long tale that focused on Boone Caudill's tortured journey from Kentucky to the mountains and streams of Montana and turned it into a competition between Jim Deakins and Boone Caudill for the charms of an older, more sexually attractive Teal Eye than Guthrie's. Teal Eye was not the twelve- to fourteen-year-old girl of Guthrie's novel, but a statuesque six-foot-tall part-Cherokee model, Elizabeth Threatt, whom Hawks had recruited from the Powers model agency in New York City. This alluring quality of the movie's Teal Eye was what upset Guthrie the most about the film as she appeared more steel-eyed than teal-eyed when any man looked her way in a languorous manner.[9]

In the film, Guthrie's engaging internal monologue, originally rendered by Dick Summers in the novel, was transferred to the novel's otherwise minor character, Zeb Calloway. Calloway was Boone's uncle in the novel, and it is he who narrates the film.[10]

One critic observed that perhaps Hawks was trying to enlarge on the competitiveness between Deakins and Caudill much as he had earlier portrayed the struggles between John Wayne and Montgomery Clift in *Red River*.[11] Only the first third of Guthrie's novel was used for the film version, and Hawks ends *The Big Sky* with Teal Eye's tribal marriage to Boone. Deakins leaves the Blackfeet village and, with keel-boat captain Jourdonnais, continues down the Missouri River to St. Louis.

In casting *The Big Sky*, Hawks had high hopes for getting Gary Cooper and Arthur Kennedy for the two lead roles, but as time went on, his list narrowed. Robert Mitchum, Charlton Heston, John Wayne, and Montgomery Clift were also considerations. Earlier, producer Mark Hellinger, while in the hospital (he passed away four months later), moved closer to purchasing the novel to release through Warner Brothers.[12] He pushed for *The Big Sky* as a Humphrey Bogart film. Ned Brown, Guthrie's Hollywood agent working in concert with Guthrie's New York agent, reported that "Mark seemed absolutely wild about the book and thinks it is one of the best he has ever read. He knows *The Big Sky* country well, having made a picture for Warners up in that part of the world. Mark told me that he also spoke to Humphrey Bogart about the book and Bogart is just as enthusiastic about it too." Aley then mused to Guthrie, "I kidded Ned about Bacall for Teal Eye and he kidded back. Naturally, neither one of us is serious. I don't think even Bogart would insist on her presence in the film."[13]

For a time Marlon Brando was seriously considered for Boone Caudill and negotiations began, but the successful star of the recently released *Streetcar Named Desire* demanded too much money. For the part of Jim Deakins, Hawks engaged Kirk Douglas, a relative newcomer to films. Douglas was eager for the part as he was looking for roles other than the young toughs and gangsters he had essayed up to that time. Ironically, Douglas's asking price of $125,000 was the same demanded by Brando. Hawks's own talent discovery, Dewey Martin (fresh from a major role in Hawks's previous release, the science fiction thriller *The Thing From Another World*), got the role of Boone Caudill. A copy of *The Big Sky* had been sent to young actor Montgomery Clift (John Wayne's co-star in Hawks's *Red River*) by Lasker, but apparently Clift did not respond positively or was perhaps otherwise committed and was, therefore, not in the running for the role of Boone Caudill.

The Zeb Calloway character, played by veteran character actor Arthur Hunnicut, stole the show. His philosophical musings, wit, and voice inflections kept the film moving. Under Hawks' direction, he was much like Walter Brennan in *Red River* and other Hawks films as a cross between a country bumpkin and, at the same time, a more steadying influence for the oftentimes conflicted protagonists.[14]

The Big Sky was a box office hit shortly after its August 1952 release, and in September it was the number-two grossing film in the country. But, perhaps because of the strong competition from *High Noon,* also in release, it lost its "legs," as the insiders put it, and failed to return its high $2.5 million production cost.[15] In a lengthy and unusual cover-story in *Saturday Review,* critic Hollis Alpert praised *The Big Sky* for its use of the majestic Wyoming location on the Snake River against the backdrop of the Grand Tetons. Admitting that the film had action and Indians, as did so many other cliched Westerns, Alpert wrote that Hawks's film was "something a good deal more than a Western. It explores a real tradition, and thus becomes almost the first true Hollywood attempt to equate with some honesty, the events with the geography. . . . What is so heartening about *The Big Sky* is that it pits its people against nature herself, and in the doing helps re-create an aspect of our frontier, our folklore, and our history." Alpert then stepped out of his role as film critic to praise Guthrie's novel, even though Guthrie himself was not involved with the film. "It takes boldness to get out of any particular Hollywood groove," Alpert concluded, "and it has also taken the talents of Mr. Guthrie and the immense popularity of his novel to show the true way West."[16]

Guthrie, in spite of the praise by critics for the film's realism and the absence of showdown-type gunplay, was adamant in his dislike for a scene purporting to be a novel game delivery system in the old West. Caudill and Deakins strap a slain deer on a small aspen tree, pull the top back, and on signal give it a quick-release, sending the deer skyward on a trajectory that lands fresh venison right in front of the *Mandan* going upstream. Years later, Guthrie still cringed at Hollywood's attempts to add engineering feats to his wily frontier characters. "I think the film is a turkey," he told an interviewer in 1984.[17]

The film's original length was a protracted two hours and eighteen minutes. After the first two months of its initial release, because of lagging box office receipts and the desire to squeeze in an extra daily showing, the film's distributor, RKO, edited out some sixteen minutes from five scenes.[18] In the late 1980s, the deleted portions were discovered (although from a poor quality sixteen milimeter print) and restored to the release footage. Unfortunately, as of 2001, this version was not available on video, but has been exclusively broadcast from time to time only on the American Movie Classics and Turner Classic Movies cable television channels.

One of those restored moments is in the final scene of the film where, at night around the campfire, Jim Deakins discusses with Zeb Calloway the sudden abandonment of Teal Eye, whom Boone has just married. Zeb tells the story of a white man he had known who married a Blackfeet, but still "had a hankerin' for white men's ways" and left her for a short visit to St. Louis. When he returned, Zeb recounted, it was too late. The man's wife had already committed suicide. In the uncut print, this scene is an appropriate setup for Boone's decision to return to Teal Eye. Also cut from this scene was Zeb's conversation with Jourdonnais about what he will do with his money from the sale of the fur pelts. Jourdonnais says that he wants to live in the city, to be respected, and to "stay in the house." Zeb underscores this seemingly incongruous desire in the hearts of those who are perceived as children of the wilderness and unfit for "civilized" life: "Most of them [mountain men] are thinkin' about going home. Man gets away and then gets all het-up to go back again." The scenes embody a tone that rings of Guthrie's mountain men.

For all the criticism leveled against *The Big Sky* because of its literary license with Guthrie's novel, three aspects stand out in its favor. Its leisurely pace, its superb use of locations, and its use of a seldom-dramatized time period of America's past, convey what Hollis Alpert observed as a different depiction of the West than viewers were accustomed up to that time. But, as Hawks's biographer observes, the major problems lay in the casting of the picture (with the exception of Zeb Calloway).[19]

Shane (1953)

Whatever Guthrie said privately about *The Big Sky*, he chose not to criticize it too much publicly, a wise decision, as Guthrie later learned, as Howard Hawks himself recommended Guthrie to producer-director George Stevens. This recommendation eventually led to Guthrie's first experience as a screen writer for *Shane*.[20] His screenplay credit on the screen for *Shane* would lock Guthrie into a kind of fame—and money—previously unknown to him as a writer. That fame would bring to him all of the rewards, as well as all of the frustrations, that come with screenwriting.

Guthrie's connection with *Shane* began in January 1951, even before *The Big Sky* was in production. Guthrie's other Hollywood agent, Ray Stark, called him to report that George Stevens wanted Guthrie to write a screenplay from the popular Jack Schaefer novel. As reported by Guthrie's new literary agent, Carl Brandt, to Stark,

Guthrie "is not interested in a B production. Delighted to discuss with Stevens but must have George's slant before agreeing."[21] Guthrie wrote earlier to Joe De Yong, a fellow resident of Choteau who had become a successful consultant to Hollywood studios on authentic western lore and costumes, and confided his reservations in journeying to Hollywood. "I really have no desire to go to Hollywood, except to see old friends like you," Guthrie wrote a few weeks after the sale of *The Big Sky*. "I think I know where I belong, and it definitely isn't Hollywood."[22] A few days later Guthrie flew down to Hollywood and visited with the large, imposing producer and director of such diverse but quality films as *Gunga Din* and *A Place in the Sun.* The meeting went well. Guthrie was impressed that Stevens, in what went against the Hollywood stereotype, would ask him about ideas for the screenplay. Guaranteed a salary of $1,500 per week, Guthrie agreed to tackle the screenplay "with misgivings," as he would often say later. The Nieman Fellowship at Harvard University and his session at the Bread Loaf Writer's Conference in Vermont had assisted Guthrie in refining his skill as a novelist, but there was nothing but on-the-job experience to guide him in the complicated technique of screenwriting. Initially, he felt guilty for accepting such a high salary to read scripts for an entire week before doing any writing. He soon learned how much work was involved in fleshing out Schaefer's sparse novel to feature-film length.

One idea Guthrie presented to Stevens not in the Schaefer novel was written into the film. "I had always wondered at the absence of grief in western pictures," remembered Guthrie. "Here would be bodies strewn all around, but where were the funerals and where were the mourners?"[23] The funeral of Torrey was the setting for Guthrie's scene of extended mourning. Torrey was the hot-headed farmer who was killed by Wilson, the gunfighter hired by Ryker to drive out the "sod busters." Played out on the big screen, the funeral combined irony with sadness as it was intercut with shots of children playing with one another, seemingly oblivious to the solemn nature of the occasion. Guthrie later recounted that Stevens "seized on the suggestion" for this scene.

Guthrie's innate sense of authenticity, ingrained by his years of research on both *The Big Sky* and *The Way West*, prompted another suggestion to the veteran producer. Wrote Guthrie: ". . . [T]here was no complete right or complete wrong taken by open-range ranchers and homesteaders. Each side had its case."[24] Debating issues in film, especially in a Western, rarely plays well, and yet in *Shane*, the confrontation between cattle baron Ryker and farmer Joe Starrett, as scripted by Guthrie, is dramatic and relevant. It greatly expanded the nature of the issues involved in the traditional cattleman vs. farmer conflict. For the purposes of keeping this scene visually interesting, Stevens cuts alternately between Ryker, Starrett (Van Heflin), Shane (Alan Ladd), and Wilson (Jack Palance). However, Guthrie's carefully written dialogue remains intact.

About this scene, Guthrie later reminisced: "[T]here's a point for arguing that either way. What cattleman had the right to claim all the grass which was public land in the first place, the grass and the waterholes? It wasn't right, but I can't say it was an improvement to have all the homesteaders move in. You see that was why I tried to present a balanced view between the rancher and the homesteader, both of them speaking their piece."[25]

Shane has since become a landmark film and an item of American cultural mythology that has parlayed its central character as a Christ figure.[26] The film received five Academy Award nominations, including one for Guthrie's screenplay. President Eisenhower selected it as the best film to represent the Old West in America for viewing by visiting Russian premier Nikita

Khrushchev in 1959. In 1981, it was one of five films chosen to screen in China to represent the United States. So powerful was the story that much of it was appropriated by Clint Eastwood for his inferior film *Pale Rider* in 1985.

Ironically, during the summer of 1951, while Guthrie was at the Jackson Hole, Wyoming, location busily attending to rewrites required by Stevens during the shooting of *Shane*, Howard Hawks and *The Big Sky* crew were thirty miles away on the Snake River pushing the crew of the *Mandan* ever northward. While *The Big Sky* was released the following summer, *Shane*, for various studio-imposed reasons, was held back from release until 1953. Returning from Jackson Hole, Guthrie wrote to his agent: "Everything is well with me, though I'll confess I'm pretty tired of script writing even at the generous money Hollywood pays."[27]

The Kentuckian (1955)

Even before the Academy Awards presentation in 1954, Guthrie's name was well known. One of his Hollywood agents who worked with the Brandt Agency was already fielding offers for movie rights to his Pulitzer Prize–winning novel *The Way West*. "Bud could work anywhere in town after receiving the solo screenplay credit on *Shane* and after the success of *The Big Sky*," wrote one agent to Guthrie's agent Ben Benjamin in Hollywood. "When the picture is generally released in a few months, it may bring the price of *The Way West* soaring."[28]

Guthrie was now more in demand, but the prices paid for novels in Hollywood were steadily affected by the anti-trust decision and by the increasing competition from television during the early 1950s. Fewer films were being made, and a growing percentage were being made by a new breed of filmmaker—the independent producer. One of these was former theatrical talent agent Harold

Hecht. Hecht was responsible for not only discovering Burt Lancaster on stage, but also for making him a production partner in motion pictures.[29] Guthrie appreciated Hecht's decisiveness and the manifest talents of the third partner in the mix, writer James Hill. Hecht-Lancaster engaged Guthrie to write the screenplay for Lancaster's first and largely unsuccessful directoral effort, *The Kentuckian.* Taken from the novel, *The Gabriel Horn* by Felix Holt,[30] the story probably appealed to Guthrie, who had spent twenty-one years as a journalist at the *Lexington Leader,* years that instilled in him an appreciation for the state of Kentucky and its formative history.[31] The script he wrote was set in the Appalachian Mountains in the 1820s and concerned a young boy and his father (Lancaster) involved in a family feud, and their desire to break free and to settle in Texas. Guthrie's literate script so impressed Hecht that during the writing of *The Kentuckian* in the spring of 1953, Hecht purchased film rights to *The Way West* for an impressive $50,000. *The Kentuckian,* however, did not fare well with audiences or critics who rightfully singled out Lancaster's inability to keep the story moving.

Novels or Movies?

At the close of 1953, Guthrie was richer than he had ever been, but was also subject to increasing commitments for story conferences that involved time-intensive trips to Hollywood from Lexington, Kentucky, and then from Great Falls, Montana, and later from his boyhood hometown of Choteau, Montana. The converging and often competing tasks of starting a new novel (*These Thousand Hills),* writing magazine articles, completing more than nine months of detailed negotiations with Hecht on film rights to *The Way West,* and trying to meet Hecht's demands to show up for lengthy story conferences in Hollywood often put Guthrie at the proverbial fork in the road: "Do I write novels or screenplays?" Apparently the answer was "yes."

Work on the novel that became *These Thousand Hills* began shortly after Guthrie's return from the Jackson Hole locations for *Shane* in the summer of 1951. The publication of the novel would not occur until the fall of 1956, just over five years after the publication of *The Way West*. During those years, Guthrie was festooned with offers from many studios and producers. For example, while in Hollywood working on *The Kentuckian*, Guthrie was approached by Paramount to script an epic remake of their earlier silent film success, *The Covered Wagon*. Parrying their advances, Guthrie stood adamant. Movie offers were taking him away from his novel. Nevertheless, agent Ben Benjamin wrote to Guthrie that Paramount "had expressed deep regret they hadn't purchased *The Way West* to use as a basis for *The Covered Wagon*." Furthermore, wrote an anxious Benjamin, Paramount wants to "see if you would reconsider and come back for consultations on *The Covered Wagon*, and I imagine we could get almost any price we wanted."[32]

Other studios approached Guthrie to doctor Western movie scripts they already had. Paramount was keen to have Guthrie script their upcoming film on Lewis and Clark, a project about which they had also approached historian Bernard DeVoto. As it turned out, Hecht himself committed to Guthrie for his own Lewis and Clark film. Warner Brothers was also reportedly working on its version of the epic trans-Mississippi trek which they planned to release in the widescreen phenomenon of Cinerama. After all of the Hollywood dust settled, only one film from Paramount emerged from the fray. *The Far Horizons* was released by Paramount in 1955. Even though it was photographed in Paramount's new widescreen VistaVision process on picturesque locations, the film was not only dull, but horribly miscast. Donna Reed, in dark makeup, played Sacajawea, unconvincingly vying for the hearts of Charlton Heston and Fred MacMurray in the lead roles.[33]

Meanwhile, Guthrie continually pushed back deadlines imposed by his aggressive New York agent Carl Brandt for delivery of *These Thousand Hills* to publisher Houghton Mifflin. As Hollywood kept offering Guthrie more and more money for numerous projects and Hecht himself was proving something of a nuisance with repeated demands for story conferences, Brandt in 1954 wrote a trenchant letter to agent Ben Benjamin in response to Benjamin's report of the latest Hollywood offer to Guthrie. "I might as well let you know what we think," wrote Brandt. "Bud is one of our really creative and popular novelists, and to keep him off the market in the book world is to do all of us an injustice. Or, at least, it isn't foresighted. Unless he continues his position as a novelist, you won't be able to get the prices on the movies that you do get. Not unless he gives up everything and becomes a screen writer. But, as I say, he'll have to make his decision."[34]

Guthrie himself was likely feeling squeezed as Hecht pressured him to go beyond advising the company about the script for *The Way West* and write it himself. Guthrie had initially refused, and Hecht sought his advice soon after he purchased the property. Dudley Nichols was an early contender even though, as Hecht wrote to Guthrie, "I know that Dudley Nichols did *The Big Sky* and I am quite sure you were disappointed in it. I know that I was. I thought it a mighty poor picture, however, I don't believe it was necessarily Nichols' fault."[35] Hecht laid most of the blame on Hawks as being an "autocratic director." Guthrie was overwhelmed by the very success he had sought. In January 1955, Guthrie wrote, "[A]s I keep on writing [the novel] I get more and more critical of myself with the consequence, it seems to be sometimes, that I have to scrutinize and pinch and heft each word like a woman at a vegetable rack looking for the best head of lettuce. If Hollywood would just let me alone, I ought to be on top of the thing [the novel] by spring, though I'm chary of promises, having failed one. But there are still four weeks on *The Way West* that I have to give under contract."[36]

However, a case can be made that in fact these very film assignments—often criticized for keeping him away from his work on the novel—actually served to get him past writer's block and creative dry spells. In early 1953, Guthrie was still weighing the possibility of writing *The Kentuckian* for Hecht's company. As Guthrie wrote back to his agent, money was not the only consideration: "I would reject almost any offer immediately except that the money is a consideration at this time and that the novel is going so badly that I'm trying to tell myself I need to get away from it for a while."[37]

Unfortunately, much of Guthrie's decision at the "fork" was made for him. He continued to juggle the demands of the novel with his commitments to Hollywood. Curiously enough during this time, Guthrie himself pitched movie ideas. A story in *Publisher's Weekly* in 1955 about Guthrie's partnership with actor George Montgomery on a film brought letters from Guthrie's publisher, Houghton Mifflin, to the Brandt agency, claiming that *These Thousand Hills* still had not been finished. Only explanatory letters from Guthrie himself could calm the palpitations of publisher and agent. In his letters, Guthrie admitted that, while he had met with Montgomery about a movie deal, the article had been wildly inaccurate on other details.[38]

One film idea that has not been completely documented was what Guthrie referred to simply as an "idea for Gary Cooper," which he had sent on to the famous actor who had earlier taken out an option to make a movie based on *The Way West*.[39] Another was a film on Charles Russell, which for a time was met with interest by a few studios. Guthrie even positioned himself as an author-turned-arbitrager between studios. During the fall of 1953, while completing work on *The Kentuckian,* Guthrie met with producers at Fox on other film subjects. Guthrie, the negotiator, wrote agent Brandt about his machinations regarding the Charles Russell film: "I will almost bet you, though, that if Hecht finds I'm flirting with Fox, he'll come along with a better offer."[40]

These Thousand Hills (1959)

Guthrie's film associates, ironically enough, actually helped move along the sluggish pace of *These Thousand Hills.* After carefully reading a draft sent to him in late summer 1955, Jim Hill of Hecht-Hill-Lancaster wrote frankly to Guthrie that "there is so much lacking in character development and motivation." This caused Guthrie to rewrite the entire book. He admitted to actor-friend George Montgomery months later that "Harold Hecht and the rest were right in rejecting my manuscript. . . . The structure worked, [but] it was the language, the feeling around for what to say and where to go that operated against the story."[41]

To the great relief of Houghton Mifflin and Guthrie's agent, by the summer of 1956, completion of *These Thousand Hills* was in sight. Then it was as if the Hollywood flies scented bait. In late July, Arthur Kramer, a producer at Twentieth Century–Fox, flew to Guthrie at his home in Great Falls to present an offer and hopefully close the deal. "I shall try to excite him more, without, of course, committing myself at all," wrote Guthrie to his agent in anticipation of Kramer's visit.[42] Up to then, typescript copies of the manuscript, even prior to the printing of galleys, circulated to every major studio in Hollywood and to their representatives on the East Coast. Copies were carefully monitored by the Brandt agency. Later while Guthrie was reviewing galleys, David O.

Selznick, George Stevens, Sam Goldwyn, Jr., and others, including Hecht himself, were reviewing the possibilities of a film deal. Henry Ginsberg, who produced *Giant* that year for George Stevens, was considering *These Thousand Hills* for Rock Hudson.

Kramer sufficiently impressed Guthrie that Fox was the studio to bring *These Thousand Hills* to life—for $100,000. The sale for that amount of money was a major victory for Guthrie in one sense—financial—and a major, and painful, realization for him in another. This represented the most money his work had received for film rights. Things improved significantly when Fox asked him to write the screenplay. Guthrie hesitated and then, during December, with the promise of an additional $75,000 for a completed screenplay, accepted the assignment. Under the terms of the agreement, Guthrie would receive an initial $15,000 for a seventy-five-page treatment. If Fox approved the treatment, then Guthrie would proceed with the screenplay and on its completion receive a final payment of $60,000.

The disappointing result of Guthrie's attempt at writing the screenplay was foreshadowed by Carol Brandt in a memo to the Brandt agency's Hollywood representative Ben Benjamin about the deal: "I think that's going to be a very tough screenplay. The fact that you did miracles about that deal doesn't make it any the easier script to do. I myself hope that he undertakes another project or else gets all the money you've asked for. He will work for it."[43] And work for it he did. In the first half of 1957, Guthrie did produce a treatment, and then a screenplay. However, the first script at 176 pages was much too long. By August, it was down to 159 pages, still long, but at a more manageable length. The writing was good, but the comments from producer David Weisbart were guardedly complimentary to the Pulitzer Prize–winning author: "I have genuine respect for the script," Ben Benjamin quoted

Weisbart to Guthrie in September of that year, "and said that it was certainly close to being right."[44]

Clearly, the material about cattleman Lat Evans and his single-minded quest for wealth and social respectability was true to the spirit of the 1880s West. It was just not yet cinematic. Guthrie's foreword to the script resonates with the kind of dedication he put into the novel: "Its materials have been gathered from reminders of the early West that lingered during my boyhood, from long and rich acquaintance with many an old-timer, from the study of authentic cowpuncher chronicles as those of Con Price, Teddy Blue Abbott, and Charles M. Russell, to name but a few. It does not subscribe to that myth of the West which has every man a gunslinger and every ride a chase. Nor does it see the right as forever clear-cut and forever triumphant. The true West held—and holds—abundant drama, abundant interest, abundant actual material without falsifications particular or general. . . . I should be delighted were some vanished old-timer disposed to report; This is the way it was."[45] What a treat it would have been to have seen the movie described by Guthrie's foreword!

The filming of Guthrie's screenplay was not to be. After further attempts to, as producer Weisbart put it, "get it right," Guthrie called a halt to the process. He later wrote of the realization that had sabotaged his efforts throughout the screenwriting process: "I am in the position of having helped mutilate my own child," wrote Guthrie to Kramer after studio contract writer Alfred Hayes had taken over the script duties. "You see, I wrote the book in the hope of bringing something fresh and honest to the western story." And then he shocked the man who had campaigned successfully for his studio's purchase of the novel, "Just strike my name from the screen-play credits, if that is within my choice."[46] His request was honored. *These Thousand Hills*—initially an A-budgeted film—became a glossy-looking B production although filmed on location near Durango, Colorado, in CinemaScope and color. It was even burdened with a main title song performed intrusively on the soundtrack by teen crooner Randy Sparks.

Don Murray, who was a rising star at Fox and who had appeared in *Bus Stop* opposite Marilyn Monroe, starred as Lat Evans, the cowpuncher who deserted his old friends in search of money and position. The saloon girl Callie, from whom Evans borrowed the seed money for his first ranch and whom he abandoned when he campaigned for senator, was played by Lee Remick in this her second Hollywood film. Nevertheless, the film's theme of materialism at the expense of personal relationships was thoughtful and important in a materialist-prone America of the late 1950s. However, the release of *These Thousand Hills* in early 1959, in spite of generally favorable reviews, generated only average box office returns. For Guthrie, however, its debut in theaters was a "time for confession and penitence," as he wrote to David Weisbart. The film "astonished me agreeably," he wrote. "Though I went to it prepared to be disappointed, I came away pleased. I count it a superior western. . . . The picture is awfully tight. With a little more leeway I think it would have emerged as one of the very best of pictures of its kind, past and present, though I still wonder why some of the changes were made. But I am not kicking. I'm confessing to a mistaken prejudgement."[47]

Since its initial release, the film has been rarely broadcast and has never been released on home video, but continues to enjoy a favorable critical reputation.[48] However, writing in 1965, Guthrie's backward glance at those months on the film was colored by the challenge his own material presented, which led him to conclude: "I tried to shrink my book to the dimensions of a play. Though, after it had been doctored to order by a studio writer under long-term contract, the film version lost the values I struggled for in my novel. I'm still firm in the belief that a novelist ought to leave his novel alone. Other writers without blood ties can do it better."[49]

The Way West (1967)

The Way West was Guthrie's second novel and the one for which he received the Pulitzer Prize. When the prize was announced in May 1950, Maxwell Aley, Guthrie's agent at the time, noted that Guthrie should have received it for *The Big Sky*, then remarked that "It [the Pulitzer Prize] ought, of course, to produce an immediate motion picture sale."[50] *The Way West* was the last of his novels to be brought to the big screen even though, as previously noted, it had been purchased in 1953. Harold Hecht had repeatedly held off until an acceptable script could be written. Censorship problems with the story and finding suitable writers seemed to conspire with Hecht's changing business fortunes to delay production until 1967. Story problems centered around the character of young Mercy McBee, who is raped by the lecherous old mountain man. The script writing was variously in the hands of no less than seven writers including Clifford Odets and James R. Webb.[51] Burt Lancaster announced to the press in 1957 that he would star with James Stewart and—hopefully—with Gary Cooper, but the announcement was all that materialized from such plans. As 1959 came to a close, *The Way West* still had not been put into production. Hecht-Hill-Lancaster Productions, as it was known then, announced in June that the company would produce two final films to complete their distribution agreement with United Artists and then close down. Burt Lancaster, it was announced, would star in both films. But the company folded in February 1960 with $2.5 million worth of unproduced properties, including *The Way West*.

Hecht continued as an independent producer and in 1965 negotiated to get Charlton Heston in the lead role of wagon master Senator William J. Tadlock. On the strength of Heston's interest, Richard Widmark was signed on for the part of Lije Evans. When director Andrew McLaglen was brought to the project, Heston pulled out. Robert Mitchum and Kirk Douglas were added to fill out the lead roles of Dick Summers and Senator Tadlock.[52] *The Way West* was not a popular film when it was released to theaters in 1967. Years later Kirk Douglas simply referred to the film as "the less said the better." One standard reference book on motion pictures refers to *The Way West* as "an extraordinarily predictable and uninviting western . . . based on a Pulitzer Prize–winning novel (though you'd never know it). . . ."[53] For his part, director McLaglen claims that the head of production at United Artists demanded that the first twenty-two minutes be cut from the film prior to its theatrical release. McLaglen and Hecht were forced to discard the all-important expository footage introducing each of the characters in Missouri and whose interactions on the Oregon Trail comprised the balance of the film. "I have nightmares about what happened to that film," the director reminisced in 1998. "All of the character motivation and background was gone from the film."[54] One note of distinction, however, is that the part of Mercy McBee served as the screen debut of Sally Field. When *The Way West* finally reached the screen it was no doubt to Guthrie a sad conclusion to fourteen years of work on a motion picture that should have towered in quality above the others—inasmuch as it was indeed based on his Pulitzer Prize–winning novel.

Guthrie did entertain some film projects during the 1960s. For Columbia Pictures, he wrote a treatment based on David Lavender's book *Bent's Fort* that was never produced. Tom Gries, who directed *Will Penny,* kept up extensive correspondence with

Guthrie who prepared a screen treatment, ultimately unfilmed, for a half-hour television program called *Sun Prairie* as part of ABC's short-lived '66 series. He also advised Gries on *Will Penny.*

This Rebel Breed (1960)

One of the more unusual efforts with which Guthrie became affiliated was a film about racial strife that went under a variety of titles but was ultimately released by Warner Brothers in early 1960 as *This Rebel Breed.* Strictly speaking, this was not a "Guthrie film," inasmuch as the script was written by Guthrie's friend Morris Lee Green. However, he did permit his name to be associated with the project, and on release prints of the film, Guthrie was credited as "story editor and consultant." The film was about a "half-negro, half-Mexican" policeman who, with his white cop counterpart, broke a dope ring in a local high school. Hollywood trade papers, read mostly by those in the industry including theater owners, were split on the film's effectiveness. *The Hollywood Reporter* listed the "problems of narcotics, murder, illegitimacy and right down the line to disinterested parents, wild parties and misunderstood offspring" as "top fodder for ad-exploitation and youthful (but not too young) word-of-mouth." *Variety* panned the film, objecting to its "repeated use of crude racial terms or explicit scenes of inter-racial cruelty and violence." In a press release, Guthrie described the film as being about "hatred and brutalities that differences of color engender when reason remains undiscovered. We could have used Orientals in it, or Jews, or Puerto Ricans, and been just as true to our theme. It happened that, handier, were Mexicans and Negroes and whites, and they served. The cancer of racial antagonism grows in the whole body of man." In a most unusual revelation—especially in a press release—Guthrie admitted that his agent tried to dissuade him from his association with the film. "I appreciate his concern for me, but reject his attitude. It's good to do as you darn please sometimes."[55] The last sentiment was vintage Guthrie.

This Rebel Breed, completed and previewed in September 1959, was not in theatrical distribution until the spring of 1960. Guthrie was a prominent part of the Philadelphia premiere on March 4. Guthrie spoke on racial discrimination to packed classrooms of students at nearby Temple University. Producer William Rowland and the film's star Mark Damon were also in attendance. However, when *This Rebel Breed* went into general distribution, it went virtually unnoticed as indicated by its poor box office take, even after it was quickly—by the end of the month when it hit theaters in San Diego—retitled *Three Shades of Love.* Guthrie, proud as he was with his association with the liberal theme of the film, likely cringed at the film's advertising copy in newspapers: "When the flimsy negligee of the color-line is ripped away . . . these are the things that go on!"[56] The film's interest to movie chroniclers of the 1990s stems from the early performance of two later Hollywood stars, Dyan Cannon and Rita Moreno.

So, in conclusion, what of Guthrie and the movies? As a consumer he enjoyed the movies as a pastime, even though he disliked much of what he saw. His favorites included *Will Penny, Red River,* and *The Gunfighter.* As a writer, a visit to a movie theater with his wife Harriet in the mid-1940s resulted in an epiphany about what had been stalling progress on the writing of *The Big Sky.* They often went to the movies together when Guthrie was "most confused and sorest beset" by the writing process. During a double-bill in Boston, he later wrote, "a curtain lifted for me. I had been hamming. Plain, by-God hamming. . . . I had to show and not tell, a difficult achievement in any case and more difficult in the case of a newspaperman who had spent his life telling. . . .

Hollywood can teach dialogue and pace and the significance of expression and movement. Which is to say that, as theater, it underscores showing." But he complained about the "always present tense" required in screenwriting, about the "bare bone descriptions" of characters, and that films allow no place for Guthrie's favorite device—internal monologue.[57]

Guthrie's Hollywood work alone brought him more than a quarter of a million dollars in fees in less than a decade.[58] "I have no personal quarrel with Hollywood," he wrote in his autobiography. "I met nothing there but consideration, kindliness and generosity and would be false to myself were I fashionably snide. The wonder to me is that, from an industry so beset by difficulties, so many good pictures get made. . . ."[59]

Guthrie's involvement with the movies opened a new era of Guthrie's writing experiences. It stretched his capacity to produce a lean, visually oriented manuscript that was inspected and trimmed by not just one editor, but a team consisting of director, producer, and anyone else brought in by production personnel. Ultimately, the making of movies is by a crowd for a crowd in an often highly pressured environment and within a relatively constricted time frame. It is not a solitary creation for a narrow audience. Guthrie's rewards for his Hollywood work were high in monetary terms, and to a degree, the screenwriting assignments were, particularly with his novel *These Thousand Hills*, therapeutic for his literary output. Did the film work unduly prevent what might have been greater productivity as a novelist and feature magazine writer? The "might-have-beens" are tempting avenues of inquiry. However, retroactive prophecy has nearly always proven to be a loser's game. Rather, it is more fruitful to deal with what occurred and what resulted. Guthrie contributed authenticity in story and dialogue to a profession that too often would "print the legend" where movie Westerns were concerned. Guthrie's persistence for professional integrity as well as in the subjects of which he wrote placed him well beyond the Hollywood hacks grinding out B Westerns and collecting their checks. He was, to borrow from one of his own book titles, the genuine article. As such, his choices amidst adulation—and a swelling bank account from his Hollywood work—ultimately prevented him from an even more lucrative Hollywood career. I think that the mercurial meaning of the Hollywood experience to Guthrie is identical with a judgment he once pronounced on his typewriter. It is, he wrote, "my partner and my enemy."[60]

The author wishes to thank the Creative Projects Committee at Brigham Young University's Harold B. Lee Library for funding that assisted research for this article.

Notes

1. A. B. Guthrie, Jr., *The Blue Hen's Chick: An Autobiography* (New York: McGraw-Hill, 1965; Lincoln: University of Nebraska, 1993), 216–22.

2. Guthrie was one of many writers who worked in Hollywood going as far back as the 1920s. Historian Robert Sklar termed the period from 1929–1932 as the "Hollywood Gold Rush" as writers Ben Hecht, Donald Ogden Stewart, Nathaniel West, William Faulkner, and others were drawn by large salaries to write for the movies. "Beyond the rewards of salary—even mediocre incomes for Hollywood screen writers were higher than almost any other pay scale in writing—movie writers in the 1930s were held in considerable esteem by people in other walks of life. It was widely believed that they had brought the saving grace of literature to the movies, a view fostered by critics and scholars who understood words better than images and imagined that movies would improve if they became more like filmed plays. But writers who took that attitude to heart were in for a rude awakening in Hollywood; the men of letters who cast themselves as saviors discovered that in the power games of Hollywood

their most pressing task was to save themselves." Robert Sklar, *Movie-Made America*, rev. ed. (New York: Vintage Books, 1994), 237. See also Ian Hamilton, *Writers in Hollywood* 1915–1951 (New York: Harper and Row, 1990); and Tom Dardis, *Sometime in the Sun* (New York: Charles Scribners, 1976).

3. Letter, Maxwell Aley to A. B. Guthrie, Jr., 26 November 1945, Box 16, Folder 215, A. B. Guthrie, Jr. Papers, YCAL 60, Beinecke Library, Yale University, New Haven, Connecticut (hereafter referred to as Guthrie Papers—Yale).

4. Memo, Aley to Guthrie, 22 October 1948, Box 16, Folder 216, Guthrie Papers—Yale.

5. Memo, Aley to Guthrie, 8 December 1949, Box 16, Folder 217, Guthrie Papers—Yale.

6. The eight studios were Paramount, Metro-Goldwyn-Mayer, Twentieth Century–Fox, Warner Brothers, RKO, Columbia, Universal, and United Artists. The three minor defendants were Columbia, Universal, and United Artists. *United States v. Paramount, et al.* (1947) was the culmination of anti-trust litigation initiated by the Justice Department in the late 1930s. The two major issues involved the monopoly of the five major studios over production, distribution, and exhibition of the motion pictures they produced. The three minor studios were charged with collusion with the five major studios to restrain trade. Under the terms of the decision, the studios would confine their operations to motion picture production and distribution only. The theater chains owned by the studios, which provided an automatic outlet for a total of up to five hundred feature films per year, were sold. Thereafter, each film made by a studio had to be sold competitively to theaters no longer under their ownership or control. In this new competitive environment, and with increasing competition in a post-war America posed by radio and other forms of recreation, studio output decreased significantly. See Michael Conant, *Anti-trust in the Motion Picture Industry* (Berkeley: University of California Press, 1961).

7. Memo, Aley to Guthrie, 13 March 1950, Box 16, Folder 217, Guthrie Papers—Yale.

8. Dudley Nichols (1895–1960) was a successful journalist who began writing for films at the dawn of the sound era in 1930. He wrote a number of films for director John Ford (*Stagecoach* being the only Western) and only one other film—the hilarious comedy *Bringing Up Baby*—for Howard Hawks besides *The Big Sky*. Other Westerns scripted by Nichols were *Rawhide* (1951), *Return of the Texan* (1952), *The Tin Star* (1957), and *The Hanging Tree* (1959).

9. An amusing report to Hawks of the reaction to the first draft script from the Production Code Administration, ca. 1952, suggests some of the problems posed by aspects of Guthrie's realistic novel for adaptation to the movies: "The first and most important element has to do with the suggestion that one of the

principals, Boone, sleeps with the Indian girl, Tealeye [sic], only to wake up the next morning and find that he has married her—this, to his surprise and chagrin. . . . Some other way will have to be devised to get Boone 'married' to the girl, which does not involve his having pre-marital experience with her." The three-page, single-spaced review covered a number of "objectionable" words, scenes, and descriptions dealing with "brutality" of the script going "entirely overboard on the subject of drinking," and even down to the way Teal Eye buckles her belt. It should not, the critique pointed out, "suggest that she had divested herself of her clothes when she slept with Deakins during the night." J. A. V., "Johnson Committee Report on original script of *THE BIG SKY*," 29 August 1950, typescript carbon, Alfred Bertram Guthrie, Jr. Papers, 86M1, Division of Special Collections and Archives, University of Kentucky Libraries, Lexington, Kentucky (hereafter referred to as Guthrie Papers—Kentucky).

10. An internal studio memo suggested that this combining of characters was done for legal reasons, in order to avoid the use of the name of Dick Summers. Guthrie retained "sequel rights" to the Summers character owing to the publication of *The Way West* during the previous year. "File Note" [n.d.], in RKO Radio Pictures Corporate Archives, Los Angeles, California (now at Turner Entertainment Corporate Office, Atlanta, Georgia, hereafter Turner).

11. Todd McCarthy, *Howard Hawks: The Grey Fox of Hollywood* (New York: Grove Press, 1997), 486–87.

12. Mark Hellinger (1903–1947) spent only a few years as a film producer after being a journalist; he specialized in urban crime dramas. His film *High Sierra* (Warner Brothers, 1941) as associate producer to Hal Wallis at Warner Brothers virtually made Humphrey Bogart a star. Returning from duty as a war correspondent in World War II, he produced some of the finest crime films of the genre including *The Killers* (1946), *Brute Force* (1947), and *The Naked City* (1948). He died of a massive heart attack in January 1947 as he was making plans to purchase *The Big Sky*. It is unlikely that Hellinger would have utilized Montana locations, since his credited films are well known to have been made either in California or in the urban environment of New York City.

13. Memo, Ned Brown to Aley, 18 September 1947, Box 16, Folder 215, Guthrie Papers—Yale; letter, Aley to Guthrie, 1 October 1947, Box 16, Folder 215, Guthrie Papers—Yale.

14. In fact, Walter Brennan was suggested for the Zeb Calloway role. Memo, Edward Lasker to C. J. Devlin [vice president of Production at RKO], 9 March 1951, RKO Radio Pictures Corporate Archives, Los Angeles, California (Turner).

15. McCarthy, *Howard Hawks,* 491–92. This is the most complete account of the production and exhibition of *The Big Sky* available. The production cost was $2,546,336. Box office returns from U.S. theaters totaled $1,650,000.

16. Hollis Alpert, "SR Goes to the Movies," *Saturday Review*, 16 August 1952, 28.

17. In the videotape documentary, *A. B. Guthrie's Vanishing Paradise*, produced, written, and edited by Ronn Bayly and Susan Cohen Regele (n.p.: A Lightbound and Center for Public Vision Production, 1984), 28 min.

18. Joseph McBride, *Hawks on Hawks* (Berkeley: University of California Press, 1992), 30.

19. ". . . [T]he film is genial in the manner of several of the more relaxed Hawks films to come, deeply appealing for the innumerable times the characters help and support one another in unspoken ways, and quite successful in giving the viewer a feeling for the discovery of the land, of pushing known boundaries, physical and emotional. The film also rewards multiple viewings, offering up further riches upon deeper investigation. Truly, the problem lay in the casting; if he had made the same film with, say, Brando and Mitchum in the leads, it could have made all the difference." McCarthy, *Howard Hawks*, 493.

20. Guthrie was "enthusiastic about the artistry and naturalism of Producer-Director Howard Hawks and the photography" went a feature story on Guthrie and the film in the *Louisville* (KY) *Courier-Journal*. "He [Guthrie] also liked Hawks's choice of actors for the main roles." Paul Hughes, "*The Big Sky*," *Louisville Courier-Journal*, 14 September 1952.

21. Telegram, Carl Brandt to Ray Stark, 9 January 1951, Guthrie Papers—Kentucky.

22. Letter, Guthrie to Joe De Yong, 29 June 1950, Box 4, Folder 45, Guthrie Papers—Yale. De Yong served as the period consultant on both *The Big Sky* and *Shane*.

23. Guthrie, *The Blue Hen's Chick*, 217.

24. Ibid.

25. Harvard Heath interview with A. B. Guthrie, Jr., 25 September 1985, page 6 of typescript draft, Special Collections and Manuscripts, Brigham Young University, Provo, Utah.

26. See Michael T. Marsden, "Savior in the Saddle: The Sagebrush Testament," in *Focus on the Western*, by Jack Nachbar, (Englewood Cliffs, NJ: Prentice-Hall, 1974), 93–100; and James C. Work, ed., *Shane: The Critical Edition* (Lincoln: University of Nebraska Press, 1984), which contains the full text of Schaefer's novel with analyses dealing with the novel, the motion picture, and Schaefer.

27. Letter, Brandt to Stark, 6 August 1951, Guthrie Papers—Kentucky, quoting Guthrie's letter to Brandt.

28. Letter, Stark to Brandt, 11 March 1952, Guthrie Papers—Kentucky. Actually,

Guthrie did not receive sole credit. Because of revisions necessary in some scenes, and the periodic unavailability of Guthrie, Jack Sher contributed what the credits identify as "additional dialogue." Nevertheless, the structure of the film, as well as the majority of the script, is of Guthrie's authorship.

29. New stage actor Burt Lancaster was Harold Hecht's (1907–1986) first client when they formed Norma-Hecht Productions in 1947 (Norma was the first name of Lancaster's wife at the time). Most of the films they produced together starred the athletic Lancaster. They included *Apache, Vera Cruz,* and the Oscar-winning *Marty* (1955), starring Ernest Borgnine. In 1957, the company was renamed Hecht-Hill-Lancaster with the addition of author Jim Hill, and a string of hits followed: *Separate Tables, Run Silent Run Deep, The Unforgiven,* and their final film as a partnership, *The Birdman of Alcatraz* in 1962.

30. Felix Holt, *The Gabriel's Horn* (New York: E. P. Dutton, 1951).

31. In *The Blue Hen's Chick*, Guthrie wrote of his affection for Kentucky: "I came to feel as much at home in Kentucky as in Montana. They were in a sense opposing worlds, both known and both loved" (74–75).

32. Letter, Ben Benjamin to Guthrie, 22 December 1953, Guthrie Papers—Kentucky.

33. *The Far Horizons* was based on Della Gould Emmon's novel *Sacajawea of the Shoshones.* One critic wrote that "Adventure and historical drama are sacrificed to the cardboard romance between Heston and Donna Reed. . . ." Brian Garfield, *Western Films: A Complete Guide* (New York: Rawson Associates, 1982), 160.

34. Letter, Brandt to Benjamin, 18 August 1954, Guthrie Papers—Kentucky.

35. Letter, Harold Hecht to Guthrie, 10 July 1953, Box 38, Folder 534, Guthrie Papers—Yale.

36. Letter, Guthrie to Bernice Baumgarten, office administrator at the Brandt and Brandt agency, 5 January 1955, Guthrie Papers—Kentucky.

37. Letter, Guthrie to Brandt, 11 April 1953, Guthrie Papers—Kentucky.

38. *Publisher's Weekly*, 12 February 1955, 1073. Guthrie's explanation appears in a series of letters sent to Houghton Mifflin and Ben Benjamin between 24 February and 7 March 1955, Box 38, Folder 532, Guthrie Papers—Yale.

39. Letter, Benjamin to Guthrie, 4 October 1957, Guthrie Papers—Kentucky.

40. Letter, Guthrie to Brandt, 26 September 1953, Guthrie Papers—Kentucky.

41. Letter, Jim Hill to Guthrie, 26 September 1955, Guthrie Papers—Yale; letter, Guthrie to George Montgomery, 24 January 1956, Box 6, Folder 95, Guthrie Papers—Yale.

42. Letter, Guthrie to Bernice Baumgarten, 15 July 1956, Guthrie Papers—Kentucky.

43. Letter, Carol Brandt to Benjamin, 3 January 1957, Guthrie Papers—Kentucky.

44. Letter, Benjamin to Guthrie, 16 September 1957, Guthrie Papers—Kentucky.

45. Script, *These Thousand Hills*, first draft screenplay by Guthrie, 14 August 1957, 159 pages mimeographed, Guthrie Papers—Kentucky.

46. Letter, Guthrie to Arthur Kramer, 18 June 1958, Box 37, Folder 530, Guthrie Papers—Yale. Seven years later, Guthrie wrote: "I was too close to my novel, too committed to words and pages and characters and the turns of the story to use a knife, to divide and discard and reassemble and reduce to the size of a short story a full-length book, as moviemakers must do." Guthrie, *The Blue Hen's Chick*, 219.

47. Letter, Guthrie to David Weisbart, [n.d., late January 1959], Box 37, Folder 530, Guthrie Papers—Yale. Guthrie did not identify in this letter just what changes he had in mind.

48. "[Director Richard] Fleischer manages extremely well for the most part to integrate his theme within a good-looking, intelligently scripted, well acted and occasionally quite spectacular framework." Edward Buscombe, ed., *The BFI Companion to the Western*, rev. ed.,(London: Andre Deutsch/BFI Publishing, 1993) 304. See also John H. Lenihan, *Showdown* (Urbana: University of Illinois Press, 1980), 134-35; Jay Robert Nash and Stanley Ralph Ross, eds., *The Motion Picture Guide* (Chicago: Cinebooks, 1987), 8:3349; Phil Hardy, *The Western* (New York: William Morrow, 1983), 270; and Brian Garfield, *Western Films* (New York: Rawson Associates, 1982), 314.

49. Guthrie, *The Blue Hen's Chick*, 220.

50. Letter, Aley to Guthrie, 2 May 1950, Box 16, Folder 217, Guthrie Papers—Yale.

51. Memo, Benjamin to Guthrie, 19 September 1961, Box 38, Folder 533, Guthrie Papers—Yale.

52. Andrew McLaglen (b. 1920), son of actor Victor McLaglen, began working for John Wayne's Batjac Productions in the early 1950s and later directed *Chisum, McLintock!*, and *Cahill United States Marshall* starring Wayne. James Stewart personally requested McLaglen to direct the successful *Shenandoah* (1965), and McLaglen also directed the legendary star in two other Westerns, *The Rare Breed* and *Bandolero.*

53. Nash and Ross, *The Motion Picture Guide*, 9:3752.

54. Andrew McLaglen, telephone interview by author, 12 November 1998.

55. *Hollywood Reporter*, 4 February 1960, 3; *Daily Variety*, 4 February 1960, 3; news release, 9 February 1960, typescript original with Guthrie's annota-

tions, Box 38, Folder 541, Guthrie Papers—Yale.

56. Advertising copy enclosed in letter, William Rowland to Guthrie, 4 March 1961, Box 38, Folder 531, Guthrie Papers—Yale. The author acknowledges the kind help of Helen Guthrie Miller with information on her father's involvement with *This Rebel Breed/Three Shades of Love/Lola's Mistake.*

57. Guthrie, *The Blue Hen's Chick*, 170–71, 221.

58. This approximate figure is derived from documents in the Guthrie Papers at both Yale and Kentucky specifying the purchase price for the film rights to Guthrie's literary properties. Estimates are based on fragmentary information in the papers: *The Big Sky*, $30,000; *The Way West*, $50,000; an option on *The Way West* by Gary Cooper for $5,000; *These Thousand Hills*, $100,000. Fees paid to Guthrie for the writing of screenplays: *Shane*, $20,000 (estimate); *The Kentuckian,* $25,000 (estimate); *These Thousand Hills*, $75,000. In most cases, payments of these fees were spread over from three to five years for tax purposes.

59. Guthrie, *The Blue Hen's Chick*, 222.

60. Ibid., 200.

Scene still from Shane *motion picture, featuring Alan Ladd (as Shane) going for his gun,* 1953
COURTESY OF THE BISON ARCHIVES, HOLLYWOOD, CA

Richard Hutson

Guthrie's *Shane* and American Culture of the Cold War

The translation of Jack Schaefer's 1949 novel *Shane* to a 1953 film narrative raises some extraordinarily interesting issues. A number of scholar/critics have noted some of the important differences between the novel and the film— for instance, scenes added to the film.[1] And, in addition to the provocative issues raised by attention to A. B. Guthrie's reworking of Schaefer's narrative, there is also the issue of the position of George Stevens' *Shane* within the context of the development of the Hollywood genre of the Western during the post–World War II era. The period from 1946 to the early 1960s generated the most sophisticated narratives in the history of the genre of the Western. Thus, the complexities that can be noted in Guthrie's screenplay refer to two different sets of texts, the novel and the Hollywood genre. And I want to claim that these complexities within the film can be interpreted as expressing a number of Cold War themes. But I shall limit myself to thinking about only two features of the film narrative, features that are admittedly somewhat abstract, but which I believe have been carefully thought out in the film narrative and must be, at least in major part, attributed to Guthrie as the screenwriter. The issues I wish to focus upon are nowhere to be found in the novel, although one might argue that, with subtle shifts of emphasis, the film narrative could be construed from the materials of the novel without a great deal of distortion. Yet, such shifts and additions add up to a considerable change in the significance of the Shane story. The screenwriter, in effect, offers a major re-interpretation of Schaefer's novel.

Guthrie construed the narrative movement of the story so that it could take on the aura of a fatalistic narrative, a suggestion that providence is dispensing the action of the narrative above and beyond the actual players and actors. And he changed the nature of the big rancher by inventing a brother. Instead of Schaefer's imperialistic rancher, Fletcher, Guthrie provides us with the imperialistic Ryker brothers.[2] My claim is that these changes are highly significant for a reading of the film narrative.

According to Stephen J. Whitfield, "The movie industry was conscripted into the Cold War in 1947 when HUAC was invited to Los Angeles. The committee's host was the Motion Picture Alliance for the Preservation of American Ideals, an organization that struck a typical postwar stance in asserting that 'co-existence is a myth and neutrality is impossible. . . . anyone who is not FIGHTING Communism is HELPING Communism.'"[3] From this time on, Hollywood was the focus of hyper-patriotic attacks, stemming from a suspicion that the movie industry was infiltrated with highly influential intellectuals and actors/actresses who were ready and willing to attack, or at least ignore, what politicians thought were basic American values. Almost any kind of film could be construed as having tinges of Communism, almost any popular genre, that is, except the Western. Congressmen on the investigating mission of HUAC seem to have believed that no Western, deriving as it did—in this view—from the historical facts of the American frontier experience, could be in danger of being so tinged. The history of the West was the genuine, incorruptible American history, our true tradition. In their imaginations, the genre was set apart, exempt, from suspicion of subversion of American traditions and ideals. In this view, Westerns were thought to be politically neutral. They were just good stories coming down to us from American history. But the film version of *Shane* (released in April 1953) wears the signs of a certain anxiety, either of a superpatriotism or of a defense against superpatriotism by being about as patriotic as could be: mom, apple pie, the Fourth of July, a backdrop of mountains so visually pure as to stand for western frontier landscape in general. If Jack Schaefer's novel was based loosely on the Johnson County war,[4] this famous disturbance of 1892 had been appropriated and purified into elements of class and vocational and ideological warfare, a struggle between bigness and modesty, between a ruthlessly aggressive imperialist of land and the modest agrarian family man who dreamed of the Lockean/Jeffersonian ideology of one's own labor as the source of self-sufficiency. Guthrie, in turn, "re-accentuates" Schaefer's narrative materials, inventing a number of changes and nuances that add up to an ideological re-interpretation.[5]

Dwight Eisenhower, in his 1952 campaign for the presidency, had promoted the analogy between the needs of the Cold War and the history of western settlements and their need for defense: "An analogy can be made, with some validity, between the life we lead today and that led by the American pioneers who made their homes, raised their families, plowed their fields, and lived a full life even under the never-ending threat of attack by hostile Indians."[6] By 1946, and certainly by 1947, American policy makers and intellectuals were convinced "that Soviet behavior was offensive, not defensive, and that the United States had to act decisively if it hoped to avert repetition of the sad spectacle of appeasement of the 1930s."[7] John Ford's cavalry films of the late forties were designed, in part, to remind American audiences of the need for a strong defense against an enemy. Despite the congressional sense of the neutrality of the genre of the popular Western, major conservative, and liberal, thinkers thought that Westerns would be the appropriate popular genre to bring to attention an analogy for Cold War awareness. It is no accident that this era is the heyday of Westerns as a popular and serious genre.

Of course, *My Darling Clementine* had preceded *Shane,* but between the two film successes, Hollywood developed a powerful narrative of seemingly reformed lawmen and gunmen, hanging up their weapons, and then picking them up again. The Westerns of this period, it could be argued, are the purest narratives of Cold War ideology, to such an extent that we could also claim that Cold War ideology derived from our mythology of the frontier, as Eisenhower and others suggested. At the same time that the Turner thesis had become transformed from a historiographical theory for research into the nature and development of the United States into pure American mythology,[8] American popular culture, and Hollywood in particular, was generating highly mythic narratives to bolster the need for Cold War watchfulness, for national expenditure in a massive defense buildup, what Eisenhower would, at the end of his administration, call the "military-industrial complex."

But before we get to *Shane,* I want to go back to what I take to be the actual opening shot in this Cold War Hollywood debate, namely, John Ford's *My Darling Clementine* (November 1946), a remake of an earlier Wyatt Earp narrative called *Frontier Marshall* (1939). In Ford's version of the Earp legend, Wyatt and his brothers are driving a herd of cattle to California where they plan to settle down to become ranchers, having given up their vocation as lawmen of the cattle towns. The Earp dream of domesticity and a normal peaceful life is shattered when a brother is murdered and the herd is stolen. The Earps return to the business of being lawmen. For my purposes, thinking about *Shane* as a film of 1953, what is especially interesting is the chiasmus entailed in the switch from the patriarchal bad guys (the Clantons) and the good brotherly regime of the Earps in Ford's film to the brotherly bad guys and the patriarchal good guys in *Shane.* Although I am not entirely sure what this switch means for American culture at this time, the sense of a struggle between an organization of the brothers and the rule of the fathers always seems to be responding to something deep within the American political unconscious. These outlaw clans, especially strange family clans (brothers or uncles and cousins), appear again and again in the Westerns of the postwar era. Ford himself had used such an idea in his 1939 film *Stagecoach,* with the deadly Plummer brothers, all of whom the Ringo Kid kills in the final shoot-out. And he used a similar idea in *Wagonmaster* (1950), where a male horde led by Uncle Shiloh commandeers and terrorizes a wagon train of Mormon families on their way to a new settlement. One could suggest a history of American ideology from the Depression era to the war years to the postwar era of the Cold War by tracing the narratives of the good outlaw brothers in *Jesse James* (1939) to the good law-and-order brothers of *My Darling Clementine* to the imperialist Ryker brothers of *Shane.*[9] For the producers of *My Darling Clementine,* in 1946, as I think for the nation, the rule of the brothers represented a later stage of human and political evolution. It was seen as progressive, a more democratic expression of political order than that of the tyrannical, repressive patriarchal Pa Clanton or Uncle Shiloh (in *Wagonmaster*). *My Darling Clementine,* with the fictional death of two of the four Earp brothers, refers to the military films of the war years, a remembrance of the tragic loss of a number of brothers in the war effort.[10]

In the film *Shane,* the Rykers represent a rule of the brothers, a pseudo-patriarchy and, thus, all the more dangerous in its illegitimacy and imperialist impulse to usurp the land and role of the homesteading fathers. It is important to have the boy Joey in the narrative (rather than Schaefer's adult remembering his childhood experience) because Joey, of course, constructs Joe Starrett as a father. Even more interesting, I would say, is that Joey's relationship to Shane constructs Shane as a second father rather than, as in the novel, a hero, a heroic supplement to Bob's sense of a heroic father.[11] In fact, at one point in the film, even the elder Ryker appeals to Joey to make the important decision about joining forces with the Rykers.

The film narrative, thus, is constructed to uphold the patriarchal order of things rather than the regime of the brothers.[12] Why make the Rykers simply brothers, without any other relationships? All of the cowboys belong to this rule, forming a group of what might be referred to as "an unlimited aggressive narcissism" that knows "only aggression and hostility against those who are not fully incorporated into it."[13] And the presence of Shane as a second father may be the reason that Marion, wife and mother, appears to become enamored with him, threatening a certain postwar Puritanism about the holiness and integrity of the nuclear family. Marion, as well as Joey, has two fathers, then, as options. Her possibly erotic interest in Shane helps to confirm him as a father, who teaches Joey how to use a gun, even though it is the actual father, Joe Starrett, who says that he will teach Joey how to use a gun. Shane and Joe, thus, do not constitute a regime of brothers. They join up with other fathers in the valley to create a regime of the fathers, also known as a community (a defense system).

The prolonged fight between Shane and Joe at the end of the film,[14] a battle that would seem to threaten the agrarian order that the fathers are trying to build, as the animals break out of their boundaries, nevertheless separates the two roles or functions of the patriarchal adult male so that they cannot ever establish their own version of a regime of the brothers.[15]

I want to claim that the rule of the brothers, in *Shane,* is roughly identified with something like a militantly aggressive socialism or communism. There is a rich ambiguity about the status of this brotherly primal horde. In the argument of the elder Ryker brother, he will justify his right to the land by claiming that he was the original tamer and master of the land. But he also wishes to be the future order of the land. He claims to be both atavistic and progressive, a later stage as well as the earliest stage. (Both Ryker and Starrett argue against each other's claims to the land with versions of the Turner thesis.)

In contrast, the fatherly heroes of this narrative hold to the patriarchal order of things, which allows for the division of the fathers into their proper and distinctive roles. It will be later, in feminist thinking of the 1970s, that such a patriarchal order will be called into question, but in 1953, it can still be imagined as the legitimate American political order of things. The danger for this order is that the actual father can misunderstand his proper role, is at risk of exceeding the patriarchal division of labor in the defense of fundamental American values. He continues to believe and to state that the trouble in the valley is between the Rykers and himself, and he does not want Shane to fight his battles for him. But the sense that the troubles are something of a different order, not at all a one-to-one or "reasonable" conflict between Ryker and Joe Starrett, is the view that Shane (and the film) take, and such a view is in the service of supporting a professional order of gunmen, a defense industry separate from the needs of ordinary, hard-working, and modest American families. Once the Rykers bring in a reputable hitman, Shane's progressive move toward agrarian domestication is quickly reversed. The gun and the legendary gunman are mightier than the farmer father who has a gun stashed away somewhere and who stolidly thinks that he can outlast the Rykers in a gun battle, without even suspecting, in his naive self-identification as a "reasonable man," the "stacked deck" that the Rykers have deviously strategized for Starrett's reception.

Shane arrives on the scene at the moment of crisis. Where does he come from? He is some kind of ghost out of the deep American mythic psyche, somewhat in the tradition of Hawthorne's "gray champion." But he is in competition with Joe Starrett in the final showdown. The father's role has to be doubled, one the militant, the other the domestic. Shane can put aside his gun and his buckskins and join forces with the domestic, agrarian homesteaders. (Think of the mythic, historical force behind the image of chopping and pushing over the tree stump in an area that was legendary for having no trees.) But as a farmer, he is always violence in repose. He is the protective spirit of the ongoing American enterprise, the figure who stands uneasily both within and without the myth of the family. This is Daniel Boone or Natty Bumppo, together with the Jeffersonian frontier farmer, in a condensation of the mythic history of the American push ever westward. The archaic explorer of the virgin wild—who has pioneered the way for the later more domestic followers—now returns, fatalistically, at the moment of crisis, when the family enterprises are threatened.

As it turns out, what is really operative in the valley is the causality of fate rather than an institution referred to as the law.[16] Fate may be construed as a supplement to the law, or perhaps the actual source of the law. The institutions of the law may be a hundred miles away, but the causality of fate is present within the movement of the narrative as Guthrie has reconstructed it, within the antagonists' decisions and consequent events. The law is on the side of the small farmers, but its institutions, and, thus, the executors and the procedures of the law, are too far away to protect them from the Rykers and Wilson. Fate, as the support of the absent law, is the complex movement of life itself. Certainly, the idea of the surveillance of fate over the activities within the valley holds a narrative ambiguity. In the traditions of American and European narratives of what we can refer to as providence or fate, an action will lead to a counteraction which, in turn, will lead to other actions designed to oppose such counteractions. In this fundamental kind of narrative, according to the ancient proverb, man proposes while God disposes. Human actions lead precisely to the opposite of the goal to which they were intended. In such narratives, irony or fate or providence takes over. For instance, the Ryker cowboys set fire to the Lewis family ranch at the Torrey funeral, since the Lewises have abandoned their homestead and are on their way out of the valley. But seeing their burning ranch precipitates a change of heart and mind, and the Lewises and their neighbors rush to save the ranch from total destruction. Ryker brings Wilson, a professional killer, into the valley, but that action brings Shane out of his domestic recess and restores him to the role of the gunman. The struggle for control of the valley would seem to favor a victorious outcome for the Rykers, since they have the money and the will to use violence against the family people for whom violence tends to be successful in getting them to move out of the valley. In short, the presence of fate as the cause of the movement of the narrative may be seen as the movement of history, a kind of theoretical or pure history, a model of historical working in the idealized form of a past historical community, a depiction that must gather most of the major symbols of American identity. The invocation of the Turner thesis, in the argument between Ryker and Starrett over who has a right to the land, about the movement of history, is a theory of history as a providential working of stages of history in which the rancher will inevitably give way to the progress of the farmer.

Although this providential or progressive movement of history works convincingly within such a historical community, it also has a reference to something external to that community. It brings out the rich paradox of an action that at once lies within a coherent social entity—a valley that is more or less self-contained with the forces of opposition within it—and that must refer to a global movement. I would say that such a narrative is, for these reasons, a deeply consummate representation of a necessary paradox of Cold War ideology, the sense that, within American fantasies of self-sufficiency, there will always be a reference to the global relationships of these local autonomies. The causality of fate reconciles the local and the universal, the internal and the external. It demonstrates that the workings of history are on the right side.

The concept of the causality of fate is a deeply reassuring notion, a sense that a providential history will reveal itself as validating and favoring a certain side of a conflict. The one aspect that perhaps has to be ignored here is thinking of the Rykers as a representation of a new sense of a corporate America, the next stage of history over the Jeffersonian agrarian stage rather than as a representation of an atavistic or regressive stage.

Is it possible that any of the characters can become self-conscious about the workings of fate? Yes, and that person is Shane. In his final encounter with Ryker, just before the shoot-out, Shane tells Ryker that his days are over, to which Ryker asks, "What about you, gunslinger?" Shane's response is that the difference between the two of them is that "I know it." Shane's self-reflection here is a tragic reflection on the causality of fate. Ryker, and even Joe Starrett, are unable to reach this kind of knowledge about themselves. Shane is able to understand that both of these men have flawed views about themselves, and he has, in the end, to fight both of them, although Joe Starrett and his family have to be fought in order to be saved, whereas the Rykers have to be fought in order to be destroyed. Like Natty Bumppo, Shane recognizes himself as an instrument of the movement of history, as a sacrificial figure whose task is to protect the patriarchal Jeffersonian social order.

This West of the Starretts, thus, is a profoundly symbolic or mythic setting, a Jeffersonian setting, which "celebrated independence and underlined the close connection of hard work, self-sufficiency, and rural life to political democracy and freedom."[17] The screenwriter felt that he had to remind Americans of these simple, school room "hard facts" of American life. The Starretts celebrate their tenth anniversary on the Fourth of July, as if their joining themselves in a family is itself a mythical repetition of American independence. (To illustrate just how mythical the Jeffersonian agrarian myth could be: The late forties and early fifties witnessed the greatest migration of rural farming people into the cities of any time in American history. The agrarian myth as well as the frontier myth might have gained status as myth, but the realities supporting the original ideas had either disappeared by this time or were rapidly dissolving.) One can think of John Ford's project, from 1946 to 1960, as essentially using film to "print the legend" rather than the facts of past American life. What is so revealing and brilliant about Ford's ideas is that he understood that the legend and the facts will never coincide. Thus, Ford feels an obligation to print the legend. The facts are secondary, although in *The Man Who Shot Liberty Valance,* Ford does present the so-called facts as well as the legend. "Facts" and legends can be included in a coherent narrative. He, thus, openly promotes the need for the legend against the facts of history, a view that many people later felt precipitated the U.S. into a crisis in the 1960s and the war in Vietnam. Certainly, the film version of *Shane* is openly, thoroughly, shamelessly, unembarrassedly committed to the legendizing of the West, to redeploying basic myths of American history. But of course, it is simultaneously striving to overcome some of the anxiety of postwar Americans about who they were and what they stood for. The construction of Cold War ideology is as much about the need for Americans to establish self-definition as about the need for military readiness.

In a retrospective review of *Shane* in 1968, Pauline Kael complained that "It's overplanned and uninspired: the Western was better before it became so self-importantly self-conscious."[18] She does not stop to consider what forces might have generated this generic self-consciousness. No doubt, the context of anxiety in the formative period of American Cold War history is easy to forget or misremember. Films like *Shane* or *High Noon* point to how deep the anxiety was.

Notes

1. This point is made by James D'Arc in his essay, "A. B. Guthrie, Jr., in Hollywood: Variations on the Writing Experience," delivered during the "*The Big Sky*—After Fifty Years" conference and included in this book.

2. Jack Schaefer, *Shane: The Critical Edition,* ed. James C. Work (Lincoln: University of Nebraska Press, 1984), 62.

3. Stephen J. Whitfield, *The Culture of the Cold War* (Baltimore: Johns Hopkins Press, 1991), 127.

4. Chuck Rankin, "Clash of Frontiers: A Historical Parallel to Jack Schaefer's *Shane,*" in Schaefer, *Shane: The Critical Edition,* 3–15.

5. M. M. Bakhtin, "Discourse in the Novel," in *The Dialogic Imagination: Four Essays by M. M. Bakhtin*, ed. Michael Holquist, translated by Caryl Emerson and Michael Holquist (Austin: University of Texas Press, 1981), 421: "The historical life of classic works is in fact the uninterrupted process of their social and ideological re-accentuation. Thanks to the intentional potential embedded in them, such works have proved capable of uncovering in each era and against ever new dialogizing backgrounds ever newer aspects of meaning; their semantic content literally continues to grow, to further create out of itself."

6. Dwight D. Eisenhower, *Mandate for Change*, 1953–1956 (Garden City, NY: Doubleday & Company, Inc., 1963), 445.

7. James T. Patterson, *Grand Expectations: The United States*, 1945–1971 (New York: Oxford University Press, 1996), 113. Cf. also Melvyn P. Leffler, *The Specter of Communism: The United States and the Origins of the Cold War*, 1917–1953 (New York: Hill and Wang, 1994), 62: "American policymakers saw themselves waging a geopolitical battle over correlations of power in the international system, a battle whose reverberations carried enormous implications for the political economy at home."

8. The history of this development is given its consummate statement in Henry Nash Smith, *Virgin Land: The American West as Symbol and Myth* (Cambridge, MA: Harvard University Press, 1950).

9. Richard Slotkin has done something like this in *Gunfighter Nation: The Myth of the Frontier in Twentieth-Century America* (New York and Toronto: Atheneum and Maxwell Macmillan, 1992), 278–400.

10. In films such as *The Fighting Sullivans* (1944), for instance, five brothers are killed in the war.

11. In the novel, the teller of the story is named Bob.

12. I take this term and idea from Juliet Flower MacCannell, *The Regime of the Brother: After the Patriarchy* (London: Routledge, 1991).

13. Ibid., 34.

14. This fight is not in the novel.

15. Does the doubling of the fathers, in fact, the dissemination of the fathers in general, strengthen or weaken the patriarchal order? We might recall Erik Erikson's famous essay, "Reflections on the American Identity," in *Childhood and Society*, 2d ed. (New York: W. W. Norton and Company, 1963 [1950]), 285–325. In this view, thanks to the "frontier" American experience, among other causes, Americans developed a highly "fragmentary 'Oedipus complex,'" which dispersed and displaced the strong European experience of the patriarch (296).

16. For the political and narrative implications of the "causality of fate," I am indebted to J. M. Bernstein, *Recovering Ethical Life: Jurgen Habermas and*

the Future of Critical Theory (London: Routledge, 1995), 82–85, 177–82.

17. Philip Fisher, *Hard Facts: Setting and Form in the American Novel* (New York: Oxford University Press, 1987), 12.

18. Pauline Kael, "*Shane:* Review," in Schaefer, *Shane: The Critical Edition,* 270.

Dee Garceau

Meditations on Women in *The Big Sky*

Consider the women in Boone Caudill's universe. His mother, loyal to an abusive husband, is selfless to a fault. "She looked like a tired, sad rabbit, her eyes round and watery, and her nose twitching." Boone shrinks from the memory of her pathetic figure: "The tired face rose before him. . . . He saw her in his mind without wanting much to see her sure enough." Boone's sister-in-law Cora marks the opposite extreme. Opinionated to the point of self-righteousness, she "was a strong-minded woman, . . . a fool, laying everything to God and the devil. . . ." Neither do we find a laudable character in Nancy Litsey, the Kentucky neighbor who flirts with Boone. Boone tells us, "This was how it was with a white woman. She put talk in the way and made up piddling dodges, pretending all the time not to know the prime thing that brought a man and woman together."[1] Whether doormat, virago, or hypocrite, white women appear as negative caricatures in *The Big Sky.*

Native women fare little better. Boone's journey west was peopled with nameless "squaws," distinguished only by their sexual promiscuity or by a kind of crude domesticity. Witness Boone's memory of an Arikara camp on the upper Missouri: "It wasn't dark yet. . . . But the boatmen and the squaws didn't care. In the open grass behind the clay huts they made moving heaps, the men writhing over the squaws, . . . [and later] Boone heard again the sounds that came from the rutting back of the village."[2] The implication is that these unnamed Indian women functioned at the level of animals, "rutting" in "moving heaps." Even for native women in domestic situations, the degrading images persist. Once again they are unnamed squaws, as in the following scene from Boone's visit to a Piegan camp: ". . . Heavy Runner lay in front of his lodge with his head in his squaw's lap. The squaw was going through his hair with her fingers, looking for lice and cracking them between her teeth when she found any." With images like these, Guthrie reduced native women to stereotypes as negative and one-dimensional as those of white women. Boone summed it up when he mused, "Squaws lives weren't much no matter what."[3]

Boone spoke for Guthrie, insofar as *The Big Sky* is clearly a masculine story. Women appear as backdrops, scenery against which masculine dramas are played out. In this respect, Guthrie preserved the conventional wisdom of his day, the assumption that the history of the American West was a story of white men's dreams, white men's migration, and white men's losses and gains.[4] Only later, decades after Guthrie wrote *The Big Sky*, would revisionist scholars challenge these assumptions. Guthrie's treatment of women in *The Big Sky* is striking in that it reminds us of the mutability of history, for Guthrie's female characters have little to do with the experience of nineteenth-century women, white or Native American. Instead, women in *The Big Sky* emerge from two templates. First, Guthrie drew from Euro-American tradition depicting the Indian woman as squaw or princess.[5] Second, Guthrie's female characters, both white and Native American, can be read as artifacts from post–World War II America.

"History," wrote Wallace Stegner, "is an artifact. It does not exist until it is remembered and written down; and it is not truly remembered or written down until it has been vividly imagined."[6] Stegner praised Guthrie for his rendering of mountain men's lives in *The Big Sky.* In Boone Caudill, Guthrie created a man whose wild spirit connected us to the mysteries of river and mountain, sky and plain, even as his savagery repelled or saddened us. Guthrie did not romanticize Boone. Rather, he dramatized both the vitality of individualism and its perils—rootlessness and isolation. In the end, Boone's violent nature is his downfall; he destroys the very relationships that sustained him. Through Boone, Deakins, and Summers, Guthrie evoked the paradoxical nature of Anglo migration westward. Both our violence and our need for order would compromise the sense of possibility that drew us up the Missouri in the first place.

If Boone Caudill's life is a meditation on freedom and restraint; if Jim Deakins fell victim to this frontier of the spirit; and if Dick Summers managed to bridge the wild and civilized worlds, where does Teal Eye fit in? Along with Deakins and Summers, Teal Eye became part of Boone's loosely constructed western family: Summers, the father-mentor; Deakins, the affable brother figure; and Teal Eye, the ideal wife. For a short idyll, Boone and Teal Eye share an inchoate love. Guthrie makes it clear that Boone and Teal Eye's marriage bore no resemblance to such unions in white society.[7] But the idea that Boone symbolically marries the wilderness when he marries Teal Eye is too easy a conclusion if one wants to understand Guthrie's portrayal of women. The fact remains that Guthrie's fictional women lack the humanity of his male characters, raising questions about *The Big Sky* as history. Stegner holds that Guthrie gave voice to our collective memory in this novel. And Guthrie did capture some essential truths about mountain men and about the beauty and brutality of a life lived in the open.[8] But Guthrie's depiction of women reminds us that memory is tricky. It behooves us to ask which century gave rise to Guthrie's memory of women? Women in *The Big Sky*, even the desirable Teal Eye, remain flat types who bear little resemblance to actual women of the historic Plains or Mississippi Valley. Instead, Guthrie created a post-World War II landscape of women. Copyrighted in 1947 and reprinted during the 1950s, *The Big Sky* betrays gender tensions present in postwar American culture. Guthrie's camp squaws, farm wives, Kentucky sweetheart, and Blackfeet princess more accurately reflect a discourse about gender that followed World War II than they do the experience of mid-nineteenth century women.

Since the 1970s, multicultural and feminist perspectives have changed our understanding of women's roles within nineteenth-century Plains and Rocky Mountain tribes. If Guthrie had had access to such knowledge, he would have seen the American West redefined as a meeting ground of cultures rather than as a white frontier. He would have read about the trans-Mississippi West as a crucible of intertribal diplomacy as well as encounters between First Nations and Spanish, French, and English colonizers, Hispanic and Anglo emigrants, and European immigrants.[9] Guthrie also would have been introduced to the concept of gender as a category of analysis. No longer do scholars assume a masculine West in which historical significance was defined by the activities of men alone. Instead, historians now ask how gender systems evolved on this multicultural ground. They argue that western history offers vivid case studies in race relations, cultural brokerage, colonialism and conquest, and their relation to changing gender systems.[10] Without the questions posed by revisionists, Guthrie's images of native women mirrored the perceptions of nineteenth-century white men whose journals, letters, and diaries served as principal sources of information.[11] Lewis and Clark, George Ruxton, Osburne Russell, Thomas Farnham, and other Euro-American men recorded their impressions of Native American women. These diarists created a disparaging view of Indian women as "sexually lax," "beasts of burden."[12] Only after Guthrie's time would scholars point out the cultural bias inherent in these judgments. As Katherine Weist explained it,

> Some of these [nineteenth-century expedition journals] were straightforward reports based on what Euro-Americans had actually witnessed and heard. Others were largely moral pronouncements deeply rooted in the observers' own complex attitudes about the proper place of women. . . .[13]

When white travelers in North America confronted female sexual expression outside the bounds of patriarchal marriage, they called it prostitution. When Euro-American missionaries and traders saw native women sharing responsibility as providers and property-holders, they called such women "drudges" and insisted that farming and house-building were "men's work."[14] Biases like these gave rise to the derogatory image of the squaw.

Over time, the reports of Euro-American travelers and traders merged with legend, song, jokes, and popular pictorial images of mythical Indian women. By the late 1940s, when Guthrie published *The Big Sky,* the image of native women in American popular culture had coalesced into two types, the princess and the squaw. Rayna Green notes that these images divide into a Virgin-Whore paradox in which the Indian princess is mysterious, alluring, and chaste; while the squaw is overtly sexual, degraded, and venal. Both images reinforced white nationalism, the princess because her choice of a white husband, as in Pocahontas legend, reinforced

Anglo notions of superiority; and the squaw because her degradation represented the savagery of all Indians, thus justifying white conquest.[15] Princess and Squaw, of course, comprise "unendurable metaphors" for actual Native American women. "Perhaps," writes Green, "if we explore the meaning of Native women's lives outside the confines of myth, we will find a 'more humane truth.'"[16]

With Green's charge in mind, consider the information available today to those who study American trappers and Native American people on the nineteenth-century Plains. One source of misunderstanding about Native American sexual mores was the role native women played in intertribal and Euro-Indian diplomacy. Recent research on fur trade society demonstrates that personal relationships established through marriage or adoption had significant diplomatic value. When an outsider voluntarily entered into such a relationship with a tribesperson, the obligations of kinship bound them to peaceful, mutually beneficial relations. Thus the custom of person exchange between tribes, through marriage or adoption, sometimes cemented trade or military alliances. French and British fur traders understood the link between familial and diplomatic relations. The Hudson's Bay Company and the Northwest Company, for example, encouraged their staff to marry native women, in order to secure the cooperation of fur-supplying tribes. But if these marriages held clear political and economic benefits, neither were they coldly opportunistic. Many of them lasted long and provided the genuine emotional satisfactions of family life.[17] The metaphor of kinship was seamless, crossing from personal relations to trade and diplomacy, and back again. Intermarriage knit together the Canadian fur trade during its first 150 years.

By Lewis and Clark's time, intermarriage was on the wane in central Canada and the Mississippi Valley, as white agricultural settlement brought white women and Protestant missionaries to the territory, both of whom decried mixed marriages. On the upper Missouri and farther west, however, where white agricultural settlement had not penetrated, the offer of female companionship—a gift of hospitality which carried an invitation to kinship relations—remained a common diplomatic gesture. Captain Clark recorded one such encounter in 1804 when the Corps of Discovery reached the Arikaras:

> 12*th October Friday* 1804
> a curious custom . . . is to give handsome squars to those whome they wish to show some acknowledgements to. . . . The rickores we put off during the time we were at the Towns but 2 Squars were Sent by a man to follow us, they came up this evening, and pursisted in their civilities.[18]

Clark understood the Arikara man's offer of female company as a diplomatic move, "to show some acknowledgements" to him. But Clark may not have grasped the extent to which rituals of reciprocity shaped nineteenth-century Plains Indian diplomacy. Gift-giving and hospitality were powerful metaphors, inseparable from negotiation. A gift to a desired guest was an invitation to enter into relationship with the host. Whether the guest accepted the gift, and what he offered in return, comprised a material language of power-brokering, of defining boundaries and responsibilities between the communities that guest and host represented.[19]

In 1804, the Arikaras and the Mandans needed new allies, for both tribes had been hard hit by epidemic disease. At the time of the Corps' arrival, Arikara and Mandan settlements were in disarray, with combined refugee populations from towns decimated by smallpox. In some cases, Arikara and Mandan civil chiefs vied for influence over these refugee populations. In other cases, the

Sioux preyed on the weakness of refugee towns, forcing them into tributary trading relations in which the Sioux controlled access to British goods.[20] It makes sense that an Arikara leader would court William Clark, either to strengthen Arikara influence in refugee towns, or to strengthen the tribe's bargaining position with the Sioux. Hence his offer of female hospitality, with its potential for familial and diplomatic partnership. In American popular culture, however, the role of Arikara and Mandan women in Plains diplomacy was lost, eclipsed by the image of female promiscuity.

The degeneration of attitudes toward native women can be traced, in part, to the nature of the American fur trade in the Far West. From 1825 to 1840, American fur companies hired white trappers, dispatched them to hunt furs on the great river systems that drained the Rocky Mountains, and collected the pelts at yearly rendezvous. The rendezvous system ended dependence on Indian trappers and middlemen.[21] With marriage *a la facon du pays* no longer necessary, reciprocal ties between Native Americans and white traders declined.[22] The custom of intermarriage persisted, but in degraded form. White American fur trappers, the "mountain men," still saw advantages to an Indian wife. She could cure hides, cook meals, and share his bed, and her presence might mollify hostile tribesmen who threatened isolated trappers. However, by the 1830s and 1840s, white trappers no longer honored the obligations between kin that had formerly shaped these partnerships. As contemporary George Ruxton described it,

> The Indian women who follow the fortunes of white hunters are remarkable for their affection and fidelity to their husbands, the which virtues, it must be remarked, are all on their own side; for, with very few exceptions, the mountaineers seldom scruple to abandon their Indian wives, whenever the fancy takes them to change their harems.[23]

The term "harem" is significant, for it implied the acquisition of women for a man's pleasure, free of duty to spouse or extended kin. Ruxton went on to quote a mountain man whom he called "Killbuck," who took the harem allusion one step further, referring to one of his native wives as a "slut":

> For twenty year I packed a squaw along. Not one but a many. Irst I had a Blackfoot—the darndest slut as ever cried for fofarrow. I lodge-poled her at Colter's Creek and made her quit. My buffler hos, and as good as four packs of beaver, I gave for old Bull Tail's daughter. . . . In two years I'd sold her to Cross-Eagle for one of Jake Hawkins guns. . . . [24]

Killbuck's casual references to beating one woman, buying another, and then trading her for a gun suggest a level of transience, exploitation, and disrespect not present in the mixed marriages of earlier generations. Even if Ruxton exaggerated Killbuck's dialogue to entertain his readers, the gist of his portrait still indicates a shift away from marriage *a la facon du pays.* The metaphor of prostitution had replaced the metaphor of kinship: A Blackfeet spouse was not wife, but "slut."

Guthrie alluded to Ruxton's narrative and to the deterioration of kinship relations between white trappers and native women in the following passage from an 1837 rendezvous attended by Boone, Deakins, and Summers:

> Some of them [native women] would catch themselves a white man, and their pappies would get gifts of blankets or whisky or maybe a light fusee and powder and ball, and they would be glad to have a white brother in the family, and the white man would ride away from rendezvous with his squaw and keep her while she pleased him, and then he would up and

> leave her, and she would be plumb crazy for a while, taking on like kin had died. . . .

Summers advises Deakins, "Reckon maybe you should take one away with you, and not buzz yourself around like a bee in clover." Boone jokes, "Jim hankers for the whole damn tribe."[25]

Unfortunately, Guthrie's brief acknowledgment of white trappers' culpability in the decline of kinship relations—quoted above—is upstaged by the image of the promiscuous squaw, the unnamed native woman who represents a white fantasy of whores for free. Boone's sexual encounter with an Arikara woman is typical. Brief and impersonal, like an encounter with a prostitute, "Boone's squaw lifted her gown and sat down and lay back. There was no get-ready, no kissing or hugging or hunting with the hand. . . . Afterwards he got up without a thank-you or a how-de-do, walking away with the loose, easy fag of a man who had spent himself."[26] The cumulative effect of these images is that historical perspectives on native women regarding marriage *a la facon du pays* and its deterioration in the mid-nineteenth-century American fur trade lie buried under the stereotype of native sexual license.

Evidence abounds in the historical record of declining reciprocity between white trappers and tribespeople. A common symptom was the debasement of gift-giving rituals. Like Ruxton's "Killbuck," mid-nineteenth-century American trappers reduced the ritual of gift-giving to an economic transaction, as though they were "buying" a woman. This reinforced the prostitution metaphor. In 1839, Rocky Mountain traveler Thomas Farnham reported that a white man could buy an Indian woman by giving a horse to her parents, "a fair business transaction," he wrote. "The girl [that he] received in exchange for the horse," explained Farnham, "becomes the absolute property of the enamored jockey, subject to be resold whenever the state of the market and his own affection allow."[27] Thus Farnham presented gift-giving as a purely economic transaction. Gone was the understanding that gifts functioned as symbolic declarations of reciprocity between in-laws. Indeed, references to social ties with tribes through intermarriage virtually disappear from the records of American trading posts during this period. Instead, the record suggests the opposite. N. J. Wyeth's 1834 instructions to staff at the Fort Hall trading post, for example, reveal social distance and distrust between whites and local tribes. Staff were instructed to give credit to no one and to keep sentries on guard any time Indians entered the fort; all hands were forbidden to trade even the smallest article with Indians, on their own.[28] Gone was the social web that had stabilized relations between white traders and Native Americans for generations in Canada. In short, the deterioration of relations between traders and tribespeople in the mid-nineteenth-century American fur trade led to a devaluing of native women as wives, economic partners, and diplomats. As the metaphor of kinship eroded, American mountain men increasingly saw native women as commodities, expendable sexual partners—in the white lexicon, as prostitutes.

Another factor in the white distortion of native women's sexual reputations may have been the practice of ceremonial sexual intercourse among the Mandan, Hidatsa, and certain Northern Plains tribes. Anthropologist Alice Kehoe found that Mandan and Hidatsa spiritual beliefs included "the transfer of power from one man to another through a woman as intermediary, with sexual intimacy the channel of transfer." Among the early nineteenth-century Hidatsa, for example, a younger man wishing to obtain spiritual aid from an older, more powerful man would offer his wife to the more powerful man during the Buffalo Dance. If the elder man accepted the offer, he transmitted some of his power to the younger man through symbolic or actual intercourse with the younger man's wife. As Kehoe explained it, "both symbolic and actual intercourse between married women and the men from whom their husbands wished power were believed to reenact intercourse with the life-giving bison, ensuring a happy and prosperous life for the married pairs." The Arapaho, the northern Cheyenne, the Atsina, and the Horns Society of the Blood division of the Blackfeet Confederacy practiced modified versions, largely symbolic, of the transfer of power through sexual intercourse.[29] In 1805, Captain Clark witnessed a Mandan Buffalo Dance, a spiritual ceremony intended to call forth the bison herds. Clark grasped the concept of symbolic transfer of power, but missed some important details:

> 5*TH OF* *JANUARY* *SATURDAY* 1805 -
> . . . a Buffalow Dance . . . for 3 nights passed in the 1st Village, a curious Custom. . . .
>
> The old men arrange themselves in a circle & after Smoke[ing] a pipe . . . the young men who have their wives back of the Circle go [each] to one of the old men with a whining tone and request the old man to take his wife. . . . the Girl then takes the Old Man . . . and leads him to a convenient place for the business, after which they return to the lodge; . . . (We sent a man to this Medisan Dance last night, they gave him 4 Girls) all this to cause the buffalow to Come near so they may Kill them.[30]

It makes sense that a member of Clark's party was invited to participate, the idea being that the powers of the Corps might be transmitted to a younger generation of Mandans along with that of Mandan elders whose bison-hunting powers were well known. What Clark missed was that a married woman's sexual fidelity in everyday life guaranteed a successful transfer of power. Northern Plains tribes valued sexual fidelity among married women in civilian life, and such virtue increased a woman's spiritual power. For example, among the Blackfeet, only a woman of virtue could sponsor a Sun Dance.[31]

In short, some of the ways that Native American cultures sanctioned female sexual expression had no counterpart in Euro-American culture. Plural marriage, considered immoral by Euro-Americans, held certain advantages for mid-nineteenth-century Crow women. Those who entered plural marriage typically practiced sororal polygyny,[32] with each sister-wife having her own lodge. With a shortage of men due to equestrian raiding and warfare,

> Crow women considered polygyny to be in their best interests. Having a man in her household increased a woman's prestige and the security and welfare of her family. . . . Sororal polygyny tended to strengthen a woman's position rather than weaken it. Sisters protected one another from domestic aggression, and sisters were often able to present a united front to further their interests.[33]

Among the Crow, divorce and premarital sexual experimentation incurred negative sanctions only after the arrival of white missionaries in the second half of the nineteenth century.[34]

Alcohol and epidemic disease complicated the picture. Between the 1780s and 1830s, three smallpox outbreaks devastated tribes from the upper Missouri west to the Rocky Mountains. Political and social fragmentation piled upon loss and grief in the wake of these scourges. At the same time, alcohol use further rent the native social fabric. Historians point to the resulting poverty and instability as reasons for increased pressure on native women to exchange sexual hospitality for food or military protection.[35] What had been a diplomatic ritual of kinship and reciprocity became, under desperate circumstances, a native bid for survival that white traders and military personnel called prostitution. Upper Missouri towns also included the intertribal and international trade in war captives, some of whom were women. Sacagawea, a Shoshone woman, remains the best-known example of such a captive. The Hidatsas captured her as a girl, then sold her to the French trader Charbonneau.[36]

Aside from displaced captives or prostitutes, mid-nineteenth-century whites could not fathom female sexual expression outside the bounds of patriarchal marriage. Neither did they grasp the full import of female hospitality as an invitation to kinship, a familial, economic, and diplomatic relation of reciprocity. Nor did they respect gift-giving ritual or ceremonial transfers of power as potent social, political, or spiritual metaphors. If mid-nineteenth-century Northern Plains and Rocky Mountain tribeswomen understood such activity as vital to their communities, it seems their white contemporaries did not. Instead, they shoehorned these behaviors into that narrow Euro-American template, prositution. Hence the image of the sexually degraded "squaw."

Native women's work also met with negative judgments from nineteenth-century travelers. White journalists called native women "beasts of burden," creating the squaw-drudge stereotype.[37] Native women's narratives and recent research, however, tell a different story.[38] Anthropologists and historians sometimes refer to nineteenth-century Blackfeet society as a fierce warrior culture that subordinated women, reinforcing the "oppressed squaw" stereotype. Beverly Hungry Wolf offers another perspective, based on her interviews with Blood elders. Though Blackfeet political and social organization was patriarchal, "the work of the women was generally respected and honored, for the men knew very well that they could not live without them." Hungry Wolf described nineteenth-century gender-based divisions of labor in which men and women held complementary roles. Women made the lodges, set them up, took them down, and packed them for travel. Women sewed bedding and clothing for household members; gathered, prepared, and preserved foods; and bore and raised children. This work, done well, brought honor to oneself and one's family. "In the social life of my grandmothers," wrote Hungry Wolf, "a household was judged not only by the bravery and generosity of the man, but also by the kindness and work habits of the woman." Hungry Wolf further revealed that women held crucial spiritual responsibilities in nineteenth-century tribal life, as keepers of medicine bundles. Often a husband and wife shared responsibility for the care of medicine bundles, and for the ritual practice associated with these sacred objects. In short, Hungry Wolf's portrait of her nineteenth-century Blackfeet grandmothers admits the reality of hard physical work, but unlike the squaw-drudge trope, the meaning of such work encompassed honor rather than degradation.[39]

Native women's perspectives further refute the image of the squaw as drudge if we consult Hidatsa sources. Maxidiwiac, also known as Buffalo Bird Woman, grew up among the Knife River Hidatsa during the mid and late nineteenth century. Her narrative, as told to anthropologist Gilbert Wilson, casts new light on women's work among upper Missouri tribes. Nineteenth-century Hidatsa women excelled at farming; they grew corn, squash, beans, and sunflowers. These farm products not only supplied the towns with staple foods, they also became the basis of trade. At the great trade fairs on the upper Missouri, the Hidatsas bargained with corn, for example, to get horses, guns, and other Euro-American manufactured goods. Women participated directly in this trade, overseeing the exchange of produce for specific trade goods. Hidatsa women also built their lodges, owned and distributed products from the men's hunt, and daughters inherited their mother's fields.[40] In these ways, Hidatsa women exercised considerable initiative and control over property and economic life.

Recent research on Crow women offers further perspective on women's place in Northern Plains tribes. One common assumption among scholars has been that Plains tribeswomen's status declined with the transition from a horticultural to an equestrian society.[41] Anthropologist Martha Harroun Foster tested this assumption against the experience of nineteenth-century Crow women. She found that Crow women's work did change in response to the rise of equestrian culture, but their status did not. That is, Crow women shifted from farming in a horticultural economy to processing hides and meat in a bison economy. But like Hidatsa women, Crow women continued to control the distribution of men's products from the hunt. Moreover, their tanning skills proved essential to the fur and hide trades. A picture of economic partnership emerges, in which Crow women made skilled contributions to family and tribal sustenance. Notably, Foster's research included Crow women informants, the narrative of Pretty Shield being a principal source.[42] Once again the perspectives of native women overturn the assumption that nineteenth-century Plains tribes relegated women to demeaning work.

Similar insights come from native people of the Northern Rockies, such as the Salish-speaking cultures of the Columbia Plateau. Like Blackfeet, Hidatsa, and Crow women, Salish women made and owned their lodges. Salish women also owned and traded their own horses. Frances Vanderburg and Dorothy Felsman, enrolled members of the Confederated Salish and Kootenai Tribes in Montana, described nineteenth-century Salish women as providers. They dug camas root and bitterroot and gathered huckleberries, chokecherries, raspberries, and strawberries, as well as herbs and medicines.[43] Anthropologist Lillian Ackerman estimates that the foods Plateau women gathered provided from 50 to 70 percent of the nutrition in the nineteenth-century diet; the fish and game men hunted, 33 to 50 percent. Based on extensive interviews with Plateau women, Ackerman found that the work of both genders was judged equally valuable. "Good providers," male or female, earned political influence in council.[44]

Vanderburg and Felsman added that women ran the daily life of the village, since men often left home on hunting, fishing, trading, diplomatic, or military expeditions. Members of extended families looked to their grandmothers for approval and advice. Women suggested to the chief when to move camp and decided where to set up new camps. The *sku'malt* was an elected position in which women sometimes served as a civil chief, hearing and mediating disputes. The wives of nineteenth-century Plateau chiefs advised them on major decisions, handled leadership responsibilities during a chief's absence, and nominated the chief's successor. In council, men and women alike discussed the issues until all sides of the question had been aired.[45]

Dorothy Felsman noted that Salish women took active roles in the spiritual life of the community, as healers. Felsman told the story of her maternal grandmother who became a midwife and healer following a dream in which she was instructed how to assist with a difficult birth, including what herbs to use and where to find them. Ackerman's informants reported that female as well as male children vision-quested for guardian spirits; and that women and men each practiced a spiritual cleansing ritual followed by ceremonial offerings and requests to appropriate powers before embarking on significant provider activities—women before their first root-digging expedition of the season, and men before their first fishing expedition. Ackerman concluded that nineteenth-century

Plateau women's roles were complementary to men, but "balanced in rights," a far cry from the oppressed "squaw."[46]

Plateau societies were in flux during Boone Caudill's time, giving rise to new forces that threatened women's position within Salish culture. "The Flatheads," Teal Eye said, "have the black robes and the Book of Heaven."[47] Teal Eye referred to the influence of Catholic missions on Plateau cultures. In 1839, the Salish-Kootenai people of present-day northwestern Montana sent a delegation to St. Louis, inviting the Catholic church to establish a mission among them. They hoped the black robes would strengthen them spiritually, so that they might better hold their own against the Blackfeet. The Blackfeet had become increasingly dangerous by virtue of their control over the arms trade. In 1841, the first Catholic missionaries arrived.[48] Over the next century, Catholic missionaries tried to impose Euro-American forms of family organization on Plateau congregants. They discouraged divorce, outlawed polygyny, and urged the formation of patriarchal, nuclear family households. Some time after 1844, Father Joseph Joset confided to his diary "how difficult [it was] to establish Christian subordination" in Plateau women.[49] This, too, contradicts the slavish squaw image.

Finally, native informants and revisionist scholars report that women among Northern Plains and Rocky Mountain tribes sometimes joined military expeditions, earning recognition as warriors.[50] Though not common, it was not unheard of. Rosemary and Joseph Agonito discovered a Northern Cheyenne woman, Buffalo Calf Road, who rode into battle at the Rosebud in 1876 to rescue her brother, earning her the name, "Brave Woman." The Agonitos' investigation of Buffalo Calf Road is significant for it revealed the extent to which native women had been expunged from the historical record.

In their search for Buffalo Calf Road, the Agonitos found a trail of elusive leads and dead ends. Neither government nor newspaper reports on the Black Hills War of 1876 named Indian women as individuals. The War Department, for example, listed Buffalo Calf Road's husband, Black Coyote, in a report on Cheyenne fugitives, but referred to the women with him as "three squaws." In interviews by ethnographers with over thirty Sioux and Cheyenne warriors, the tribesmen also omitted Buffalo Calf Road from their memories of battle, the exception being Cheyenne warrior Wooden Leg, who mentioned Buffalo Calf Road's presence at the Rosebud. So, too, the Native American visual record was sparse. When the Agonitos combed through Cheyenne ledger book drawings, several depicted battles from the Black Hills War, but only one portrayed Buffalo Calf Road. Northern Cheyenne artist Spotted Wolf drew Buffalo Calf Road on horseback, picking up her wounded brother, Comes-in-Sight.[51] Ultimately the two most complete accounts of Buffalo Calf Road's exploits came from Northern Cheyenne women. Kate Big Head and Ironteeth both mentioned Buffalo Calf Road's war deeds in their accounts of Cheyenne history.[52] The Agonitos concluded that both white and native sources revealed a gender bias that rendered women almost invisible, except to the most diligent researchers. Information about native women was so often buried or forgotten there had been little in the popular record to challenge Euro-American imagery of the squaw as drudge.

⁂

If A. B. Guthrie replicated the squaw trope in his treatment of Native American women, what informed his portrait of Teal Eye, *The Big Sky's* exception to squawdom? For that matter, what shaped Guthrie's portrayal of white women—Boone's browbeaten mother, his opinionated sister-in-law, and the coy Kentuckian, Nancy

Litsey? Together, the doormat, the virago, and the hypocrite, as well as Guthrie's Indian princess, Teal Eye, mirrored a dialogue about gender that surfaced after World War II. Men's and women's roles were in flux, with competing notions of power and place. Both sexes renegotiated their peacetime identity, as veterans returned home and women left war manufacturing jobs.

After more than a decade of depression and conflict, post-World War II Americans wanted stability and security. They created abundance in the wake of deprivation and made babies in the aftermath of war. An ideal of middle-class suburban life took hold of the popular imagination, in which nuclear families cohered in the blessed details of peacetime routine.[53] A *Saturday Evening Post* cover from 1955 epitomized this vision:[54] In the background stands a suburban home, its chimney covered with climbing roses. Both chimney and roses are emblematic; the chimney, of the hearthside, a totem of family togetherness; and the roses, of the vine-covered cottage, a totem of marital bliss. In the foreground lies a white man sunning himself on a towel in his swim trunks. Behind him, his slim, pretty wife sits on the lawn, transplanting flowers from their pots to the soil. Their little boy stands by his dozing father, tilting a watering can toward Daddy's face as he dozes. Visually, the recumbent man dominates the picture, even though he sleeps. His supine form underlines the comfortable home he has provided, reminding viewers that he is both provider and head of the household. However, the suburban husband exercised benign leadership, as suggested by the boy's playful gesture with the watering can, a gentle tableaux of trust and affection between father and son. The roles of economic provider, head of household, and benign leader were centerpieces of postwar masculine role ideology.[55] Meanwhile, the wife's figure is set behind the husband's, closer to the house and turned toward it, signifying her subordinate status and her focus on domesticity. The wife's work with flower pots associates her with fertility; while the visual echo between her flowers and the chimney roses link her to that emblem of marital bliss, the vine-covered cottage, reminding viewers that wives are responsible for the quality of affective relations within the home. Subordination, domesticity, fertility, and nurturance were the key components of postwar female role ideology.[56]

Images like this *Post* cover multiplied in American popular culture after the war. But all was not rosy in the vine-covered cottage. The transition to peacetime production, the reconstitution of families, and the reconstruction of peacetime values did not go smoothly. Women who had worked in wartime industry were reluctant to leave when the war ended. Many women emerged from their wartime work experience with raised expectations and a broader sense of place. Returning veterans perceived these women workers as more powerful because of their wartime record as successful providers.[57] Government newsreels raised the specter of male unemployment, urging women to give up their jobs. "You women," intoned one film clip, "will go back to the home where you belong, as wives and mothers."[58] Psychologists, sociologists, educators, and advice columnists joined the chorus directing women "back to the home." Leading the charge were sociologists Marynia Farnham and Ferdinand Lundberg. They published *Modern Woman: The Lost Sex* in 1947, the same year as *The Big Sky.* In *Modern Woman,* Farnham and Lundberg declared that, for women, any ambition outside the domestic realm was deviant and unfeminine. They exhorted women to cleave to "unimpaired feminine strivings, for which a home, a husband's love and children are . . . entirely adequate answers." They warned against "the masculinization of women," sure to bring "enormously dangerous consequences." Women who insisted on working for wages after the war would destroy the social fabric. Their "rivalry with men," pronounced Farnham, "engenders all too often anger and resentfulness toward men. Men, challenged, frequently respond in kind."[59]

Farnham and Lundberg were right about anger in one sense. Men and women sometimes butted heads as they adapted their goals to postwar society. But Farnham and Lundberg oversimplified the case when they vilified working women. For the postwar reality was full of contradictions. Even as Farnham and Lundberg released their jeremiad, marriage and birthrates were rising; women were embracing domesticity. Moreover, those women who continued to work for wages were shunted into the low-paid service industries where they rarely competed with men. At the same time, women's literature affirmed traits like ambition and initiative, as long as women expressed such drive through homemaking, volunteer work, or the entertainment industry.[60] Not surprisingly, the postwar discourse on gender revealed tensions on both sides. Betty Friedan documented the frustrations of middle-class housewives who tried to live out the domestic ideal, in *The Feminine Mystique.*[61] Less well documented are men's responses to the reordering of gender after World War II.

Popular literature suggests that men reacted against perceived threats to masculine privilege. One reaction was to contest the expansion of female authority in the home. War work had empowered women, a fact that reverberated in domestic settings even after women lost their wartime jobs. Postwar writers addressed the uncertain balance of power between husband and wife. Another reaction was to reject suburban materialism and to blame it on overzealous housewives. This exposed tensions in the model of strict separation between provider and consumer roles in middle-class marriage. A third response was frustration with peacetime models of masculine authority. A corporate ideal of benign leadership confused the exercise of masculine power. Male unease about female authority, materialism, and the fate of masculine privilege surfaced in lampoons against women. Guthrie presaged this crisis of masculinity in *The Big Sky,* where each obnoxious female type registered a male complaint in the postwar dialogue about gender.

Guthrie was profoundly ambivalent about women's exercise of power. On the one hand, he made fun of assertive women, implicitly denouncing the empowered war worker. Specifically, in *The Big Sky,* Guthrie transformed assertive women into comic busybodies or self-righteous scolds. Neither made assertiveness acceptable in women. Witness the broom-wielding farm wife who interferes in a fight between Boone and her husband:

> "Don't you dast, Henry!" It was the woman, rushing between them while her mouth spouted words. "You stay right there. Hear?" . . . She raised the corn shuck broom. "You git! Git off our place, you—you murderin' white injun, you!"
>
> "He asked fer it."
>
> "Git!"
>
> . . . "Push'er out, Caudill," Mefford cried, chuckling. "I can stand to men's talk but not to skirt scat."[62]

This woman makes a comic figure. Rushing in with the proverbial broom, a symbol of witchiness, her mouth "spouted words." These words had no value; they were ill-timed "skirt scat," easily dismissed. Thus the farm wife wields authority ineffectively, laughably even. Less amusing, and more repellent is Boone's sister-in-law, Cora. In her, the assertive woman is a self-righteous scold. "'It was his sinnin' that killed him,'" Cora announces, in response to Pap's death. "'It was the Lord in His wrath.'" Someone chides her,

"'It ain't becomin' to talk that way, not about your man's pa.'" But Cora gets in the last word: "'All the same it was.'"[63] Here, female social authority is distorted, appearing as judgmental pronouncements, a negative version of female power. Indeed, Cora's assertiveness makes those around her uncomfortable:

> She was a strong-minded woman who never talked quite friendly but not unfriendly enough to make a ruckus about unless a body was on edge. Probably words wouldn't tame her anyway; what she needed was a good lodgepoling.[64]

In Boone Caudill's universe, assertive women were either laughable or so obnoxious they made one want to beat them into silence. If viragos in *The Big Sky* represented Guthrie's response to the empowerment of wartime women workers, he was clearly rejecting the expansion of female social authority.[65]

On the other hand, Guthrie recoiled from extremes of female submissiveness. Boone's mother is a case in point. Loyal to a cruel, tyrannical husband, she is a browbeaten martyr. "It beat all how Ma could grieve for the likes of Pap and couldn't talk about him without a sad, rabbity look and the tears leaking." Ma's resignation to oppression makes Boone feel claustrophobic at the thought of her:

> The tired face rose before him, and the misty eyes and the body worn from doing.
>
> She had been gone from his thoughts for many a year, except for just a flash now and then, and she was back. He saw her in his mind without wanting much to see her sure enough.
>
> ... Looking out at hills set small and close and the sky pale and low overhead and the trees thick enough to smother him, he was half a mind to turn about.[66]

Here, the memory of a martyr mother is linked to a suffocating landscape. The implication is that submissiveness taken to extremes is soul-killing for both women and men. Guthrie's sketches of viragos and doormats suggest the nature of men's ambivalence about women's place after World War II. They negate the expansion of women's social authority, yet they also recoil from the dispiriting oppression of women.

The postwar discourse on power relations between men and women also included prescriptions for female sexuality. According to Farnham and Lundberg, anatomy determined the psychology of gender relations. Because nature designed women to "receive the seed," it followed that women were inherently passive. Women's inherent passivity, in turn, fitted them to a subordinate social role. Farnham and Lundberg targeted their remarks at empowered women fresh from wartime work. "We should again point out to female egalitarians," they wrote, that in the sex act, the male "is playing the leading role." Sex, for men, they assured readers, was as easy as falling off a log. As for the woman, "It is as easy as being the log itself." Farnham and Lundberg urged women to embrace passivity and subordination, socially and sexually.[67]

Guthrie disagreed with Farnham and Lundberg's prescription. While Farnham and Lundberg touted female passivity as healthy and respectable, Guthrie linked it to sexual degradation. In *The Big Sky,* female passivity went hand in hand with prostitution. Consider Boone's impersonal tryst with a nameless squaw: "Boone's squaw lifted her gown and sat down and lay back. . . . The squaw lay waiting, thinking likely about the scarlet cloth her man bargained for. . . ." Here the squaw's sexual passivity is part of prostitution; she has sold herself for red cloth. In contrast, Teal Eye represents the faithful wife, whose sexuality is active. Guthrie presents Teal Eye as the more desirable and the more respectable of the two: "She [Teal Eye] was always ready for him [Boone] when his body was hungry, not lying still and spraddled, either, like a shot doe, but joining in, unashamed. . . ."[68] The phrases, "still and spraddled, like a shot doe," conjure up a dismal image of female sexuality. Thus Guthrie added to the postwar dialogue on female sexuality, rejecting the model of passivity. But if Guthrie was leery of female self-abnegation, neither did he affirm a redistribution of power between men and women. As we shall see with Teal Eye, Guthrie wanted self-respecting women—who remembered their place.

Another facet of postwar sexual mores was the code of containment. A double standard of morality prevailed, which allowed premarital intercourse for men but condemned it in women. Unmarried women could engage in some sexual experimentation as long as they stopped short of intercourse. Historian Elaine Tyler May called it the "sexual containment ethos." Responsibility for sexual containment fell upon women, in order to protect their reputations. "As one contemporary observer noted, the 'ideal girl . . . has done every possible kind of petting without actually having intercourse. This gives her savoir-faire, while still maintaining her dignity.'" Thus single women played a kind of sexual brinksmanship, "walking the tightrope between sexual allure and the emphasis on virginity that permeated youth culture."[69]

Guthrie recreates this ethos in Nancy Litsey, Boone's Kentucky sweetheart. Nancy's behavior resembles that of a post-World War II woman concerned with sexual containment. In the following passage, she flirts with Boone, then resists his advances. Boone's response could well be Guthrie's critique of sexual containment:

> She might have been speaking to the moon instead of him. . . .
> "I think I'll go to far places one day and wear a boughten dress,

> and eat off plates with flowers painted on."
>
> . . . He [Boone] let himself down in the spot he had cleared. "Best set here."
>
> "Chiggers torment me terrible. Salt and lard don't help me, or anything. . . ."
>
> "Too early for chiggers," he answered, but she still sat there on the fence. . . .
>
> This was how it was with a white woman. She put talk in the way and made up piddling dodges, pretending all the time not to know the prime thing that brought a man and woman together. A squaw, now, would own to what was in a man's mind. It would be yes or no right off, and no play-acting about it.[70]

Moments later, after giving in, Nancy asks, "When'll we be married, Boone?" When he doesn't answer, she repeats, "When, Boone? . . . We got to be married. . . . We just got to be married."[71] Nancy fears for her reputation when sexual containment fails, echoing the double moral standard of the postwar years. Boone's commentary, in turn, reveals the hypocrisy of sexual containment. Women "pretend" not to want the same thing, "make up piddling dodges," and "play-act" instead of owning up with "a yes or no right off." Implicitly, Guthrie rejects women's postwar role as enforcers of sexual containment.

The issue of female authority, and its extent and limits, also became entangled with consumerism. Postwar advertisers urged women to channel their ambitions into educated consumerism rather than wage work, arguing that housewives could exercise intelligence, managerial skill, and creativity in buying for their families. Female consumerism became central to the postwar ideal of suburban life. The husband earned a salary, and the wife used it to furnish, feed, dress, refresh, educate, or entertain the family.[72]

In this equation, material abundance expressed the husband's and wife's competence and generosity. For some men, however, consumption became a tiring round of social competition, debt, and meaningless accumulation. Popular novels like *The Man in the Gray Flannel Suit* and sociological tracts like *The Status Seekers* questioned the materialism of postwar suburban culture.[73]

The most dramatic expression of this reaction appeared in *Playboy* magazine, in an essay by Philip Wylie called, "The Womanization of America." In it Wylie unleashed a tirade against female consumerism. Like Communists threatening the free world, consumer housewives threatened the masculine world. Female consumerism, according to Wylie, revealed women's lust for power: Housewives did makeovers with a vengeance, retooling everything around them in their own image. "On some not very distant day I expect to see a farmer riding a pastel tractor and wearing a matching playsuit," wrote Wylie. "Farfetched?" he asked. "Not so very." Wylie lambasted women for feminizing male sanctuaries, beginning in the home. "Where once a man had a den, maybe a library, a cellar poolroom, ... he now found himself in a split-level pastel creation ... the beloved old place now looked like a candy box." To add injury to insult, "the cost of the new abode" kept the hapless male on a treadmill. "Too often overtime work, required to pay the mortgage on the remodeled house, brought him home in darkness—too weary for fun." Masculine retreats like bars or men's clubs offered no relief because they, too, were taken over by feminine consumer power. "Drinks began to taste like perfume ... the traditional decor soon vanished—the big stone fireplaces ... the heavy wonderful chairs ... replaced by bright chintzs ... [and] pastel works of whatever nitwitted flimsy painter held the ladies' awe." Wylie concluded that the American male had "lost his authority"; while for women, "equality meant the tyrant's throne."

Wylie's men were refugees, beleaguered by a feminine aesthetic. Like Ruxton a century earlier, Wylie used hyperbole to make his point. But even allowing for exaggeration, Wylie conveys a shift in relations between men and women. In Wylie's case, the theme is a crisis of masculine authority, symptomized in the excesses of female consumerism.[74]

In *The Big Sky,* Guthrie presaged Wylie's lament with Boone's distrust of white women as usurpers of masculine spaces. "It gave him a pinch when he thought back to last year and remembered the white women that a couple of crazy preachers had brought to rendezvous on Horse Creek, bound on across the Columbia. . . . White women! . . . They figured to spoil a country. . . ."[75] Boone sees the Far West as a free, masculine space. So, too, Wylie longs for a "society dreamed up by males, by males pioneered," where a man "could talk and think of himself as a sportsman, a lover, an adventurer"; where a man "could openly acknowledge that his true, male feelings did not, in his opinion, make of him the beast that 19th Century Society [sic] claimed he was."[76] Wylie longed for the world that Guthrie created in *The Big Sky.*

Guthrie echoed Wylie's hostility toward women as consumers. In a conversation between Teal Eye and Jim Deakins, middle-class women who spend their husband's wealth are derided as "weak and lazy":

> In Blackfoot Teal Eye said, "We thought Red Hair had taken a white squaw."
>
> "Not me," said Jim. "Too fofaraw, them bourgeways are. I got things to do besides waitin' on a woman. . . . The white men in their big villages do not have squaws like you. The women are weak and lazy."[77]

"Too fofaraw" meant too greedy for consumer goods. Just as Wylie's postwar American man resents living in thrall to a suburban wife's material demands so, too, Guthrie's mountain man has "got things to do besides waitin' on a woman."

While Wylie pinned the crisis of masculine authority on female consumerism run amok, others laid blame on postwar corporate culture. With the G.I. Bill, male enrollment in higher education jumped during the late 1940s and continued high through the 1950s. Thousands of college graduates entered the white collar world. As manufacturing boomed, corporations expanded and administrative positions multiplied. A vast corporate culture emerged and with it, new models of leadership. The Victorian model of the irascible individualist, a self-made man, gave way to the Organization Man. The Organization Man personified adaptability to group norms. He subordinated individualism to the needs of the group. He favored persuasion over confrontation, cooperation over competition.[78] Organization men tried to "motivate" their underlings rather than "boss" them. As one middle manager confessed to sociologist David Reisman, "Everything was done in an atmosphere of extreme amiability. No one ever does anything to rock the boat, and everyone keeps smiling. Honest to God, my face was sore at the end of the first month there, smiling at everyone."[79] Authority was disguised as sociability. Open displays of power were taboo.

The Organization Man's affability extended to family life as well. Husbands and fathers who ruled like Victorian patriarchs drew criticism. Instead, masculine authority was tempered by the ideal of "togetherness." Husbands and fathers were admonished to share leisure time with their wives and children.[80] The recumbent man on the suburban lawn of the *Post* cover represented surrender to family sociability; he took his lying down. In short, the corporate model of benign leadership also contributed to postwar gender tensions. At the very time when masculine privilege was threatened by women's wartime empowerment, American men faced a new leadership style that masked authority.

Guthrie implied an interesting resolution to this dilemma. He hinted at respect for those women who functioned as economic providers, but only if they also embraced homemaking and left male authority intact. In the character of Teal Eye, Guthrie combined provider activity with domesticity and subordination to men. Revisit Jim Deakins' comparison between Teal Eye and white wives:

> "The white men in their big villages do not have squaws like you. The women are weak and lazy. They do not dress skins and cut wood and pitch and break camp. They are not like Teal Eye."
>
> Boone could see Teal Eye was pleased.[81]

If we superimpose this scene onto the postwar discourse about gender, Deakins' affirmation of Teal Eye's work sounds like respect for women as economic providers. However, Teal Eye never challenged masculine authority. "It was one of the things he [Boone] prized her for, that she didn't argue. . . . He spoke his mind, and that was that, and he didn't have to fuss about it. It saved a man a heap of bother." Unlike the Organization Man at home or office, the mountain man exercised authority without apology. He asserted his will over women without negotiation or sociability—as Guthrie put it, without "a heap of bother." In this respect, Guthrie's mountain men were like fictional antidotes to the Organization Man's confusion about masculine authority. Further reinforcing masculine privilege was the fact that Teal Eye was a dutiful homemaker. Boone's lodge was "kept as well as anybody's," for Teal Eye was "neat by nature and knew how to keep a lodge right."[82] Wylie would have traded his pastel tractor for a woman like Teal Eye. She was the ideal wife for the post-World War II American male: domestic but not materialistic; economically productive, yet obedient.

In sum, Teal Eye was not the only fifties idol in nineteenth-century clothing. Guthrie's sketches of women, from the farm scold to the squaw drudge, belong to a post-World War II dialogue about gender. Recent research on Native American women reveals an unbridgeable gap between Guthrie's fictional "squaws" and the actual lives of mid-nineteenth-century native women. Guthrie cannot be faulted for lacking perspectives on native women that emerged decades after *The Big Sky* was published. But neither is his rendering of the squaw trope a neutral or innocent function of ignorance. There is an adamance to Guthrie's caricatures of women, native and white, that suggests strong feelings about gender and power in American society. Women in *The Big Sky* register men's unease with the shifting ground of postwar gender relations. Most striking are the ways Guthrie tried to reconcile elements of female equality with protection of male privilege. If Guthrie spoke for American men after World War II, they saw economic productivity and active sexuality as desirable traits in women, if only such traits did not challenge male authority. Like Boone, then, Guthrie leaves us to ponder the contradictions stirred in his wake.

Notes

1. A. B. Guthrie, Jr., *The Big Sky* (New York: William Sloane Associates, 1947; Boston: Houghton Mifflin, 1974), 7, 349, 363, 362, 374.

2. Ibid., 127, 130.

3. Ibid., 258, 324.

4. Susan Lee Johnson writes, "Of all the regions people have imagined within the boundaries of what is now the United States, no place has been so consistently identified with maleness—particularly white maleness—as the region imagined as the American West." Susan Lee Johnson, "'A Memory Sweet to Soldiers': The Significance of Gender," in *A New Significance: Re-Envisioning the History of the American West,* ed. Clyde A. Milner II (New York: Oxford University Press, 1996), 255–78, 255. See also Susan Armitage, "Through Women's Eyes: A New View of the West," in *The Women's West,* eds. Susan Armitage and Elizabeth Jameson (Norman: University of Oklahoma Press, 1987), 9–18.

5. Rayna Green, "The Pochahontas Perplex: The Image of Indian Women in American Culture," *Massachusetts Review* 16 (Autumn 1975): 698–714; Patricia Albers, "New Perspectives on Plains Indian Women," in *The Hidden Half: Studies of Plains Indian Women* (New York: University Press of America, 1983), 1–16; Donna J. Kessler, *The Making of Sacagawea: A Euro-American Legend* (Tuscaloosa: University of Alabama Press, 1996).

6. Wallace Stegner, foreword to Guthrie, *The Big Sky*, ix–xiv, x.

7. Jim Deakins tells Teal Eye, "The white men in their villages do not have squaws like you." Guthrie, *The Big Sky*, 265.

8. Stegner, foreword to Guthrie, *The Big Sky*, ix–xiv.

9. Richard White, *"Its Your Misfortune and None of My Own": A New History of the American West* (Norman: University of Oklahoma Press, 1991), 613–32; William Cronon, George Miles, and Jay Gitlin, "Becoming West: Toward a New Meaning for Western History," in *Under an Open Sky: Rethinking America's Western Past,* ed. Cronon, Miles, and Gitlin (New York: W. W. Norton, 1992), 3–27; *A New Significance.*

10. Morrissey, "Engendering the West," in *Under an Open Sky,* 132–44; Elizabeth Jameson and Susan Armitage, introduction to *Writing the Range: Race, Class, and Culture in the Women's West,* ed. Jameson and Armitage (Norman: University of Oklahoma Press, 1997), 3–16.

11. Guthrie drew from the journals of Lewis and Clark, George Ruxton, Osburne Russell, and Thomas Farnham, among others. In some cases, incidents in *The Big Sky* appear to be lifted almost verbatim from these nineteenth-century trappers and travelers' diaries. At a rendezvous, for example, Boone, Summers, and Deakins witness an altercation with some Bannocks that Russell described in his account of a rendezvous in *Journal of a Trapper, or Nine Years in the Rocky Mountains,* 1834–1843 (Boise: Syms-York Co., 1921), 62–64. See Guthrie, *The Big Sky*, 199–200.

12. Katherine Weist, "Beasts of Burden and Menial Slaves: Nineteenth-Century Observations of Northern Plains Indian Women," in *The Hidden Half,* 29–46, 29. See also Robert Berkhofer, *The White Man's Indian: Images of*

the American Indian from Columbus to the Present (New York: Vintage Books, 1979).

13. Weist, "Beasts of Burden," 30.

14. Ibid., 31–41. See also Kathleen Brown, "The Anglo-Algonquian Gender Frontier," in *Negotiators of Change: Historical Perspectives on Native American Women,* ed. Nancy Shoemaker (New York: Routledge, 1995), 26–48; and Theda Perdue, "Women, Men, and American Indian Policy: The Cherokee Response to 'Civilization,'" in *Negotiators of Change,* 90–109.

15. Green, "Pochahontas Perplex," 17–21.

16. Ibid., 21.

17. Sylvia Van Kirk, "The Role of Fur Trade Women in the Creation of Fur Trade Society in Western Canada, 1670–1830," in *The Women's West,* 53–62. See also Sylvia Van Kirk, *"Many Tender Ties": Women in Fur Trade Society,* 1670–1870 (Norman: University of Oklahoma Press, 1980); and Weist, "Beasts of Burden," 44.

18. Reuben Thwaites, ed., *Original Journals of the Lewis and Clark Expedition,* 1804–1806 (New York, 1904), 1:189.

19. Albert Hurtado, "When Strangers Met: Sex and Gender on Three Frontiers," in *Writing the Range,* 122–42, 131; Raymond deMallie, "Touching the Pen: Plains Indian Treaty Councils in Ethnohistorical Perspective," in *Ethnicity on the Great Plains,* ed. Frederick C. Luebke (Lincoln: University of Nebraska Press, 1980), 38–51; James Ronda, *Lewis and Clark Among the Indians* (Lincoln: University of Nebraska Press, 1988), 62–64.

20. Ronda, *Lewis and Clark Among the Indians,* 42–112.

21. White, *"Its Your Misfortune,"* 46–47; Ray Allen Billington, *Westward Expansion: A History of the American Frontier,* 4th ed. (New York: MacMillan, 1974), 384–87.

22. *A la facon du pays* means according to the custom of the country, that is, in keeping with local customs.

23. George Ruxton, *Life in the Far West* (1848; reprint, Norman: University of Oklahoma Press, 1951), 95–96. See also William Swagerty, "Marriage and Settlement Patterns of Rocky Mountain Trappers and Traders," *Western Historical Quarterly* 11 (April 1990): 159–80. From a sample of 312 cases, Swagerty found that 90 men had more than one wife, or 28.8 percent. However, one must read these statistics with caution, since some unions formed and dissolved without record. Swagerty acknowledges the decline of reciprocity between trappers and Indians during the "competitive and tumultuous period of the late 1830s."

24. Ruxton, *Life in the Far West,* 192.

25. Guthrie, *The Big Sky,* 198, 199.

26. Ibid., 128.

27. Thomas Farnham, "Travels in the Great Western Prairies, the Anahuac and Rocky Mountains, and in the Oregon Territory," in *Travels in the Far Northwest, 1839–1846*, ed. Reuben Thwaites (Cleveland: Arthur H. Clark Co., 1906), 1: 255.

28. N. J. Wyeth, "Instructions to Robert Evans" (Fort Hall Trading Post, 1834), in *Major Problems in the History of the American West*, ed. Clyde A. Milner II (Lexington, MA: D. C. Heath and Co., 1989), 177–80. Further evidence of deteriorating relations between white trappers and Indians is seen in Russell, *Journal of a Trapper*, 62–64. Russell described an altercation with some Bannocks, ending with the comment, " . . . the best way to negotiate and settle disputes with hostile Indians is with the rifle, for that is the only pen that can write a treaty which they will not forget."

29. Alice Kehoe, "The Function of Ceremonial Sexual Intercourse among Northern Plains Indians," *Plains Anthropologist* 15 (May 1970): 99–103.

30. *Original Journals of Lewis and Clark*, 1: 245.

31. Kehoe, "Ceremonial Sexual Intercourse," 100–102; Weist, "Beasts of Burden," 44. For a description of women's role in the Sun Dance, see Walter McClintock, *The Old North Trail: Life, Legends and Religion of the Blackfeet* (1910; reprint, Lincoln: University of Nebraska Press, 1992), 284–324.

32. Sororal polygyny refers to the practice of a man marrying several women who are sisters.

33. Martha Harroun Foster, "Of Baggage and Bondage: Gender and Status Among Hidatsa and Crow Women," in *American Indian Culture and Research Journal* 17 (Spring 1993): 121–52, 134.

34. Will Roscoe, "'That is My Road': The Life and Times of a Crow Berdache," *Montana The Magazine of Western History* 40 (Winter 1990): 46–55, 53–54.

35. Hurtado, "When Strangers Met," 129–37; Colin G. Calloway, "Horses, Guns, and Smallpox," in *Our Hearts Fell to the Ground: Plains Indian Views of How the West Was Lost* (Boston: Bedford Books of St. Martin's Press, 1996), 37–46; Ronda, *Lewis and Clark Among the Indians*, 52–54.

36. Kessler, *The Making of Sacagawea*, 52–58; Hurtado, "When Strangers Met," 131.

37. Beverly Hungry Wolf, *The Ways of My Grandmothers* (New York: William Morrow, 1980), 109–11; Weist, "Beasts of Burden," 30.

38. For discussion of the role of Native American oral traditions in revisionist history, see Angela Cavender Wilson, "Power of the Spoken Word: Native Oral Traditions in American Indian History," *Rethinking American Indian History*, ed. Donald Fixico (Albuquerque: University of New Mexico Press, 1997), 101–16; and Donald Fixico, "Methodologies in Reconstructing Native Ameri-

can History," in *Rethinking American Indian History,* 117–29.

39. Hungry Wolf, *Ways of My Grandmothers,* 110, 74–79.

40. Gilbert Wilson, ed., *Buffalo Bird Woman's Garden: Agriculture of the Hidatsa Indians* (St. Paul: Minnesota Historical Society, 1987), 9–28, 42–58, 68–78, 82–85, 87–97, 113–18. See also Weist, "Beasts of Burden," 42; and Foster, "Of Baggage and Bondage," 133.

41. See Alan Klein, "The Political Economy of Gender: A 19th Century Plains Indian Case Study," in *The Hidden Half,* 143–74.

42. Foster, "Of Baggage and Bondage," 131–33, 139–45. See also Frank Bird Linderman, *Pretty Shield: Medicine Woman of the Crows;* originally published as *Red Mother* (New York: The John Day Company, 1932; Lincoln: University of Nebraska Press, 1972).

43. Frances Vanderburg, interview by author, Missoula, MT, 6 August 1998; Dorothy Felsman, interview by author, Arlee, MT, 14 August 1998.

44. Lillian Ackerman, "Complementary but Equal: Gender Status on the Plateau," in *Women and Power in Native North America,* ed. Laura Klein and Lillian Ackerman (Norman: University of Oklahoma Press, 1995), 74–100.

45. Vanderburg interview; Felsman interview; Ackerman, "Complementary but Equal," 92.

46 Felsman interview; Ackerman, "Complementary but Equal," 80–85, 91–97; Lillian Ackerman, "The Effect of Missionary Ideals on Family Structure and Women's Roles in Plateau Indian Culture," *Idaho Yesterdays* 31 (Spring-Summer 1987): 64–73, 71.

47. Guthrie, *The Big Sky*, 267.

48. For history of the Catholic missions in the Northwest, see Wilfred P. Schoenberg, S.J., "Missionaries: The Jesuits," in *Religion in Montana: Pathways to the Present,* ed. Lawrence F. Small (Billings, MT: Rocky Mountain College, 1992), 1:47–76; Jaqueline Petersen, *Sacred Encounters: Father DeSmet and the Indians of the Rocky Mountain West* (Norman: University of Oklahoma, 1995), 83–133; and *Jesuit Fathers, St. Ignatius Mission* (Missoula, MT: Gateway Printing, 1977), 1–7. For discussion of Blackfeet control of the arms trade, see Calloway, "Horses, Guns, and Smallpox, " in *Our Hearts Fell to the Ground,* 37–47.

49. Ackerman, "Effect of Missionary Ideals," 67–71; Joseph Joset, S.J., Box 1351, Folder M, Joset Papers, Oregon Province Archives of the Society of Jesus, Crosby Library, Gonzaga University, Spokane, WA.

50. Hungry Wolf, *Ways of My Grandmothers,* 59–62; Foster, "Of Baggage and Bondage," 132; Ackerman, "Complementary but Equal," 90.

51. Rosemary and Joseph Agonito, "Resurrecting History's Forgotten Women: A Case Study from the Cheyenne Indians," *Frontiers: A Journal of Women's Studies* 6, no. 3 (1982): 8–16.

52. Ibid., 10.

53. Peter Filene, "The Long Amnesia: Depression, War, and Domesticity," in *Him/Her/Self: Sex Roles in Modern America* (Baltimore: Johns Hopkins University Press, 1986), 148–76.

54. Front cover, *Saturday Evening Post*, 4 June 1955.

55. Filene, "The Long Amnesia," 171–75.

56. Ibid., 165–66; Ruth Schwartz Cowan, "Homogenizing Housework," in *More Work for Mother: The Ironies of Household Technology from the Open Hearth to the Microwave* (New York: Basic Books, 1983), 196–216.

57. As the war drew to a close, 86 percent of women in war industries surveyed wanted to continue working in the same industrial group during peacetime. See Women's Bureau, *Women Workers in Ten War Production Areas and Their Postwar Employment Plans*, Bulletin 209 (Washington, D.C.: Government Printing Office, 1946). For discussion of pressures on women to leave industrial work during demobilization, see Susan Hartmann, "Returning Heroes: The Obligations of Women to Veterans in 1945," *Women's Studies* 5 (1978): 223–68.

For discussion of tensions in popular images of postwar family life, see James Davidson and Mark Lytle, "From Rosie to Lucy: The Mass Media and Changing Images of Women and Family," in *Women, Families, and Communities*, ed. Nancy Hewitt (London: Little Brown, 1990), 210–23; Nancy Walker, ed., *Women's Magazines, 1940–1960: Gender Roles and the Popular Press* (New York: St. Martin's Press, 1998); and Joanne Meyerowitz, "Beyond the Feminine Mystique: A Reassessment of Postwar Mass Culture, 1946–1958," *Journal of American History* 79 (March 1993).

58. Connie Fields, producer and director, *The Life and Times of Rosie the Riveter* (1980), film. Sponsored by the National Endowment for the Humanities.

59. Marynia Farnham and Ferdinand Lundberg, "Women Today," in *Modern Woman: The Lost Sex* (New York: Harper Brothers, 1947), 201–41, quotes from 239–40, 235, 237.

60. See Elaine Tyler May, *Homeward Bound: American Families in the Cold War Era* (New York: Harper Collins, 1988), 3–15; Douglas Miller and Marion Nowak, *The Fifties: The Way We Really Were* (Garden City, NY: Doubleday, 1977), 147–81; and Stephanie Coontz, *The Way We Never Were: American Families and the Nostalgia Trap* (New York: Basic Books, 1992).

61. Betty Friedan, *The Feminine Mystique* (New York: W. W. Norton, 1963).

62. Guthrie, *The Big Sky*, 351.

63. Ibid., 362.

64. Ibid., 363.

65. In a later novel, Guthrie edged closer to making his peace with women's wartime empowerment, using the metaphor of women as reserve labor on the Overland Trail. In *The Way West,* published in 1949, Guthrie commented that women's broadened work roles drew respect and increased their influence with men: "... the women did their part and more. They traveled head to head with men, showing no more fear and asking no more favor.... They had a kind of toughness in them that you might not think, seeing them in a parlor. So, on the trail, women came to speak and men to listen almost as if to other men.... They'd never quite believe again a woman was to look at but not listen to." A. B. Guthrie, Jr., *The Way West* (New York: William Sloane Associates, 1949; Boston: Houghton Mifflin, 1993), 295.

66. Guthrie, *The Big Sky,* 362, 349.

67. Marynia Farnham and Ferdinand Lundberg, "The Failure of Modern Sexuality," in *Modern Woman,* 263–97, quotes from 278, 275.

68. Guthrie, *The Big Sky*, 128, 260.

69. May, "Brinksmanship: Sexual Containment on the Home Front," in *Homeward Bound,* 114–34, quotes from 115, 121–23.

70. Guthrie, *The Big Sky*, 374.

71. Ibid., 376.

72. Friedan, "The Sexual Sell," in *The Feminine Mystique,* 206–32.

73. Sloan Wilson, *The Man in the Gray Flannel Suit* (New York: Simon and Schuster, 1955); Vance Packard, *The Status Seekers* (New York: David McKay, 1959).

74. Philip Wylie, "The Womanization of America," *Playboy*, September 1958, 51–52, 77–79, quotes from 51, 77, 52. Prior to this essay, Wylie had published a book in which he indicted mothers for exercising too much power in the home. See *Generation of Vipers* (New York: Rinehart, 1955). Wylie was what you might call an "unfriendly witness."

75. Guthrie, *The Big Sky*, 177.

76. Wylie, "Womanization," 52, 77.

77. Guthrie, *The Big Sky*, 265.

78. William H. Whyte, Jr., *The Organization Man* (Garden City, NY: Doubleday, 1956); May, *Homeward Bound,* 78; Filene, *Him/Her/Self,* 169–71.

79. Miller and Nowak, *The Fifties,* 127–31. See also David Reisman, *The Lonely Crowd: A Study of the Changing American Character* (Garden City, NY: Doubleday, 1950), 17–48, 151–66, 299–308.

80. Filene, *Him/Her/Self,* 171–75.

81. Guthrie, *The Big Sky*, 265.

82. Ibid., 283, 264.

Sue Hart

Some Recollections of and Reflections on A. B. Guthrie, Jr., and His Work

Guthrie as Journalist

Many years ago, I attended a meeting of the Montana Historical Society in Bozeman, Montana, where my father-in-law, Sam Gilluly, a long-time Montana journalist and director of the Historical Society, was on a panel on weekly newspapering with Montana's two Pulitzer Prize winners, Bud Guthrie and Mel Ruder (whose award was for his photo-journalism coverage—in his newspaper, *The Hungry Horse News* [Columbia Falls]—of the 1964 floods in northwestern Montana).[1]

This was one of the few times that I saw Bud listened to with reverence for his news sense and journalistic knowledge, rather than for his status as a world-renowned author. And listening to him then, it was apparent how important his grounding in journalism was as a foundation for the creative work that came later in his life: He learned to satisfy his own curiosity about the how and why of events in covering or assigning stories; he learned not to jump to conclusions, but to investigate situations fully and fairly; he learned the importance of accuracy and even-handedness; he learned that what everybody knew to be the truth often wasn't; he learned that the big tragedies and triumphs in life can best be understood by focusing on one individual out of the hundreds or thousands that might have been a part of the larger picture; he learned that small but telling details contribute a great deal to the impact of a story; he learned that news stories are not about happenings or ideas, but about people—always about people, about how they may be affected by, how they have been affected by, how they have contributed to, supported, or stood in the way of whatever the ostensible topic may be.

All this is important information not only for a journalist, but for a novelist as well. One of Bud's stories that illustrated this very well concerned an event he had witnessed, but not fully understood until it was nearly over: He was at a place in the mountains where there had been some problems with a bear. Finally, as a safeguard for the people staying there, a ranger was called in to handle the problem. Guthrie watched the young man with his gun; he watched him take aim and fire at the bear; he watched the bear fall; and he assumed that the young man was proud of his prowess with the weapon, was feeling like a mighty hunter. But as he followed the ranger to view the bear, he heard the young man mutter, "Goddamn such a job anyway!"

All of the panelists on the program had had lengthy and distinguished careers as journalists—Bud mainly in Kentucky; Mel and Sam on small-town Montana weeklies—and thus were well suited to discuss the topic of weekly newspapering. Not only were they experts in the field, they also loved the work they did and recognized the value of it. But they saw the downside of hometown boosterism, too. In fact, one thing they all agreed on was that many a small town editor had ultimately contributed to the demise of his community by campaigning for improvements, such as better roads to bring people to his town. What such editors failed to recognize was that the good roads in also lead out, and thus make it possible, even inviting, for the citizen of Small Town, Montana, to drive to the nearest "Big City" to shop, seek entertainment, conduct business, doctor, etc. When small town businesses go broke and close shop as a result of all the editorializing, lobbying, and cajoling on behalf of "progress" in their local newspaper, the community often dries up and blows away, writing "30" ("the end," in reporter's parlance) to any chance it had of growing and/or surviving.

It was a familiar theme, not only to the panelists, but also for most of their audience, a theme that some of them had lived and that many others may have been introduced to in Guthrie's *The Big Sky,* whose audience is asked—forced—to face up to the various kinds of destruction that occur in the wake of human "advancement." "She's gone," Uncle Zeb Calloway tells his nephew Boone Caudill about the wilderness Boone has run away to find, the home he hopes to claim as his own.[2] "Gone, by God, and naught to care savin' some of us who seen 'er new."[3]

Uncle Zeb is exaggerating the despoilment of the wilderness, but at this point in the novel, he's the expert, and he speaks as one who should know the extent of the damages inflicted on the land, which was "man's country onc't. Every water full of beaver and a galore of buffler any ways a man looked, and no crampin' and crowdin."[4]

As one of the first wave of mountain men, he contributed to the beginning of the end of the western frontier. As a raconteur spinning tales for eager young listeners, such as his nephew, of all the wilderness had to offer, including freedom from the shackles and societal mores of a "civilization" that was often ugly, as Boone's homelife demonstrates, he paved the way for what first would be trails and then superhighways bringing more and more people to seek the very space and beauty their presence was bound to alter and perhaps destroy. So by his own lights, as one who greatly prized the freedom, the beauty, the promise he found in the untrampled, untraveled territories of the western reaches of this continent, specifically in what became Montana, he is not only speaking the literal truth as he sees it, but sounding a lament reiterated in Boone's own report to Dick Summers at the close of *The Big Sky,* a motif that continues to reverberate through the literature of Montana and the West: "It's all sp'iled, I reckon, Dick. The whole caboodle."[5] In both cases, too, the destruction referred to moves beyond the physical landscape into the realm of the psychological.

The Big Sky has aged well—better, perhaps, than the natural world that serves as its setting—and fifty-plus years after publication its influence is obvious in the echoes of Uncle Zeb's message to Boone in the works of such newcomers on the writing scene as Norman Maclean[6]—who told his stories to preserve "the world just before this one, the world of hand and horse, hand tools and hand crafts" and to help his readers "imagine how beautiful Montana was at the beginning of this century";[7] Thomas McGuane, in whose *Nobody's Angel* the grandfather of the protagonist bemoans that fact that Montana "is not like it used to be";[8] Ivan Doig, whose Montana stories of a generation or two ago, leave readers, like the author, reaching out to touch the spirits of those who have gone before; James Welch, who so eloquently expresses the losses suffered by the Native American populations as a result of the settlement of what had been their homelands in such works as *Fools Crow* and, in a contemporary setting, *Winter in the Blood;* Peter Bowen, whose Gabriel Du Pré draws constantly on the past history of his people, the Métis, for inspiration and consolation; Mary Clearman Blew, who often reminds us of what we have lost in poignantly simple statements made by the characters in her stories. (This is just a brief sampling of countless authors who could be included in this list.)

When we remember the nostalgic title of Charles M. Russell's collection of stories of the Montana he knew, *Trails Plowed Under,* we realize that Guthrie is not the first Montana author to sound the alarm about how easily we can lose that which we most prize, but he is probably the best known and most widely read.

Many of Guthrie's contemporaries also recognized the spoilage that had been underway for a century or more when they began writing about it. Thomas Savage's first novel, *The Pass,* published in 1944, introduces Jess Bentley, a young rancher, who begins "to resent the future and everything it meant" when he realizes the railroad will encroach on the valley where he has settled. Another character in this novel notes that "all the new things, all the new ways, spoiled something."[9] In Dorothy M. Johnson's "A Time of Greatness," an aged Jim Bridger–like mountain man walks and talks with the men he knew in the Montana mountains of his youth, and the Northern Cheyenne grandfather in "Scars of Honor" tries to pass on the traditions of his tribe's past. Further depictions of the changes forced upon the native populations who lived on the lands that became Montana are provided by D'Arcy McNickle, whose most stunning literary achievement, *The Surrounded,* speaks to the loss of freedom and culture suffered by Native Americans, and Frank Bird Linderman, who records the lament of Pretty Shield in his book of the same name: "[T]imes have changed so fast that they have left me behind. I do not understand these times. I am walking in the dark. Ours was a different world before the buffalo went away, and I belong to that other world." "I am trying to live a life that I do not understand."[10]

Still, it is Guthrie, in his creation of Boone Caudill, who best sums up in a single being the ruination of the very qualities of landscape and promise that drew first adventurers and profiteers and then pioneers to the West. (Boone belongs in the first two groups himself; and in agreeing to guide Peabody through the mountains to establish a "trail" for the wagon trains that are poised to begin the westward trek, he helps open the West to settlement.)

Boone's personal qualities aid in this portrayal of "the mountain man as he really was," which was Guthrie's aim in writing *The Big Sky.* He is not a polished easterner; he lacks the social skills to do well in "civilization." In fact, in his at-times brutish responses to the taunts of others (he "prit' near killed Mose Napier" because Napier had "deviled" him) he not only demonstrates his inability to live in close contact with others, but foreshadows what is to come later in the novel when he is again "deviled" by the taunts of Teal Eye's people which feed his own suspicions.[11]

Guthrie's portrait of Boone is certainly psychologically sound: Boone had grown up in a household with a mean, abusive father, and he was the product of his upbringing. One time when we were talking about *The Big Sky,* I asked Bud if the last name—Caudill—had been chosen to suggest caudle, a tail-like appendage, which might reflect Boone's brutish, animalistic side. (This had occurred to me because the names Dick Summers and Jim Deakins seemed so appropriate for the characters: Summers, the "old man," at thirty-three, past his first youth, entering the fall and winter seasons of his life; Deakins, the philosopher, wondering and worrying about God and the afterlife.) Bud was kind enough to consider the question quite seriously, and then confessed that he'd picked that name simply because it was a common one in Kentucky. (He did have some fun naming his characters, though; the name chosen for the patron on the *Mandan,* the keelboat that brings Boone to the West, probably was "borrowed" from E. L. Jourdannais, publisher of the *Choteau Acantha* from 1919 until 1926. Guthrie's father served briefly as the *Acantha* publisher in the early

1900s, and Guthrie himself went to work for the paper when he was fourteen.)

In his relationship with Jim Deakins, Boone reneges on the one rule of behavior he himself has insisted upon: Company is all right if it's in the form of "a body" he could "trust"; if that companion were someone who would "stand by a man, come whatever."[12] Even though he has shown himself capable of just such devoted friendship, in the end jealousy and suspicion—and the tendency to lash out—win out, and Boone truly destroys his own mountain paradise. For the second time in the novel, Boone runs away from "home" after killing Jim, and he soon discovers that he does not have a home in the world he left behind anymore than he does in the mountains of the West. By his actions—uncivilized and unacceptable in either world—he truly has "sp'iled" it all.

Bud and Carol told me a story one time about a young man from an eastern university who showed up on their doorstep one evening and asked if Mr. Guthrie was home. "Well, there he was, sitting in plain sight of the door," Carol said, "so I couldn't very well deny that he was there." So she invited their unexpected visitor in, and his first words to the author he'd come to find were, "What happened to Boone?"

Guthrie countered by asking, "What do you think happened to him?" and went on to explain that he was "finished with that book." So it was interesting in *Fair Land, Fair Land* that he chose not only to return to the site of "that book," but to reintroduce Boone as well—perhaps to satisfy the many readers who had asked him that same question. Whether those who wondered were happy with the fate that Boone meets in *Fair Land, Fair Land,* I don't know, but certainly showing him preying on others and finally losing his life in a violent fashion was "right" or "appropriate," given what readers know of him from *The Big Sky.* (The young man who came in hopes of discovering Boone's fate apparently was so awed by the presence of Guthrie that he couldn't tear himself away; Carol finally solved the problem by going to the next room and returning with a leash. She told him she was sorry, but it was time for them to walk their dog, so they'd have to say good night. Their "guest" took his leave, apparently not finding it at all strange that people would walk a dog that had nearly all of northwest Montana as his romping grounds!)

Guthrie on Writing and Women Characters

At another time, Bud and I were talking about the women characters in his books, particularly in *The Way West,* his Pulitzer Prize–winning novel. I had always used *The Big Sky* in my "Montana Writers" class, but at the time, I was preparing for a class on "Women and the Frontier Experience," and I planned to use *The Way West* early on in the course. As we began our discussion, Bud told me that he had a favorite question he posed whenever the topic of pioneer women was introduced: "I wonder," he asked, "how many men would have gone West had they been women?"

That question became the underpinning of the "Women and the Frontier Experience" class—along with another question one of the students discovered on a notecard: "If I had lived then, would the strength of my dreams have brought me West with the pioneers?"

Rebecca Evans, the main female character in *The Way West,* struggles with both questions as she prepares to leave the life she has known for the uncertainties of life on the trail: "It was like men to be excited and not to feel with their excitement such a sadness as a woman did at saying goodbye to her home. . . ." Despite her sadness and reluctance, though, Becky goes West, following her husband's dream as though it were her own. "A woman ain't cut like a man," she thinks. "Not so adventuresome or rangin' and likin' more to stay put—but still we foller 'em around, and glad to do it, too."[13]

That kind of sentiment did not sit well with some readers and reviewers who accused Guthrie of not being sympathetic toward his women characters. "I think I am," he countered. "When I wrote *The Way West,* for example, I began to think about Rebecca Evans, a rather hefty woman, jouncing over the plains, and I thought 'that must have been hell on her breasts'—and I put that in the book to express in a physical way the hardships those pioneer women endured."

"Of course," he continued, "the pioneer women, largely unacknowledged, were real heroines. They made the westward trek, often with babies, always with more concern for their children or menfolk than for themselves. By and large, maybe the westering experience was easier for men. I'm not sure, though, that the men had more fun. They weren't burdened with such drudgery as the women had to contend with, but still, if they were good men and concerned about their wives and their families, they had a big burden on them, too. . . ."

Guthrie spoke frequently during our talks about turning to the historical record for character prototypes and dramatic episodes for his novels. "Everything is based on record," he said, to underscore the historical accuracy of his work. "Not my characters, necessarily, but I try to be totally honest to history. I don't like to put words in the mouths of people who have actually lived and are now dead. That seems to be a little like disfiguring headstones. So I won't do that. But still, I try to be true to the time, the events, the techniques, the experiences of people of that time."[14]

That attitude is probably Guthrie's best defense against those who would read an anti-women bias into his work. The attitudes he expresses were current in the mid-1800s. One scene in *The Way West* demonstrates the conventions of the time with a touch of humor—and with a tip of the author's hat to the women as well, as expressed by one of his characters. The men on the train meet to discuss an issue of propriety: Wood for cooking fires is scarce; is it proper for women to collect and cook over buffalo chips? The men will decide what should be done and let the women know. When a Mr. Byrd expresses his opinion that "it's not a lady-like thing," Higgins, another man in the party, is amused:

> It struck him that Byrd and some of the others, for all that they knew better, stuck to some queer ideas of women, not liking to think of them as flesh and blood and stomach and guts but as something different, something a cut above earthly things, so that no one should let on to them that critters had hind ends. . . . [15]

Higgins suspects that the women in the party—who are not privy to the meetings of the male leadership, of course—would find this whole discussion very amusing because, in his opinion, "women had harder heads than men liked to believe."[16]

Guthrie gives the job of summing up the contribution of women on the westward trek (and of expressing his own admiration for those women) to Becky Evans's husband:

> Raw or not, the women did their part and more. They traveled head to head with men, showing no more fear and asking no favor. . . . They had a kind of toughness in them you might not think, seeing them in a parlor. . . . It was lucky for the pride of men that few traveled with their wives to Oregon. They'd never quite believe again a woman was to look at but not to listen to.[17]

While this view of women's capabilities was realistic in Guthrie's eyes, it did not necessarily bring about major changes in women's status and standing in their newly formed frontier communities. "The early westerner was very courteous to the womenfolk," he said, commenting on the passage above. "I think that was half out of convention, but it also was a way to keep seeing women as needing protection, etc."

There was also the clash between women's desires to "civilize" the West, and the wishes of at least some of the men who sought sanctuary there from the law and society to keep it untamed. The arrival of Guthrie's wagon train at Fort Laramie allows the author to offer the differing views his characters might have on "civilization."

Dick Summers, who was first introduced in *The Big Sky* and who was destined to return again in *Fair Land, Fair Land,* has led the train this far, but soon will leave it to seek the freedom of the mountains. As they approach the fort, he is disturbed by a sign of the changes taking place in his beloved West: "A cornfield, even like the sorry patch by the fort, didn't belong with war whoops and scalping knives. It belonged with cabins and women and children playing safe in the sun. It belonged with the dull pleasure, with the fat belly and the dim eye of safety."[18]

Contrast Summer's attitude with that of Rebecca Evans:

> She sighed inside, thinking it would be good to stay at the fort for the rest of her life and so be done with dirt and hard travel and eyes teary with camp smoke and the back sore from stooping over a fire and the legs cramped from sitting on the ground. . . . Her face, she knew, was a sight, reddened by the sun and coarsened by the wind until it was more man's face than woman's. For all that God had made her big and stout and

> not dainty, she wanted to feel womanlike, to be clean and smooth skinned and sometimes nice dressed, not for [her husband] alone, but for herself, for herself as a woman, so's to feel she was a rightful being and had a rightful place. . . .[19]

Guthrie explained his ability to speak through these two very different characters with the ring of truth by noting that he builds his characters "by thinking, by transposing myself, if that is possible, by trying to think as they might think. You will note in my books that I always try to be totally with the character whose viewpoint I am expressing, whose sensibilities, understandings, or lack of understandings are right there. I have the feeling that if the author extrapolates his imagination enough, he can really understand everybody, even the other sex."

The Loss of a Friend

When Bud died in April of 1991, the *Billings Gazette* asked me to write a piece about his importance to the state, to the literary world, and to his family and his many friends. It was a hard task. I had known that he was not well—in fact, my son and I had planned to visit the Guthries to videotape an interview with them, but the trip was postponed when Carol called to say that Bud just wasn't up to it at the moment. Still, even though he had lived a long and amazing life, I wasn't ready when word came of his death.

The tribute ran in the May 5 Sunday paper, and before much time had passed I began receiving notes of appreciation from Guthrie family members and fans of his work, like Bruce Kennedy, president of Sage Publishing, which published several Wyoming newspapers. Kennedy wrote that it was hard for him to believe that more than forty years had passed since he first read the words of A. B. Guthrie, Jr. "They always meant so much to me," he added—a feeling I could well understand.

It seems to me fitting that I include portions of that *Gazette* piece in this collection of recollections and reflections:

> Bud left us at that tantalizing season when hope grows with the new grass and joy surges at the sound of birds' songs, and so his loss seems keener, somehow, and speaks more eloquently of the end of a literary era.
>
> For several decades, Guthrie was the dean of Montana literature. He was honored by prestigious groups and awarded prestigious prizes, among them the 1950 Pulitzer in literature for *The Way West,* which chronicled life on a wagon train bound for Oregon. *The Way West* was the second title in a series of novels which explored the opening and the settling of the West, particularly Montana; it followed *The Big Sky,* which many consider Guthrie's masterpiece, and set the stage for *These Thousand Hills, Arfive,* and *The Last Valley.* Guthrie returned to that series and to some of the characters first introduced in *The Big Sky* and *The Way West* in 1982 when, in spite of having declared himself through with [the series], he produced *Fair Land, Fair Land,* a story that follows *The Way West* chronologically and follows much of Guthrie's personal history emotionally and creatively.
>
> In *Fair Land, Fair Land,* Dick Summers, former mountain man (*The Big Sky*) turned wagon train guide (*The Way West*), returns to the West of his earlier adventures, renews his friendship with the Indian woman Teal Eye, a character first introduced in *The Big Sky,* and, although she is much younger, marries her. Together they build a good life—until their happiness is destroyed as a result of increasing settlement on and near Indian lands. Guthrie often said that he had never been as productive in his life as he was in his years with his second wife, Carol; and, indeed, much of the credit for his longevity and continued creativity goes to her. The world literary community

owes Carol Guthrie a great debt—a debt which I believe Guthrie acknowledged in writing of the "revitalization" of Dick Summers in *Fair Land, Fair Land,* and crediting most of what was good in Dick's new life to his happy relationship with Teal Eye.

The cautionary note first sounded in *The Big Sky*—that men can destroy that which they love most, as the mountain men did in the trapping out of the territory; as guides, such as Dick Summers, did in leading settlers into the open West, to fill it with towns and cities and more and more people—is heard through all of Guthrie's work. "It's all sp'iled," characters in *The Big Sky* say. But, of course, it—the majestic mountains, the open spaces, and the quality of life which could be lived under the big sky—was not "all sp'iled," although man continues to have a go at spoiling what is left. That, in fact, became an increasing concern to Guthrie, and his efforts on behalf of the land and the landscape which were always so important in his work are part of his legacy.

His body of work—the novels, the poems, the articles and essays, the autobiography, his letters—will continue to excite readers, to entice them into the experience of the West, to entreat them to do their part to preserve that which perhaps they will only come to know through his words. That's the comfort in loss—that so much of the man lives on in what he has written.

But the loss of the man himself cannot be compensated by a shelf of books, even though the books are important, eminently readable, and enjoyable. Bud Guthrie meant so much to so many people, not only in this state, but throughout the world, both personally and professionally, that there's a void now that will not be filled. With his death, too, the literary leadership in Montana passes to a younger generation of writers . . . and Bud would be the first to say how happy he was to know that the Montana literary community was growing—that there were younger, talented writers taking up the same concerns and subjects that he wrote of, although he may well have wondered at anyone pursuing such a frustrating career. "There's no pleasure in writing," he told me once. "The pleasure is in having written well."

He wrote well. He lived long. His voice will continue to be heard through generations to come. But every spring will bring a reminder of his death. One of his last letters to me ended, "The sun shines today, and no wind blows, but the snow drifts are pretty high from the weather of two days ago. But the days are lengthening, and the first birds are about due to arrive. By late or middle February the gophers start trying the outside air, and I know that spring is coming."

The Honors and Accolades Continue

In the summer of 1994, Bud's professional colleagues inducted him into the Montana Journalism Hall of Fame at their annual meeting in Great Falls. Carol Guthrie attended the ceremony and thanked Bud's fellow journalists and writers for honoring him in this fashion. Sam Gilluly, his old friend and fellow panelist at that Bozeman meeting two decades or more before, had been a Hall of Fame inductee a few years earlier, and Mel Ruder (who died in November 2000) will certainly join that select group at some point as well.[20] Bud would have appreciated the applause of his peers; they were the people who could rightly judge his work, and knowing that he had found favor with them would have pleased him. And as for his fellow Hall of Famers—many of whom he knew well—he'd count himself in good company.

For my daughters and me, that evening of tributes to Bud served as a memorial service. There were some tears shed, some stories told, some hugs shared. But as the assembled newspeople spoke of the influence Bud Guthrie had had on their lives, there was joy, too, similar to the feeling I get when one of my students, newly introduced to Bud's work, comes in with eyes shining to express his or her admiration and enthusiasm for whatever novel we've just read. What a gift he was to us—and what gifts he has provided for future generations in his novels and stories!

Notes

1. This was years before Chinook resident Richard Ford received the award for *Independence Day* and journalist Eric Newhouse of the *Great Falls Tribune* was awarded a Pulitzer for his year-long, twelve-part series, "Alcohol—Cradle to Grave."

2. The following reference to Boone's "home in the wilderness," from page 123 of *The Big Sky,* is interesting in part because it is one of the few places in the novel where Boone's attention (and ours) is directed toward the title element; in most instances, Boone and the other mountain dwellers, in the interest of self-protection and survival, have their eyes fixed on the ground or are looking straight ahead or around, not gazing upward: "Boone lay on his back and looked at a night sky shot with stars. They were sharp and bright as fresh-struck flames, like campfires that a traveler might sight on a far shore. Starlight was nearly as good as moonlight here on the upper river where blue days faded off into nights deeper than a man could believe. By day Boone could get himself on a hill and see forever, until the sky came down and shut off his eye. There was the sky above, blue as paint, and the brown earth rolling underneath, and himself between them with a free, wild feeling in his chest, as if they were the ceiling and floor of a home that was all his own."

3. A. B. Guthrie, Jr., *The Big Sky* (New York: William Sloane Associates, 1947; Boston: Houghton Mifflin, 1992), 150.

4. Ibid.

5. Ibid., 385.

6. Even though Norman was close in age to Guthrie, he did not begin his writing life until he had retired from the University of Chicago. In writing years, he was definitely a "newcomer." I first heard about Norman from Bud. We had picked up Carol and Bud at the Billings airport and were driving them to their hotel when Bud asked me if I'd read—or even heard of—*A River Runs through It.* When I told him I'd never heard of the book or its author, he assured me that I'd love the book (how right he was—and I came to love the author, too, even though he could be grumpy at times!). Bud wasn't surprised

that I hadn't heard anything about *A River Runs through It:* The only review thus far, he said, had been published in *Fly Fishing* magazine. This gave him an opening for one of his favorite topics: the Ineptitude of Eastern Critics and Reviewers. To illustrate, he shared a favorite story on the subject. A reviewer complained about *The Way West* by writing, "How tired I am of drunken preachers in western novels!" Bud was happy to explain how tired he was of East Coast reviewers who either ignored or apparently didn't read the books with a western flavor they'd been assigned to review. There was no drunken preacher in *The Way West.*

7. Maclean in a talk at Eastern Montana College (now Montana State University–Billings), July 14, 1977.

8. Thomas McGuane, *Nobody's Angel* (New York: Random House, 1981), 61.

9. Thomas Savage, *The Pass* (Garden City, NY: Doubleday, Doran and Co., 1944), 235.

10. Frank Bird Linderman, *Pretty Shield: Medicine Woman of the Crows;* originally published as *Red Mother* (New York: John Day Company, 1932; Lincoln: University of Nebraska Press, 1972), 70, 24.

11. Guthrie, *The Big Sky,* 4.

12. Ibid., 20.

13. A. B. Guthrie, Jr., *The Way West* (New York: William Sloane Associates, 1949; Boston: Houghton Mifflin, 1993), 171.

14. A good illustration of how successfully he was able to transform records and historical accounts into good fiction concerns *These Thousand Hills.* In preparation for that novel, Bud had read the journals of Con Price, a well-respected rancher. A mutual friend took Mr. Price, by then quite an elderly gentleman, a copy of *These Thousand Hills* and reported back that Price was confounded by how much that "young whippersnapper" Guthrie knew about early-day ranching.

15. Guthrie, *The Way West,* 92.

16. Ibid., 93.

17. Ibid., 297.

18. Ibid., 138.

19. Ibid., 140–41.

20. A journalist is eligible for induction into the Montana Journalism Hall of Fame five years after his/her death. (In Bud's case, the five-year requirement was waived in order to hold the ceremonies at a Great Falls convention.) Pictures and biographies of those honored are displayed in the School of Journalism Building on The University of Montana campus.

James Welch

The West from Two Perspectives

Bud Guthrie has always been one of my heroes. He was a very good friend. We did a lot of things together. A couple of stories illustrate how our friendship began.

The first one happened at Bill Kittredge's house many years ago. There was a literary conference in Missoula, and it was a zoo. Ken Kesey came, John Hawkes, Marge Piercy, and a whole bunch of people, and after one of the sessions there was a party over at Kittredge's house. It was so packed that my wife Lois and I found ourselves pinned against the living room wall. We couldn't even make it into the kitchen to get a drink. This guy was standing next to me, and we started chatting about the conference and so on. He wanted a drink, too, but he couldn't get anywhere, so we just talked for a little while. Then he and his wife, Carol, left, and I and my wife, Lois, left, and it wasn't until a few months later that I discovered I'd been talking to A. B. Guthrie, Jr., who was probably the most luminous literary light at this conference.

The other story that I thought was kind of fun was once at a dinner at Ripley Hugo's house when her husband, Dick, was out of town on a reading trip. Bud and Carol were again in Missoula. I think Bud was signing books or doing something at a conference.

Afterwards we went to Ripley's house for dinner, and there were Bud and Carol and Ripley and again Lois and me. *Winter in the Blood* had just come out, and so Bud started talking about it at the table. He gave me a kind of report card: A minus for characters, A for landscape and descriptive writing. Then he gave me a C minus for plot. It was kind of interesting because everybody jumped on him: Carol, Ripley, and Lois. They said, "What do you mean, C minus?" But I knew exactly what he was talking about. *Winter in the Blood* didn't have a plot. And I think what he was saying to me was, you can get away with that once, but don't try it again.

I think it took courage and a real act of imagination to write *The Big Sky.* Up until that time nobody had done anything like it. It really was a new look at the West, a dark look, and that took courage. For in the 1940s and just after the Second World War, we were in a very patriotic time. We had just won the war. People were feeling good about themselves. Books and movies reflected this feeling of intense patriotism in this country. One movie I always think of is *They Died with Their Boots On,* which was the story of the Little Bighorn, or at least Hollywood's version, starring Errol Flynn, Ronald Reagan, and Anthony Quinn as Crazy Horse. This was a time of intense patriotism. I think American literature of the time reflected that and righteousness. We were invincible. And when *The Big Sky* came along, it deflated this notion that we were invincible, that we could do no wrong. I think it was controversial back then because suddenly Americans were in the wrong out here on the frontier. And furthermore they were kind of fumbling around. They didn't quite have an idea what they were up to. So I think it did take a lot of courage to write that book, and it took a lot of historical study and imagination, too.

When I wrote *Fools Crow,* I had to put myself into the period of the 1860s up to 1870. It was very difficult. As I sat at my typewriter, I would just sit there, day after day, just sit there. Nothing would come because I was intimidated. I knew once I wrote the first sentence I was pretty much committed. And I didn't know if I wanted to commit myself, even at that point. But finally, after about a week of this, I got a sentence, and then a paragraph, and then it started coming. It started flowing. And suddenly I was back in that period. For the rest of the novel and all the drafts that followed, every time I would sit down I would be instantly transported into that period. So it became easier as time went on.

I imagine Bud encountered that same kind of problem. When you're writing contemporary fiction, you're writing about the world you see around you. You don't have to recreate a period. But Bud did. He got the courage and re-created that period, and frankly I don't see anyone who could refute him, because when I wrote *Fools Crow* I suddenly was the expert on that period. I knew more about the Blackfeet of the 1860s than anybody else in the world, because I was doing it. I was re-creating it. That was a pretty exciting thing to think about. It wasn't a history book. It didn't describe what it was like out there. It didn't give you the facts. There are facts in there, certainly, but for the most part it was a re-creation of that period. And whether I was right or wrong, I was the expert. And so I think Bud pretty much became the expert of the West, the frontier of the 1830s, the Upper Missouri country of *The Big Sky.*

The title of this essay is "The West from Two Perspectives," one white and one Indian. As I said, in the 1830s this was pretty wild country—the Upper Missouri, probably from Fort Union on out into Montana. For these trappers and traders to come in was quite an event. They would essentially change the country. As Uncle Zeb says, “She’s gone, goddam it!” when Boone and Jim and Dick are sitting there talking to him at Fort Union. Uncle Zeb has been reduced to a meat hunter now for the fort, and he doesn’t like it. All he really likes anymore is whiskey. He doesn’t like people. He came into the country in 1820. And in those ten years since he saw it all disappear—the wildness of the country—there’s hardly a place where you could go that hadn’t been trod on before. And for an old mountain man like Uncle Zeb, this was the end of innocence, or the end of pristine wilderness, pristine country. It was all gone for him. And I found that pretty interesting because 1820 was only fifteen years after Lewis and Clark. Of course the French had been in this country. The British had been in this country. And so there probably were a lot of footprints out there, boot prints I guess you could say, out there on the plains and in the mountains.

From the Indians’ perspective, of course, they had always been there. Their creation stories were centered out on the plains and in the mountains of this country. I know a lot of people say the Indians came from Asia on a land bridge. But the Indians don’t say that, because it’s quite clear through their creation stories, and all of their other stories and traditions, that they came from this country. And so this was their territory. They dealt with it. It was quite easy to live on. The game was here. They knew how to live here. The white people coming in had a more difficult time, I think—partly because of the Indians. Sometimes the Indians didn’t particularly like them coming into their territories, and especially later, when the Oregon Trail and the Bozeman Trail were created, and they started to divide the buffalo herds. From what I understand, the country for miles on either side of those trails was pretty much a barren country. All the grass was overgrazed and gone, and therefore the buffalo herds soon dwindled and were gone. Firewood was gone. These were pretty serious encroachments into

Indian territory, and it is no wonder that Indians resented this kind of thing even though they'd welcomed these people originally. They just didn't know how many of them would keep coming and coming and destroy the land.

But before the settlers came, there were the mountain men and the traders. As Bud points out in *The Big Sky,* they felt they were pretty much on their own. They seemed to get along fairly well with Indian people, especially the traders. But I think it's clear during the course of the book that that's not the case. The theme of Bud's work, as far as I can figure out, is "She's all gone." And again this is 1830, if you can imagine. Here we are in 1997 and it's still not gone. But maybe part of that wilderness, that wildness, is gone. The feeling of setting the first boot print in a particular area, say the South Fork of the Teton River, where Bud lived and wrote and set a lot of his actions, that's forever gone.

The book that I think, though, rather than *The Big Sky,* that more closely parallels *Fools Crow* is *Fair Land, Fair Land,* Bud's later book that completes his saga of the mountain men. Actually Dick Summers, to me, was probably the most interesting character of them all. He didn't consider himself a real mountain man. He wasn't hard enough. He wasn't cruel enough. In *Fair Land, Fair Land* it almost cost him his life. When he finally meets up with Boone again, they're going to get this matter settled of Boone shooting Jim and abandoning Teal Eye with a blind baby. During the course of their confrontation, of course, Boone—being the headstrong man that he is—lunges at Dick and practically strangles him to death. Dick, being the kind of man he is, could reach for his knife. He could stab Boone. But he doesn't. He feels everything going dark. It's only his buddy Higgins who actually shoots Boone. Otherwise Dick would have died even though he could have killed Boone. I think in some ways that makes Dick a much more interesting character. He has this complexity. On the one hand, he can go back to Missouri and farm. He can lead settlers out to Oregon. But always his heart is in this country, even though he admits he cannot live here as a mountain man. Eventually he doesn't. He marries into the Blackfeet tribe when he marries Teal Eye. He settles into a fairly nice life, even though he continues to see the country going, the game disappearing. Even though this troubles him quite a bit.

If the theme of Guthrie's work was "it's all gone," to the Blackfeet the country was going. They had to learn to cope with this going. But they did it because they were a tribal society. I think any society works better than individuals do. They'd lived in the country for a long time. They knew how to do it. And there were certain mores that allowed them to live in harmony with this country. They didn't fight it. They lived with it.

To them, the idea that the country was going meant to them, how do we survive now? They learned to cope—of course, they were put on reservations and so on—but even that was a part of the survival. Actually, the survival goes on today. It reminds me of a story that my wife tells about her grandmother. She was a tiny woman. She was in the hospital in pretty bad shape. I guess you could say she was on the verge of dying. She was in one of those beds that have motors in them, and somebody pressed the wrong button and this bed started folding her up. Here she is in all these mattresses and sheets and pillows and everything. You can't even see her. They were trying to free her and they heard this little voice say, "I'm still here."

That's kind of like the way the Indians are. They're still here. This new book I'm writing is about the Indians who accompanied Buffalo Bill's Wild West Show to Europe in 1889, and one in particular.[1] I've done a lot of research into the European attitude toward these Indians. And the Europeans, of course, loved them. One of the reasons they loved them was because the Indians were a dying race. They felt this was the last time they were going to see these Indians alive because they would vanish from the face of the earth. A lot of the newspaper stories I've read have reflected this kind of attitude, but it was curiously mixed with the idea that these Indians were almost sub-normal. They weren't quite human. One article I read talks about their "brick-red faces" and how there's no intelligence behind these faces. Like they're just not quite human beings. So it's a curious attitude they had toward Indians. On the one hand they thought they weren't quite human. On the other hand they were still noble people—but perhaps only because they were going to die out as a race.

I think the Europeans had a better attitude toward Indians than people in this country, because around the turn of the century the people of America did want the Indians to disappear. It wasn't just a romantic idea. It was a very real idea. I won't use any inflammatory words like extinction or that kind of thing, but the idea was to kill the Indian and save the man—that's quite a famous quote. In other words, take the Indianness out of the Indians so they could assimilate into the mainstream, and that way they would disappear. I think religious groups as well as the government played a big role in this. But what's really amazing to me is that here, in 1997, very few Indian tribes have gone. Most of the tribes are still here. It's incredible. The culture, after reaching the nadir probably from the turn of the century on to the 1950s, is now coming back stronger than ever. Indian people realize they have to save the language. They have to save the traditions and the culture. So the Indians are still here. The people who are gone are the white people who came into the country originally—the trappers, the traders, a lot of the settlers. They couldn't make a living on this land so they went away. In their stead came other people, of course. This audience probably has a lot of people who are third- or fourth-generation Montanans, or westerners at least. And so eventually a lot of people did stay.

I think one of the reasons that the Indians did survive is because they were adaptable. For better or for worse, they pretty much embraced a lot of the white culture. Where the mountain men in *The Big Sky* seemed to reject the materialistic world of people back in civilization, back in America, the Indians pretty enthusiastically accepted things that could make their life easier: horses, guns, sugar, mirrors, steel knives, trade cloth, and unfortunately, whiskey. The Indians really accepted the white culture, or the things that the white culture brought them. These things did make their lives easier. They became used to drinking coffee. That was good. They became used to adding sugar to their coffee. That was even better. And of course the mountain men enjoyed whiskey and coffee and salt and so on, but the rest of it they pretty much rejected. I think that may be emblematic of the difference between the Indian perspective on the West and the white perspective. The Indians accepted things. These early white people rejected things. And that made a difference in the way they looked at the country.

In *Fair Land, Fair Land,* the book that's most akin to *Fools Crow* just because of the proximity of history, Bud does talk about how Summers and Higgins came to live with the Blackfeet. But it's kind of interesting, they still had this attitude of separateness from the tribe. They preferred to live by themselves instead of joining the tribe. It's only toward the end when everything is pretty much gone—it's hard to find game, etc.—that they actually join the tribe. And unfortunately they join Heavy Runner's band, which was killed at the massacre on the Marias on January 23, 1870. To me that's pretty significant. Just from a personal standpoint, and as related to Bud, because we both ended our books with that massacre. Mine goes on to the spring, but his ends right there. Bud's book ends with Summers getting killed, and his wife Teal Eye leaving the group forcefully. Actually, Summers kicks her out of the lodge and says, "Run," and gives her a couple of blankets. And so in a sense my book ends with the thunder pipe ceremony in the spring, which occurred when they heard the first thunder and the rains came. And it was a time of renewal. It was a time when the grasses grew and the buffalo came back and the berries ripened, so it was a kind of hopeful ending to that book, even though a lot of people still focused on the massacre and the smallpox epidemic. But that was my attempt to say that Indians will go on. They will survive.

Even though Bud's book is very graphic about the massacre and the attitude of the soldiers—they go through the lodges cutting the teepee strings and burning the people inside—I think when Teal Eye runs it kind of leaves just a little bit of opening for some sort of hope for the future. We don't know what happened to Teal Eye. Realistically, it's January 23 in one of the coldest winters ever, and she's going out by herself. We hope she's going to survive. People did survive that ordeal. And that's a note of hope. So I think both novels maybe do end on a note of hope. Even though when Summers dies, it's kind of the end of the mountain man tradition, Teal Eye living is kind of another way of saying that the Blackfeet culture will continue. So I felt quite akin to that particular book.

I think Bud was a very important writer. This has to do with attitudes. A lot of people have criticized *The Big Sky* for attitudes toward Indians. There are squaws and bucks and papooses. Women are there basically to serve the men, from the squaws at the rendezvous and around the forts, to the women they become involved with on a longer term. Use of the word "nigger" is everywhere.

And so I've heard a few people criticize this book because of this. But if you look in *Fools Crow,* you'll see a lot of prejudice from one Indian group to another. The Blackfeet hate the Crows. They hate the Snakes. They do anything in their power to make them suffer. So there's a form of what you might call racism, a kind of scorn for these other tribes. I've received some criticism about the women in *Fools Crow* being there again basically to serve the men. So I think each of these books has had some criticism along those lines. But what you have to keep in mind is that's the way things were back then. It wasn't the 1980s and 1990s. These mountain men were very hard men. That's why they succeeded out here. That's why Dick Summers always felt he wasn't a real mountain man, because he wasn't that hard, he wasn't that cruel. It was this very nature that we might find distasteful by today's standards that allowed them to survive out in the West. And I imagine some of them even prospered in those early days. Some of those people were fortunate enough to go back home before all the beaver were trapped out. In *Fools Crow,* I know from reading about the historical Blackfeet society, it was a very male-oriented society. The women basically took care of the camp. They went to get the firewood and the water. They cooked while the men sat around and gambled and told stories and worked on their equipment. This was the attitude back in those days. It's not to be confused with the author's attitude.

I met a woman at a conference out in Eugene, Oregon, recently. She was a Cree from Canada. We got along famously out there, and she just sent me a letter a couple of weeks ago in which she talks about both *Winter in the Blood* and *Fools Crow* and the way Crees are treated in both. In *Fools Crow,* the Blackfeet call them, "The Liars." This didn't sit well with her. In *Winter in the Blood,* the young woman whom the narrator brings home is a

Cree, and the narrator's grandmother, an old lady, sits there and thinks she's a Cree, an enemy. The Crees were no good. They opened their thighs for the Long Knives. So this woman raked me over the coals for denigrating the Crees in such a way. And I'm going to write back to her. She's going for a master's degree, so she should know that you can't attribute this kind of stuff to the author. This is a fictional situation. These are fictional characters. It's not particularly the author. I mean, the author may feel that way about the Crees, but in the fiction it's the character who feels that way about the Crees. So I think it's important always to separate the story from the role the author plays in creating the story. I think you'll find that it's all fictional, and that the author's usually a pretty nice guy who has nothing against anybody. And that's what I thought when I met Bud, and that's why I liked him and *The Big Sky.*

Notes

1. This book, *The Heartsong of Charging Elk: A Novel,* was published by Doubleday in 2000.

The Circle 8 Ranch outside of Choteau, Montana
Left to right: unidentified, Grandfather Heffelfinger with cane,
Jeanne Everett, Mildred Walker Schemm, George Schemm,
A. B. Guthrie, Jr. (smoking), Charles Everett,
Joseph Kinsey Howard (with hat), Dr. G. A. Sexton, Ripley Schemm
(Hugo) (sitting, with saddle shoes), unidentified, n.d.

COURTESY MONTANA HISTORICAL SOCIETY
PHOTO ARCHIVES, HELENA

Jo-Ann Swanson

"Rattling the Teacups" of His Hometown: Guthrie's Grizzly, His Grocery List, and Other Tales of Choteau Life

"Some men escape and some renounce their origins. I didn't want to. Most of me was what I had been; most of what I had been I would always be, son of a scholar, boy explorer of field and stream, part book man, part aborigine, and the core of me Choteau, Montana."

—A. B. Guthrie, Jr., "Town to Be a Boy In,"
Venture: The Traveler's World, October 1964

Once upon a time in the West, at least sometime before 1985, a grizzly bear reportedly broke into the Guthrie cabin on the Rocky Mountain Front west of Choteau, Montana.

The grizzly busted down the front door, got into the kitchen, and pulled a table over against the kitchen counter. In short order, the kitchen was confettied with sugar, salt, and flour; cans went rolling across the floor; and honey and syrup flowed everywhere.

The table collapsed. The grizzly got its head wedged inside a cupboard and—in its struggle to extricate itself—managed to pull the entire cupboard from the wall. In panic, the grizzly, still trying to fight off this overpowering headdress, endured a boxing match with the doorway. Finally, it lumbered into the living room and crashed its way outside—smack through the living room picture window.

It's a funny story. Readers will note the colorful details, fitting tribute to Guthrie himself. Readers will notice, too, some lack of specifics. No mention is made in the story about whether the grizzly invasion took place at the old family Guthrie cabin, Twin Lakes, or at the nearby Barn, which Guthrie and second wife Carol built in 1975. No one who tells the tale seems to know exactly when the altercation occurred.

Instead, the locale is almost mythological, "the Guthrie cabin," even if listeners don't know which one, there, on the spectacular rim of windswept plains that rise face-to-face to meet the rugged Rocky Mountains.

This tale has circulated for some time and is told by a few locals, gossip repeated on the main street of Choteau, a tree-lined town of 1,740 souls some forty miles northwest of Great Falls. It's told with zest and relish. Some might say malice; after all, humor, as Sigmund Freud noted earlier this century, contains elemental forces of hostility. The tale is cautionary—about a man who deals with Nature, with forces he cannot control. It's a story of Nature's revenge, ironic because it repeats Guthrie's message at Guthrie's expense. This time the cupboards are turned; the joke is on Guthrie, who loved a good joke as much as anyone else.

Only one problem exists with this oft-repeated tale—the story is not true. The only bear Guthrie's wife Carol has seen on the Guthrie home place on the Front was a black bear, which quickly disappeared from sight. The collective imagination exhibited in this story may explain why Guthrie, in a fit of pique with Choteau, once wrote on a book jacket that he hailed "from Teton County."

Here's another colorful story about Guthrie. However, this one is true: Bud Guthrie and some friends were fishing the Teton River just down from his place when Alice (Mrs. Ken) Gleason, one of his neighbors on the Front (who died in the fall of 1997), stopped to ask if he needed anything from town. Guthrie's reply was characteristic, if the Guthrie legend is worthy of anything at all.

"Bread and bourbon."

Succinct, alliterative vernacular with echoes of Omar Khayyam. Worthy of Guthrie.

Missoula writer Bill Kittredge recalls Alice Gleason's telling of that tale at Guthrie's ninetieth birthday party at the Pine Butte Swamp Nature Conservancy at the site of the Gleasons' former home, the old Circle 8 Ranch. "At Pine Butte, he was clearly dying. As a matter of fact, he died that winter. All of these Choteau people got up and spoke. People loved him," says Kittredge.

Such stories keep alive the Guthrie mythos and machismo. The reality appears somewhat more complex. He was a man of contradictions who inspired ambivalent emotions. Guthrie was loved by many—and not loved by others.

Clearly, he was not always understood. Guthrie may have written about the wilderness in a powerful manner and spent years in research, as he did at Harvard in preparation for *The Big Sky*, but he didn't like to "rough it," notes Mary Helen Sexton.

"People he wrote about had great adventures, yet he was not an outdoorsman." Her parents Dr. George and Helen Sexton were good friends of Guthrie's, and she had known Guthrie since childhood as a neighbor on the Front. She recalls that his packing trips into the Rockies were "always first-class."

"He sat. He was not an outdoorsman," concurs son "Pete" (Bert), with whom Guthrie waged open disagreement over environmental policy, some of which centered upon Guthrie's causes of saving the grizzly from extinction and opposing development on the Rocky Mountain Front.

The dilemma is an old one, not limited to small towns where writers grew up—the writing being mistaken for the writer. Guthrie was no Boone Caudill, his defeated adventurous anti-hero of *The Big Sky.* Instead, Guthrie was a writer. Nearly the last seventeen years of his life, he pounded a Smith Corona in his loft office of the Barn, behind a window overlooking Ear Mountain four miles away, chain-smoking Camel straights. Some argue that he was less productive than in earlier life, yet many say those last years were the happiest and most peaceful of his life.

Great Falls Tribune files indicate that Guthrie spent a mere one-fifth of his life, his first eighteen of ninety years, in Choteau, proper. He came "home" permanently in the early 1950s (he had spent summers at his Twin Lakes cabin on the Front, which he had bought in 1947) to, first, Great Falls and then Twin Lakes—but he never returned to Choteau again.

After Guthrie and second wife Carol married in 1969, they built the Barn, modeled on the original barn at the Guthrie home in Choteau, in 1975. There, he continued to live the final seventeen years of his life on his beloved Front. In total, he spent some forty years in the Choteau region.

Why did Guthrie return to Choteau? Great Falls author Dan Cushman asserts that Guthrie originally returned from his journalism career in Kentucky (where he had spent some twenty-seven years) because of his close friendship with journalist, historian, and crusader Joseph Kinsey Howard. Neither of Guthrie's children, Pete of Choteau nor "Gus" (Helen) Miller of Butte, or wife Carol give too much credence to Cushman's recollection, however. Daughter Gus says Guthrie's return was pragmatic. "He always said that when he got two thousand dollars ahead, he would return to Montana. And he did." The success of *The Big Sky* in 1947 had led to *The Way West* in 1949, which was awarded a Pulitzer

Prize, and he then completed the screenplay for *Shane* in 1953, winning an Oscar nomination.

Yet Guthrie's friendship with Howard appears to be pivotal. The Great Falls area would become a mecca for Montana writers in the 1940s and 1950s—a state forerunner to the Missoula success that began with Richard Hugo's immigration in 1964—and would include Mildred Walker Schemm, Cushman, himself, and Western writers Norman Fox and Robert McCaig. Several state writing conventions noted both Guthrie and Howard on their rosters: The Writers Conference of 1949 at Montana State University, in Missoula, listed Howard as director and among the seven featured writers was "A. B. Guthrie, Lexington, Ky." Later, both Guthrie and Howard would lecture at the Bread Loaf Writers Conference led by poet Robert Frost in Middlebury, Vermont.

The idea gives an intriguing image of friends in close proximity, however short-lived, in early 1950s Great Falls. Guthrie was a hard-working and tough-talking former journalist and writer, working in the studio behind his house at 520 Third Avenue North, near downtown Great Falls. Howard was a journalist, writer, and intense crusader who lived with his mother, a Christian Scientist, about three blocks away at the corner of Third Street and Second Avenue North, in a two-room corner apartment on the third floor. Howard, a hub of the Great Falls writing scene, would fall one vote short of a posthumous Pulitzer Prize in 1953 for a book that drew some of its early inspiration from the Choteau area—*Strange Empire* about Louis Riel and the Métis people.

Carol Guthrie recalls that Guthrie was one of the last people to see Howard alive. "Forty minutes before he died," Bud Guthrie had told a *Great Falls Tribune* reporter in the 1980s, "Joe stopped by my place and wanted to know if there was anything he could get me." Howard's mother had bought a cabin on the Gleasons' Circle 8 Ranch in the 1930s, so the Howards and Guthries were neighbors on the Front for many years, along with Mildred Walker Schemm and her husband Dr. Ferdinand Schemm.

Howard was driving New York editor Helen Everitt and her son to the Great Falls airport from a writing conference in Missoula that Guthrie and Howard both had attended. Howard suffered a heart attack eight miles outside of Choteau; a second attack at Teton County Medical Center killed him.

Today, many of Guthrie's closest friends and neighbors are also dead—his first wife Harriet Larson, neighbors Alice and Ken Gleason, Dr. George and Helen Sexton. A few contemporaries and mostly sons and daughters of Choteau tell the old tales.

Choteau was town; the Front was country. Never would the two meet. "We are country people," stressed Carol Guthrie, using the present tense, in 1997 at the Barn, some twenty-five miles west of Choteau. "We were very happy here. With our thirty-year differences in ages, it was implicit he would die before I did. We were together the entire day. We liked it that way. A lot of stories go around, but our neighbors know and understand us." Even today she uses the present tense.

"If we were in trouble, people would come," Guthrie had told Nicholas O'Connell ten years earlier in an interview in the book *At the Field's End* in 1987.

Former Circle 8 Ranch owner Alice Gleason pronounced unequivocal judgment a month before her death in the fall of 1997: "We were neighbors and good friends for many, many years," she avowed in a telephone interview. "He was a very good neighbor."

Yet, in Guthrie's 1991 obituary, Melody Martinsen, *Choteau Acantha* editor who grew up in the Choteau area, noted, "While Guthrie gained national fame and praise for his writing, he developed an uneasy relationship with his hometown, a conservative, agriculture-based community."

Mrs. "Shorty" (Mabel) Crane, now in her eighties, shows off a bookshelf of signed Guthrie editions, but is more blunt about her neighbors: "I think the feeling in Choteau was they didn't like him."

Several Choteau residents provided major reasons, several of which are interrelated, that led to Guthrie's "uneasy" relationship with his hometown:

Morality, or Whose Morality Is It, Anyway?

1. Guthrie played to a tough crowd. In *Dakota,* Kathleen Norris's book about living on and writing in the Great Plains, Norris addresses the difficulty of trying to write unpopular truth in a small town, where some families rely on legend or half-truth. Guthrie's use of locals for literary material may have added to his distance from townspeople. Roy Jacobs of Choteau recalls that "He modeled his characters on people he knew in town." Guthrie's children Pete and Gus, as well as Sexton, agree. "Years back, a lot of old colorful people resided in these small towns. My dad used them in his books," says Pete.

Writer Cushman also addresses Montana gender constituencies in his autobiography of growing up in north-central Montana, *Plenty of Room and Air*; the genteel women's "civilized" town society conflicts with the men's wilderness-based taming of the frontier.

The idea is not new. In the John Ford film *Stagecoach,* the "schoolmarm" brings civilization, education, all the amenities, sometimes unwanted, to the rough-and-tough male frontier, a world that Guthrie portrayed in his early modernist novels of Montana (realistic, yet still romantic and sexist, to our late twentieth-century eyes).

Even though Guthrie was writing about relationships in an earlier time, some local women today disapprove of his books. Some of these local readings appear to be of the fundamentalist kind, lending themselves to literal interpretations. After all, *The Big Sky* can be seen as a moral and resounding indictment of greed—one of the Seven Deadly Sins.

"Guthrie was too raunchy," says Mrs. (Mabel) Crane of his writing. "He didn't understand women. He was a man's man." Crane alludes to his depiction of unmarried sex and his use of profanity, recalling that Guthrie's religious father, Bertram, was a bit "ashamed" of Guthrie's first book for these reasons. But another local, Patricia Otness, asks, "What's all the fuss about?" She wryly quotes a phrase a local had called "raunchy" in *The Big Sky:* "In the setting of the Mountains, Tetons, named by a lonely Frenchman thinking of a woman and her breasts." By today's standards, not risqué, indeed. Others seem inclined to dismiss, rather than discuss, Guthrie's books. Ironically, some critics place *The Blue Hen's Chick,* his gentle autobiography of early Choteau life, among his best books.

2. Guthrie took on the Bars vs. Churches. His father Bertram, the young first principal of Teton County Free High School, was a staunch Methodist (non-smoking, non-drinking) in a town not characterized as "church-going." He "ruled with an iron fist" was the cliché repeated by several locals. Guthrie, one of nine children, was the oldest of three who survived. The family was educated, well respected, and upwardly mobile. The Protestant work ethic clearly was functioning. In fact, Bertram insisted that all three of his children, Bud, Jane, and "Chick" (who later became a well-respected journalist) earn journalism degrees so they would have "something to fall back on."

In contrast, here is the Choteau that Guthrie portrays in the afore-quoted *Venture* article: "However much in need of grace, Choteau then [1859] and later was pretty well content to go its way to hell. A state that by 1896 had but one church for every 866 people and one saloon for each 107 might be a challenge to evangels, but it hardly wore the face of ready opportunity. . . . Today the count of churches and bars [in Choteau] give the churches a majority of one" (9–10).

3. Guthrie had a high profile in a hard-drinking era. Despite Guthrie's hard-living reputation, probably as much a by-product of the times he lived in as his individual proclivity, his approach to drinking in his last twenty years was disciplined and limited to beer and wine. He even gave up cigarettes in his eighties. Wife Carol says she never saw him drunk during their years of marriage. "He was not a drunk." In the past, during his divorce and Hollywood years, some locals say he was unhappy and drinking heavily. Of course, in today's more prohibitive climate, it's easy to forget that heavy drinking was common and socially acceptable during the 1940s and 1950s.

Community, or As a Role Model, He Was Human.

1. Guthrie married into the First Family of Choteau. He married Harriet Larson, the youngest daughter of long-time state senator Tom Larson, to whom Guthrie dedicated *The Big It, and Other Stories* ("To the memory of Tom Larson"). The influential senator and his eldest daughter drank often and well, although younger sister Harriet Guthrie never drank at all until later in her life, around the time of her divorce from Bud. Guthrie was blamed for his abandonment of Harriet, a First Daughter of Choteau. She died at a relatively young age in Great Falls in 1968. Their 1963

divorce and Guthrie's second marriage a year after Harriet died (he met second wife Carol Bischman in 1967 after the divorce) led to estrangement from children Pete and Gus.

2. Guthrie remarried and turned remote. Guthrie's second marriage brought him some of the happiest years of his life, yet a few old friends and his earlier family felt left out. Guthrie was an introvert and his second wife, not a local, came from North Dakota. His first wife Harriet had been an extrovert who connected him socially to the area, notes daughter Gus. Ironically, Carol, thirty years younger than Guthrie, was a similar age to Gus. Carol saved a sexist Missoula headline that proclaimed the 1969 marriage: "Writer, 68, marries woman, 38." The two opted for a more idyllic and isolated life at the Barn.

Money, or the Distrust of the Somewhat Doubtfully "Filthy Rich"

1. The classic Montana dilemma—Environment vs. Jobs. Guthrie's defense of the grizzly and opposition to development on the Rocky Mountain Front created a sense of betrayal and hard feelings with conservative ranchers, including one of his most vocal opponents, son Pete. Many Choteau locals felt forced to take sides. In a classic Montana showdown, some favored development and economic survival over saving the Front. Many national environmental groups supported Guthrie, which further alienated locals. Guthrie, of course, had foreseen the future, which was the underlying lesson of *The Big Sky* ("It's all gone," as Uncle Zeb proclaimed).

2. The Front for a few. In the late 1970s, the neighboring Gleasons and the Guthries sued against a development on the Front that would have included a dense clustering of some thirty houses. Although

they won the suit, some locals harbored hard feelings about the Front being an elite community and keeping other locals out.

3. The Green-Eyed Monster. Small towns, it has been observed by some of those who, themselves, hail from small towns, work best when everyone is about average, at the same level, in order to mitigate envy. Indeed, several local criticisms of Guthrie were tempered by a soon-familiar refrain, "Of course, some of it was jealousy."

"He was arrogant," declares long-time foe, the Bynum-area educator Ira Perkins, whose letters to and from Guthrie entertained readers of the *Choteau Acantha* in the early 1970s. Others felt Guthrie's Hollywood years made him impatient with small-town life and people. Perkins recalled a time soon after Guthrie was named "Foremost Citizen of Choteau" by *Time* magazine. Perkins saw Guthrie strolling down Main Street. "Two-thirds of the people didn't know him, wouldn't even say hi to him." However, this statement could more accurately reflect Guthrie's lower public profile, advancing age, and lessening community involvement in his later years. Like many communities, Choteau has seen a large influx of newcomers. Still, Roy Jacobs maintains, "Seventy percent of the people living in Choteau go back generations."

4. He was one of the "Summer People." "He mellowed in time, but he had a public persona: A. B. Guthrie who . . . didn't live here year round," is how Jacobs characterizes the writer. "He really wasn't a local figure." Roy's father, Cyril "Gotch" Jacobs, was a bartender and bar owner in Choteau during some of Guthrie's heavier drinking years. In typical local style, Guthrie frequented all three Choteau bars: the now-defunct Pioneer run by Jacobs; the Legion; and the Anchor. Of course, Guthrie had returned to the area permanently in the early 1950s. But small towns have long memories.

5. Some thought he was "filthy rich." "Of course, Choteau thought he was filthy rich," reports daughter Gus. Those well-publicized $100,000 advances were paid over ten years. Guthrie lived well, yes, but some family members claim he was a poor manager of money. Son Pete concurs with wife Carol that Guthrie continued to write into his eighties for financial reasons. A somewhat humbling thought.

Despite divergent points of view and emphasis among Choteau locals, some points of agreement emerge:

a. Guthrie was respected by most locals, but several disagreed vehemently with his opinions. Says Sexton, "Realistically, he did good things, but he was human."

b. Some of Guthrie's best characters had their roots in Choteau. Several were based on old-timers who used to drink and tell stories at the Pioneer Bar.

c. Many private libraries in Choteau contain autographed Guthrie volumes, which indicates support. Also, many locals say they have read all his books. That fact's not shabby for a place about which Guthrie once said, "Montana has a hell of a lot of people who don't read."

Guthrie left a large mark not only on Choteau, but the state, itself.

"I think his central book was *The Big Sky.* Everything around it is much smaller," notes Bill Kittredge. "Guthrie was one of the people, despite some people's misgivings about period racism and sexism, who led us through the revolution, who broke the western mindset. Guthrie, in the mid-century, tore the edifices down and let us westerners start building our own literature."

Daughter Gus recalls best Guthrie's legendary sense of humor and vitality. "He liked to 'rattle the teacups,' as his younger sister used to say. His sense of humor was so magnanimous you could forgive him anything."

In September 1997, a reception and exhibition at the Old Trail Museum in Choteau was spearheaded by then-director Eva McDunn and included cooperation between townspeople and Guthrie's two families. Fifty years since *The Big Sky* finds Choteau more conciliatory and forgiving than in the past.

The next step may be for one brave biographer to chronicle the colorful life of a writer who put Choteau on the literary map of Montana.

Guthrie ended his *Venture* article with ambivalence about his hometown, a resounding "yes" tempered by a "no" that remains indexed to the future, or at least some progress the future has wrought:

> And if I had the choice, I would choose Choteau for the years of my boyhood—unchilled, as I am chilled now, by the presence in Teton County of eighteen missile bases, eight of them within fifteen miles of the town (15).

Fifty years after *The Big Sky,* A. B. Guthrie continues to rattle the teacups of the town.

Scene still from Shane *motion picture, featuring Alan Ladd (as Shane) and Van Heflin (as Joe Starrett),* 1953

COURTESY OF THE BISON ARCHIVES, HOLLYWOOD, CA

MARY CLEARMAN BLEW

Shane Rides into the Millennium

FROM THE GRAVELED COUNTY ROAD, a mile of dirt track through sagebrush leads to a log house, shaded by a box elder tree and fenced with barbed wire, on a bluff over the Judith River. And if we follow this dirt track, into the past like a film in reverse, we will be struck by what isn't there. No power poles, no telephone wires, no satellite dish or antennae. No plumbing, only a pump in front of the log house and an unpainted outhouse in back. There is a Ford pickup, faded from its original dark green to the color of a mirage, but it spends most of its dusty days parked by the fence to save gasoline and bald tires. The muscle of this small cattle ranch is still provided by horses and the cow dog and the men and women who live here.

I woke to first consciousness, with a child's conviction of the certainty of things, in this log house on this sagebrush plain. Change was a concept expressed over my head, around the supper table by kerosene lamp, in the stories of my mother and father and grandmother, who looked back to the beginning of our time in the West. My mother was the child of homesteaders who had come to Montana during the 1910 land rush. My father was the son and grandson of ranchers who had come earlier, in 1882. His father had been a genuine cowboy, who had known and ridden with Charles M. Russell. Russell, according to family legend, had painted him in watercolor in one of those scenes where horse and rider are being jerked down by a steer at the end of a lariat. The rider's face is turned, but the brand on the horse's flank is the Open A L, brand of the old Huffine cattle outfit, for which my grandfather rode rep.

If my family's past was legendary, my childhood present was mundane. I filled dull days playing with cats and badgering hard-pressed adults for stories, and if no one had time to tell me a story, I substituted fantasy, which became farther reaching and more romantic as I learned to read the novels my father read. Fiction almost always seems more compelling than a life lived by ordinary daylight, and my father's favorites seemed to me, as I think they seemed to him, like personal history. The novels of Zane Grey and B. M. Bower and a host of tattered Westerns described a lost past, our past, a time when bravery and heroic actions were possible and landscape stretched forever.

In my teens I read all the novels of A. B. Guthrie, Jr., that were then available. *The Big Sky, The Way West,* and *These Thousand Hills*—the latter novel spoke the most urgently to me, because it described the halcyon days of the great cattle empires on open range, which my grandfather had lived and my father tried to live up to. Those glory days were gone forever. The beaver were trapped out, and the mountain men had faded into twilight. Covered wagons crossed the plains, and Dick Summers looked down from a hilltop and said, they're coming in like ants, and if they keep on like this, nothing can stop them, and this land will never be the same, and a few years later Lat Evans watched the narrowness of law replace individual morality and the possibility of valor as his life became as fenced in as the open range. Gone forever, gone for good. . . . It never occurred to me that, if I really could return to the past, like a film in reverse, I would be struck by what wasn't there, and much of what wasn't there would be glamour.

⁂

For the past twenty years, our best novelists, essayists, and historians have been telling us that the past is far more complicated than the old stories would have it. The complexity of the present convinces me that human experience has never spun itself in a single, untangled strand. The gadgets with which we festoon ourselves, of course, are another matter. My great-grandmother never had to struggle with the quirks of an uncooperative computer. All she had to do was adjust the damper on the wood stove, gather the twigs to get her hot fire going, test the oven by thrusting her hand into it, and bake her perfect biscuits made of flour and lard she probably had rendered herself. The real complications that I experience are not mechanical but personal. As the mother of two teen-aged daughters, one of them a foster daughter, I'm part of a web that stretches endlessly into webs as dense as the dark corners of my great-grandmother's root cellar, and if I'm banning boyfriends or reassuring social workers one hour, I'm negotiating the arcane passages of university faculty committees or counseling anxious graduate students the next, until I turn in relief to my undergraduate class, where we are reading *Beowulf* and discussing the ancient values, loyalty and valor, that have been immortalized by the telling of them.

An escape into a past world of plainer virtues, however, is not the reason why I still return to *Beowulf,* after all these years, with a shudder at the bone for the terrible vulnerability of the young warrior and the old king who bravely face monsters and dragons and the incomprehensible darkness. One reason is that, even through the filter of the prose translation in the Norton anthology and my half-forgotten Old English, the language sweeps me into that other time and place. Another reason is that in my time and place, in the Rocky Mountain West on the verge of the millennium, when the landscape itself is threatened by poisons and erosion and clear-cuts and concrete, when the living things that share the air I breathe are falling like dominoes into extinction, when I feel as though my children are about to be tested on a brink as perilous as Grendel's Mere, I can remind myself that one lived to tell that ancient story and some may live to tell ours.

But can I return to *Shane?*

In that last glimpse of Shane, where the peaks of the Tetons reflect the fading sunlight and the child's cries are unheeded, is the hero, mortally wounded, riding backward into a romantic story we no longer believe in?

Is there any sense in which he rides forward?

What would a re-make of the George Stevens film be like?

Most of the answers to this last question sound grotesque in the telling, even if some of the plots and casting might reflect the "new story of the West" that we've heard so many calls for. Sweet Jean Arthur turned "assertive" with guns strapped to her hips. Van Heflin minus his core of decency, Shane cast as any one of a number of dirty-blond leading men—"Who's the actor playing Shane? He's sure good looking," one of my daughters asked when we watched the video in connection with a Liberty Fund Colloquium on the western hero in film that I was planning to attend during the fall of 1998. No, the contemporary films that shy away from sentimentality by substituting violence are too depressing to consider. Besides, we've seen them all, or at least we've seen the previews, or read the reviews, or heard our friends complain about them. Even when, like Clint Eastwood's *Unforgiven,* which I watched in connection with the same Liberty Fund Colloquium, they contain a theme (in the case of *Unforgiven,* a parody of classic western films, *Shane* in particular), they're just as distant from the gritty West I grew up in as anything Gene Autry ever starred in. Dirty realism is likely to be no realism at all.

An aside is necessary here: why *Shane?* Its basis is the Jack Schaefer novel of that title, and as a movie, of all art forms, its ultimate shape is carved by any number of hands, perhaps least by the screenwriter's hand, and yet *Shane* has become so strongly associated with the A. B. Guthrie screenplay that I, at least, have come to think of the film as not Schaefer's or Stevens' or even Alan Ladd's, but as Guthrie's masterpiece, his most perfect achievement. This assessment surprises me even as I write, in part because *Shane* is such a departure from Guthrie's novels; its spare elegance compared with the sprawl of *The Big Sky* or the ruminations of the *Arfive* series; its glorious Wyoming mountain peaks and plains, so sweeping and lush and somehow unassailable, in contrast with Guthrie's obsession with the disintegration of landscape; and most of all, in place of the romantic despair that characterizes all the novels, the film's theme of courage as affirmation of the human condition and sacrifice as the basis for hope. Where the novels bear out Guthrie's apocalyptic vision—*each man destroys what he loves best,* he said, famously—the film reaffirms decency, loyalty, community. If Shane is dying in that final sequence that everyone remembers, when he turns his back on the frantic pleas of the young Brandon de Wilde and rides away toward the Tetons, it is not just because the homesteaders cannot go on living with the violence and the sexual threat of the gunman (another moment in the film that everyone remembers is the expression on Van Heflin's face when Alan Ladd dances with his wife), but because the sacrifice of the gunman sustains the community.

It seems to me that any re-make of *Shane* would have to investigate whether the film's values—the enduring vision of landscape, the power of marriage and community to resist disorder, and the efficacy of sacrifice—still have meaning as we enter the millennium. All of us have heard so much, in recent years, about community and family values that the very words have had their force wrung out of them, and we're unlikely to hold much faith in the simplistic goodness of the homestead wife as portrayed by Jean Arthur. And what can we say about landscape, which for generations has provided writers in the West with their sense of place that postmodernism has declared dead? Idaho, where I now live, has more congressionally designated wilderness land than any state apart from Alaska and California, a total of approximately four million acres; and yet in Idaho we daily read about the loss of wild salmon and other species, the threats of landslides, flooding, erosion, loss of topsoil, accumulation of pesticides, and the devastating effects of clear-cutting the national forests in a culture crazed with greed. Many of our most distinguished environmental scientists and science writers offer slim or no hope at all that the future we bequeath to our children and grandchildren will bear resemblance to the present, and fiction writers like my colleague Lance Olsen, in his futuristic novel *Time Famine,* envision a scene that implodes from our near-total capitulation to the worst, a scene all the more disturbing because we don't have to travel into the future to find its model in the Western Hemisphere:

> Within half an hour Anna and Lon had crossed the Spokane River steaming with chemicals under the amplifying sunlight, and centimetered into the snarl of meter-wide alleys lined with shoulder-high shacks made of packing cases, sheet metal,

> shards of grease-stained translucent plastic, huge soggy appliance boxes, cracks stuffed with rags and insulation from the landfill sites several kills to the east—six thousand new inhabitants arriving every week, farmers from down south, the diseased, the elderly, city dwellers whose ever-precarious credit lines had just crashed, refugees from other shanty towns and other semi-states. Campfires smoldered in doorways. Coppery smog churned close to the packed-dirt earth, stinking of rotten vegetables, fouled roach meat and the stringent petroleum distillates. People in smocks stood in long lines selling cheap polluted blood at mobile units, ushered in by people in khaki fatigues, rubber gloves and respirators. Skeletons squatted by overturned trash cans and oily puddles and hawked these new nano-drugs at bargain credit.

Worse than Dick Summers' worst nightmare as he watches the covered wagons lurching westward, worse than the fouled and filthy Oregon that Lat Evans flees for the thousand hills of Montana, worse than Mort Ewing or Ben Tate of the *Arfive* novels ever dream, *Time Famine* fast-forwards to a time when the loss of landscape has dulled every feeling, diluted every emotion that we can call human. And lest in reading *Time Famine* we become overly nostalgic for the past, we're given the example of the unfortunate Ulysses Cysop-of-the-Plains, a Nez Perce Indian who, zapped back in time to nineteenth-century Nevada, finds himself in the midst of the starving Donner party. Which of their number, they are arguing, should they butcher for the sake of the others?

> "I refuse," said Sarah.
>
> "I as well," said Mary. "I won't be part of such an enterprise. We are not savages."
>
> "... Your innocence will be the death of you, girl. This is no time

for fancy thoughts. We are in the midst of a situation that demands nothing less than practicality."

Then they notice Ulysses.

"Well, way I see it, there's another source of food here, good one, too."

"Pray tell us your meaning, Mr. Foster," Mary said.

"Source of food ain't got no soul either, Miss, near as I can tell."

Can we still believe in the power of sacrifice after such a passage, with its echoes of Calvinist dialectics on women's and Indians' lack of souls?

Or—a harder question—can we believe in the redemptive power of sacrifice after hearing a story told to me by Kim Barnes, a story she afterward included in her memoir *In The Wilderness*, about the minister of a charismatic church that her family attended, in the mountains of north Idaho, and about the minister's eldest son, a young man of great promise who went hunting one fall day with others from his family and from the congregation, but never returned. They found him three days later with his neck mysteriously caught in the cleft of a tree, where he had somehow hanged himself or been hanged. This story, with its unconscious echoes of legends of the Green Man and the Sacred Tree, looks back to an earlier time and earlier vision of wilderness as *horrentique atrum nemus imminet umbra,* of bristling trees and shadows, a landscape where Grendel might well walk in torment and where the sacrifice of the brightest and best might be the terrible toll to be paid in a place where nothing is certain and nothing guides us but our own lost footsteps. "We rocked in the comfort of their ministry," Kim Barnes writes, "until those last few months when one died, another dreamed of demons so horrible he purged his body of food and trembled in his wife's arms to stand and sing God's praises and another locked himself in an earthen cell with only a few jugs of water and a Bible, praying for a sign, deliverance for us all."

And yet, and yet. Out of the entire body of A. B. Guthrie's works, I will remember Shane in his fringed buckskins as he rides toward the mountains, not in despair but in the assurance that he chose valor and loyalty as freely as Beowulf did, and that his sacrifice made possible a place where the sobbing child might grow to sober manhood. Caught as I am in the complications of my cluttered contemporary life, stricken as I am by the damage done to my world by a few generations of my own kind, I don't expect to be rescued by the kind of sacrifice Shane made for that ill-assorted homestead community of Guthrie's screenplay. I know that the Rocky Mountain West in the millennium could no more endure Shane and his code of individual action and violence than those homesteaders could.

Shane for me is an emblem of the possible, of what we might mean to each other, of what we might pass on to our children, of what remains of beauty. His story reminds me that valor is indeed only a word, hollow as wind; and yet words can be as forcible as the wind. Words tell us that we can still act, that we still have choices, that we need not wait for the destruction of our world as passively as those old Danish warriors who feared Grendel as they did their own shadows. After Beowulf saved the Danes by killing the monsters, he went home to Geatland and ruled for a long time as a responsible king until, in his old age, another monster required his sacrifice by threatening his people. The story tells us that what he did was worthwhile, even though he died. Shane's story says something of the same thing to us. As long as stories are told, hope remains.

Scene still from The Big Sky *motion picture,*
featuring Kirk Douglas (as Jim Deakins), Arthur Hunicutt
(as Zeb Calloway), and Dewey Martin (as Boone Caudill), 1951

COURTESY OF THE BISON ARCHIVES, HOLLYWOOD, CA

Is It "All Sp'iled"? Moving beyond Guthrie's View of Nature

Ear Mountain and the Rocky Mountain Front from the hill behind Guthrie's house, mid 1950s
Photograph by Konrad Deligdisch.
COURTESY OF RIPLEY SCHEMM HUGO

Dan Flores

Mountains on Center Stage

The greatest happiness possible to a man . . . is to become civilized, to know the pageant of the past, to love the beautiful . . . and then, retaining his animal instincts and appetites, to live in a wilderness.

The great Texas writer J. Frank Dobie said that more than half a century ago. To my mind Dobie's paragraph expresses a set of ideas common among (although by no means confined to) the generation of western writers of which the Texans Dobie and Walter Prescott Webb, the cosmopolitan westerner Wallace Stegner, and the Montanan A. B. Guthrie, Jr., were all part. All of them were eminently civilized, yet all were more-or-less symbolic pioneers in that they embraced the western past as a kind of lodestone of regional identity. They each lived, at least for stretches of their lives, in what seemed to them some reasonable facsimile of purifying wilderness—the Texas Hill Country 'round about Friday Mountain for Dobie and Webb, California's Palo Alto Hills for Stegner, in Guthrie's case some wild and exotic place called the Rocky Mountain Front of Montana. And they all most certainly were under the spell of the sensuous, in love with the beauty of the world around them in all its forms.

In their different ways and with their different sorts of books, this generation of writers made the West and its history known to us, parsing it into specific places easier for our primate minds—accustomed for millennia to a life of bounded locales—to grasp, to fix in a colloidal suspension of images, scents, and feel. Dobie's place was the Tamaulipan Desert of the Texas/Mexican border, popularly called the Brush Country, and he made it hard for subsequent generations to think of Longhorns or wild mustangs without conjuring a background of tangled mesquite and a riot of cactus (as one early explorer put it) like "waving snakes rising from a Hindu juggler's carpet." The place Webb not only rendered to the world but also helped make one of the most pondered landscapes on the continent was the Great Plains, the boundaries of which he bent eastward to include his Friday Mountain Ranch. Stegner, too, wrote about the Plains, especially those northern reaches where the wolf willow grows, but the specific West he really brought to notice was dry, scoured Utah and the redrock country of the Colorado Plateau—and he did that two decades before Edward Abbey ever translated a couple of seasons as a park service ranger into *Desert Solitaire.*

For Guthrie, of course, "the Place" was that intersect of horizontal yellow sweep and gray verticality he made us think of as the Rocky Mountain Front. That naming is a kind of trick, of course, since the Plains front the Rockies across most of an 1,800-mile stretch from Alberta to New Mexico. But Guthrie gave us a latitude fix for a *ne plus ultra* Front, and it was Montana. In his six historical novels about the West, along with a slew of autobiographical writings and environmental essays, Guthrie gave us to understand, as no other writer did, that mountains meant bliss, that altitude equaled beatitude, that more than anywhere else in the West, all those qualities of mountain history, mountain glory—

and mountain environmental problems—arrived with their full freight of power in Montana.

At least that's the way a southern kid, growing up with Spanish moss dangling from my ears on the banks of the Black Bayou in Louisiana but facing the sunset and devouring book after book on the West, apprehended Montana. Until I was twenty-three and saw the place for myself, when I thought of Montana it was in terms of *The Big It*—paint ponies; shocking winter blizzards; beaver trappers who seemed plucked, vocal inflections and all, straight from the nutria swamps of my childhood and then plunked down in the grandest wilds on the continent.

Guthrie once asked rhetorically, "Where is the voice of Montana? Whose is the voice?" He knew that the West was made of words—it still is—and he surely knew that the best-known and -read Montana voice of his time was Bud Guthrie, Jr., himself, sitting there in his frame house outside Choteau with Ear Mountain and the Bob Marshall Wilderness hanging over him as personal totems, his own limestone-backboned muses, which he contemplated daily in order to "borrow a bit of Everlasting," as he put it. Guthrie was Ear Mountain's voice, making sure that when the world paused to reflect on Montana, it thought of the Rocky Mountains and their very specific history. Or, to borrow from the title of a poem he quoted approvingly in an essay he called "Our Lordly Mountains" (it accompanied a batch of Ansel Adams photos), the lives Guthrie wrote about lay grand among the hills.

What I'd like to address, now that I live among the grand hills of Montana myself, is not so much Guthrie's career as a committed environmentalist—which I admire whenever I read him, and like a lot of other contemporary western writers and artists have probably unconsciously attempted to emulate—but, more prosaically, whether or not Guthrie got it right. That's a very different thing from talent as a stylist, a drive to produce a body of quality work, intelligence, or even commitment to place. "Of this world speak you well and truly," Jack Kerouac once admonished the writer's voice within himself. Guthrie, I think we all agree, conveyed his world and its past very well. But what about the "truly" part? If Guthrie was for half a century the voice of Montana, what was his message? And did he get it right?

I wouldn't deign to speak for or paraphrase Guthrie, although in a foreword to *The Big Sky* Wallace Stegner once did and distilled the message to this: "Bigness, distance, wildness, freedom . . . victim. [And] innocence, anti-civilization, savage and beautiful and doomed . . ." From what I and others read into the tension that consistently informs the novels, and that is there in a very unvarnished form in the environmental essays, Stegner got it about right if you perhaps underline "victim" and "doomed" five or six times. Guthrie could certainly be optimistic, but about Montana's history and future he rarely was. To him, Montana represented the Last Best Eden, not just of America but of the world, and he was witnessing its devouring before his eyes.

I want to let Guthrie speak for himself, though. So listen once again to his voice, the quotes culled from a slew of sources, and many of them, perhaps, from their wombs untimely ripped. But here's what he said about Montana:

"Wild. Wild and purty, like a virgin woman." (That's Dick Summers describing the Upper Missouri country in *The Big Sky.*)

"This was a man's country onc't. . . . and no crampin' and crowdin'." (Zeb Calloway in *The Big Sky.*)

"It's all sp'iled, I reckon, Dick. The whole caboodle." Here it's Boone Caudill speaking in *The Big Sky*, to which Summers replies in a classic Guthrie comment on human nature: ". . . everything we done it looks like we done against ourselves and couldn't do no different if we'd knowed."

And this is a conversation between Higgins and Dick Summers in *The Way West:* "I got it in my head you're fightin' shy of people." Summers replies: "They spoil things. . . . Like ways of living."

And this one is Ben Tate talking to old salt Jap York in *The Last Valley:* "But Jap, you can't stand in the way of things. In your own lifetime you've seen a lot of changes." Jap's response: "Can't call to mind any good ones right now." Later Guthrie elicits this from another character in *The Last Valley:* "At every turn, sometimes it seems to me, man fucks himself."

In an essay on Montana in 1950, Guthrie had this to say: "The Montanan, especially the old-timer, is apt to sniff and ask what things are coming to. . . . He finds it hard to imagine a crowded world, difficult to think of humanity en masse. . . . You feel isolated [in Montana], happily isolated, free of the frets of our time. . . ."

Five years later, in a piece titled "The Rockies," he put it this way: "Mine is the young land, the young, raw, hardy land. . . . Here, for a fact, was the way for a man. Here was the free way for free men. . . . Possibly no other people are so pleased with place as residents of this inland West. . . . What really captivates the Western man is living room. . . . A large degree of privacy. A sort of spatial isolation from other human animals. He can go out and listen to silence. He can picnic without having to mix with picnicking strangers."

In 1959, in a foreword for a new edition of Joe Howard's *Montana: High, Wide, and Handsome,* he quotes Howard approvingly: "This sums up what I want in life—room to swing my arms and to swing my mind. Where is there more opportunity than in Montana for creation of these broad margins. . . ?"

And in 1969, in an introduction to a book on Lewis and Clark: "What say about a world known by no one save fractionally by aborigines? How get the feel of first-trod spaces? . . . How bring home the awe of finding rivers never charted, much less named?" On that same theme in 1983 he quoted this passage: "When the first colonists arrived in North America they encountered . . . virgin forest virtually untouched by the ambitions of mankind."

I could go on with this, for passages similar to these continue right through 'til Guthrie's death. But I won't. I'll just mention two more, a pair that provide an entree to answer my question, did Guthrie get it right? One is this, a theme that informed everything he wrote for fifty years, and from at least 1974 on—in conservation essays where he took on every aspect of the pillaging of Montana—he had his personal axe to grind, as he said. It was his "outlanders" and "invaders" theme, and it goes all the way back to *The Big Sky*. Here was Montana, in a nutshell: The Indians' "virgin land," appearing so new and unspoiled to the fur trappers, had been partly done in by the trappers themselves, then finished off by Oregon pioneers. Then the pioneers' world had been spoiled by miners and cattlemen, and their's spoiled by dryland farmers and environmentalists. Now the Montana of Guthrie's time was being spoiled by amenity migrants from California, "outsiders who not so long ago regarded Montana as a poor and frost-bitten land," but now, "jammed elbow-to-elbow in their concrete canyons . . . look on us covetously." "It must have occurred to you that man is a parasite," he told an audience in 1974.

Now, as one of those "outsiders" who has only been in Montana for less than a decade, I wouldn't dare imply that I know Montana the way Guthrie did. But as Guthrie himself said many times—and I'm quoting him here again—"remember that all of us are influenced, if unknowingly, by Scripture and by the frontier." As someone who lives off-the-grid thirty miles from town and two miles from my nearest neighbor, I identify almost entirely with all those deeply internalized notions that informed Guthrie's worldview, so my questioning of whether he got it right is also a probing at what I myself have long embraced (I've assumed) instinctively: That Montana represents the last of a Garden straight from the Divine hand of God (or evolution). That humans are essentially parasites and can do nothing but screw up the world. That a life in nature is pure and ennobling, and cities—while fun to visit—are unnatural and give play to all the base aspects of human nature.

So, is that a correct view of the world? With all due respect to Guthrie and those of us who think so, I confess I am now dubious, and that mostly because of the origins of the notions. Ignore if you wish (many can't) that the Montana Guthrie projected was on its face exclusively a male world, a holdout against masculine fears of a feminization of society. Guthrie kept abreast of new ideas, and I think his voice, now, would speak to the issue of women in Montana, if he could. But even more fundamentally, don't ignore—because you simply can't under the weight of today's evidence—that his conception of a "virgin" Montana and a "young, young world" of unnamed rivers and untrod places was a pure fantasy of the Euro-American imagination, literally the Paleolithic mind hoping for one last untouched hunting ground and convinced it had found Eden on a continent where animal populations were at unprecedented levels because our diseases had devastated the ancient inhabitants.

In the previous five centuries before Guthrie's ancestors had arrived, at least 150 million Indians had inhabited and extensively managed the landscape of his so-called "virgin" America. And in Guthrie's own country of supposed unnamed rivers and untrod places, a dozen different buffalo-hunting cultures had been transforming the place with fire, camps, gathering strategies, and hunting pressure for eighty centuries before Guthrie's own midwestern (I almost said "outsider") family showed up and saw untrod Eden along the Rocky Mountain Front. A young country? Montana is an old place. People have been coming and going and changing it forever.

While I enormously admire Guthrie's commitment to challenging change in Montana that is motivated by greed or selfishness, informed by ecological stupidity, or immoral from the standpoint of biodiversity, there's one last thing about the worldview he gave voice that I stand wary of. For most of his life he railed at the Biblical idea that the world was made for humans, a tragic and megalomaniacal view to be sure. But implicit in that view that humans are at base evil, destroyers, parasites, lies a companion Judeo-Christian and puritanical belief (stretching back to the Fall) that the flesh is suspect, that our species somehow is outside nature rather than a manifestation of it.

I love A. B. Guthrie's voice, and I still read him. But I have to say that the world as he saw it may not be our best vision for a twenty-first century Montana. And here's why.

For all the poetry and grace Guthrie brought to an environmentalist worldview, it seems to me that he stopped short of following the logic of ecology to its natural end. For what ecology truly insists is that the split between humanity and nature that Guthrie's generation saw is in fact a chimera—one so profound it could blind Guthrie, even Stegner, to the ancient impress of the human hand on Montana, the West, and America—but a chimera nonetheless. And that means that Guthrie's argument, that Montana was grand because it lacked people, whose arrival and presence are now killing the Last Best Place, is a conclusion flawed at its core.

My admiration for Guthrie doesn't interfere with my certain

convictions that humanity and nature are one. But this kind of human self-respect argues for an extension of Guthrie's idea that nature—in its Montana form, indeed universally—is the very manifestation of the Divine, deserving of our awe and respect. The extension translates into a new kind of environmentalism wherein our own regard for ourselves as nature's children implies (in a celebration of kinship) new respect for the rich diversity of our fellow creatures in place.

What I'm finally saying is that in this new century of history in Montana and the West, we ought to recognize that our presence by no means always ruins the world. Indeed, we are instrumental in making this planet what it is, and have been for a million years. Our task is to pull it off so well that the next generations will do exactly what Guthrie did: Look at a Montana shaped by the previous inhabitants and pronounce it Paradise.

Alan Weltzien

The Last Best Place: Economic Opportunity or Wilderness Solace?

A. B. Guthrie Jr.'s *The Big Sky* constitutes one of the most central texts in modern Montana literature; it inscribes potent ambivalences and contradictions that resonate down through the present. A canonical historical novel that James Welch's *Fools Crow* later rivals, *The Big Sky* serves as a prism through which much subsequent Montana literature, both fiction and nonfiction, refracts itself. To vary the figure, the text of *The Big Sky*, particularly its self-consciously mythic attitudes about the Montana area, is repeatedly rewritten by and in newer literature. And to vary the figure yet again, *The Big Sky* initiates a diverse conversation that later literature extends in several directions. Perhaps it stirs little debate to claim Guthrie's most famous novel as the definitive fictive treatment of Montana's fur-trapping period, particularly the 1830s. The implicit tensions crystallized in *The Big Sky* exist between those two superlatives, "last" and "best," claimed in the thoroughly immodest title of Montana's centennial literature anthology—an attitude unofficially endorsed by many Montanans, at least judging from my students.

According to *The Big Sky*, notions of Montana as the last place and the best place compete with one another. The pessimistic, cynical Uncle Zeb Calloway embodies the former view and the optimistic, idealistic young Boone Caudill, the latter. Can the last place ever be the best place as well, over time? Of course, Guthrie has Caudill changing position by Parts IV and V, particularly through the contrasts advertised in Elisha Peabody, the eternal voice of development. Peabody enormously extends, in fact, agendas of development within Caudill. Guthrie's protagonist contains conflicting ideologies, but the lover of the new land gives ground to the exploiter. Perhaps the only one who believes "We'll find beaver. Always have"[1] is Caudill, and by Part V he knows, at least dimly, that the finite supply of and demand for beaver matches the finite time of the mountain man. He has outlasted his time, a broken anachronism whose company includes the fenced cattlemen in *Shane,* Cooper's Mohicans, and Scott's Highlanders. More seriously, he is never given to acknowledge and understand his acceptance of Uncle Zeb's flawed, self-flattering determinism in which "best" slides into "last," as if the mountain man controls the forces of change. Guthrie's mountain men exist communally only rarely and sporadically; development, by contrast, is always communal. The illusion of endless beaver is replaced by the threat of endless people transported by rail and heralded by Peabody.

If Montana as the last best place poses another test case of the American garden of Eden, it lends itself to diverse interpretations, two of which strain increasingly against one another. On the one hand, Montana exists as the site for economic opportunity, as much of our history and texts such as *The Big Sky* endorse. On the other, it exists as a site for utopian vision or wilderness communion—regaining paradise by gently cultivating the garden rather than exploiting it. The first attitude is developmental, pragmatic, economic, active; the second is static, spiritual, aethestic, quietistic. If the former has held sway most of the time in modern Montana history, we may, more recently, be undergoing a paradigm shift to the latter. In Guthrie's novel, his unflattering protagonist appeals most to us when the promise of place defines his potential self. Certainly much western American literature aligns itself with Caudill's transcendental union of landscape and expansive self, a regional essence:

> By day Boone could get himself on a hill and see forever, until the sky came down and shut off his eye. There was the sky above, blue as paint, and the brown earth rolling underneath, and himself between them with a free, wild feeling in his chest, as if they were the ceiling and floor of a home that was all his own.[2]

The serpent in Caudill's house of sky—the delicious lure of ownership, of private property—forces his expulsion such that he wanders far from "the whole shitaree," forever homeless. Since *The Big Sky*, many literary voices, both fictional and nonfictional, have proposed less possessive and exclusive definitions of home.

Though the West as resource base characterizes texts such as *The Big Sky*, the West as wilderness is increasingly inscribed in more recent Montana literature. I want to focus on two Montana writers who have gained prominence in the 1990s and who well represent this paradigm shift from resource base to wilderness: Pete Fromm and Rick Bass. Pete Fromm has now published five collections of short stories and a novel; *Indian Creek Chronicles* (1993), which won the Pacific Northwest Booksellers Association Book of the Year award, stands out as a classic American text given its subtitle: *A Winter Alone in the Wilderness.* Fromm's experience wintering just southwest of Montana's Bitterroot Valley while guarding 2.5 million salmon eggs for the Idaho Fish and Game Department places him in archetypal literary territory. He dresses Boone Caudill down to size by picturing his naive, younger self as a Twainian Innocent Abroad, the greenhorn target awaiting our laughter—and sympathy—and a real education in woods survival. Just five pages in, this anti-heroic tyro confesses, "When I read A. B. Guthrie's *The Big Sky* I walked around in a daze, the next Boone Caudill, waiting to explode," and he participates in a romping pseudo-rendezvous with other boys-pretending-to-be-mountain men in Jackson Hole.[3]

This "Boone Caudill" learns a different way than his fictional predecessor, one in which he exists as a part of the wilderness rather than apart and above it—even though, in a splendidly short, ironic epilogue, Fromm confesses that the resource he guarded four winters earlier ends up at least as scarce as Guthrie's mountain men's beaver.[4] Fromm punctures Guthrie's heroic view, and the Daniel Boone mythology antecedent to it, by naming his runt of a dog Boone, whose frisky presence ironically distinguishes Fromm's valuation of wilderness from Guthrie's gospel of development. Like the earlier Boones a solitaire in the woods, Fromm measures himself differently; he breathes new life into the man-and-dog-alone-in-wilderness cliché. For example, he learns to be a decent hunter, bagging a moose and putting up the meat. That self-education could not differ more from the purposes and style of the mountain lion guides, Cary and Brian, and client, Phil: trophy seekers whom Fromm tries to understand even though they cannot understand the magnificence and power of the animal Phil manages to shoot.[5] Temporary intruders marked by their whining snowmobiles, they are not local citizens in the way Fromm comes to be.

In *Indian Creek Chronicles,* one reward for Fromm's dedicated local citizenship in the Selway-Bitterroot Wilderness Area is a full solar eclipse. Fromm and Boone climb atop a snowy pinnacle from which, like all mountaineers and spiritual seekers, he fulfills a vision quest, surveying "his" country as if for the first time:

> But still I circled, tingling on my little perch, trying to see what was no longer there, what I had not had enough time to see in those too full few minutes—trying to take in all that I had looked over for months, as if the second dawn had shed light on more than just mountains.
>
> I shouted. I raised my fists above my head and shouted. As I continued my demented circling on that spire, I knew that everywhere I could see, and far beyond that, on everything the sun had just transformed, the only footprint on the land that wasn't some animal's was mine. I shouted again, big enough to burst.
>
> Whooping, I slid off the pinnacle and Boone charged in. We wrestled around on the crusty snow and then we just flat out ran, as if there was nothing in the world that could ever stop us.[6]

In this privileged, quintessential moment, a trope of epiphany, Fromm becomes the younger Boone Caudill, "explod[ing]" and "burst[ing]" like his namesake dog with the promise of oneself under this broad house of sky. But the ecstatic affinity measures difference; this comic, mountain-man descendant practices ecology rather than spoilage (cf. Caudill's final sentences in *The Big Sky* about the "sp'iled" Teton River country), even though well over 99 percent of "his" salmon eggs don't survive to spawn back in Indian Creek after four years. Possibly Guthrie's unreflective devotion to exploitation (i.e., of resources) inevitably leads to his characters' gloomy lament of waste and loss. Contrasting voices offer characters retaining and celebrating an abiding sense of wonder and excitement—about a mountain lion or a solar eclipse—which nurtures careful stewardship, not resource depletion.

Rick Bass's prolific career shows him growing increasingly angry and alarmist about resource depletion. The author of seventeen books in sixteen years (including *Fiber*), Bass has become a major voice in contemporary western American literature, one that steadily extols wilderness and lambastes the older paradigm of unreflective consumption of Montana's forests and game populations. In his most important autobiographical essay to date, "Crossing Over," Bass describes his first reading of Edward Abbey's *The Monkey Wrench Gang* as a conversion experience in which he abandoned the Hollywood cowboy West of his childhood and replaced it with the wilderness West. His unfolding career attests to a steadily deepening environmentalism, one in which he explores the affinities between wilderness as an idea and National Park System fact, and residual traces of wildness within and without us. Bass takes his text from the Thoreau of "Walking." In promulgating a kind of ecological mental health and ethics, for example, Bass writes about the core value of island populations and genetic corridors; as with other nature writers, he studies the ways in which surviving populations of wolves and grizzly bears, for example, exist as profound exemplars for our own instruction and adaptation.

For Bass, Guthrie's Elisha Peabody has divided and multiplied like a voracious cancer, and he wears many faces by the twentieth century's end. Bass replaces the ironized Midwest domesticity of Dick Summers at the end of *The Big Sky* with the notion of sustained communion in and with wilderness. Instead of Summers' pitiful decline and fall marked by plowed corn rows, hog meat, and a nagging wife, Bass argues that his contemporary descendants, disabused of inflationary romanticism and schooled in ecology and stewardship, need never leave Montana's garden. "The Valley," probably the least fictitious story in *In The Loyal Mountains* (1995), begins, "One day I left the South, fled my job, and ran to the heart of snow, the far Northwest. I live in a cabin with no electricity, and I'm never leaving."[7] All these details ring true for Bass and family, except that several years ago they bought their own place that includes electricity. "The Valley" is, of course, Bass's

Yaak Valley in Montana's northwesternmost corner, and it figures for him as synecdoche for the West, particularly debates between wilderness preservation and resource exploitation, in this case continued large-scale logging. At the close of "The Valley," the autobiographical narrator smugly celebrates, "I wake up smiling sometimes because I have all my days left to live in this place. I hike up into the hills, to a rock back in the trees, and sit there and just look."[8] This is Bass's chronic celebration: As a writer, he discovered a semi-wilderness setting so perfectly matching him that he can thrive indefinitely through the ceaseless new discoveries of/in this marriage of self and place.

But the complacency of "The Valley" is more than offset by the threats to the same valley found in "Days of Heaven," one of Bass's starkest stories protesting development. The sympathetic narrator, like the younger Bass a ranch caretaker, faces two antagonists: a New York stockbroker owner and his sidekick, a Billings realtor. These descendants of Elisha Peabody never earn our sympathy, contrary to their prototype; they remain caricatures, and at moments the story treats them savagely. Contrary to Fromm's mountain-lion trophy seekers, they pose a permanent grave threat, as the story's opening sentence announces: "Their plans were to develop the valley, and my plans were to stop them."[9] With the narrator we enjoy mocking and sabotaging them, yet his powerlessness eventuates in a futile fatalism, as the story closes: "All I could do was wait. I sat very still, like that owl, and thought about where I could go next, after this place was gone. Maybe, I thought, if I sit very still, they will just go away."[10] The narrator's final bid for stillness, a delusive piece of wish fulfillment, contrasts markedly with the angry activism characteristic of Bass's most recent nonfiction.

The narrator, the one who knows the ranch, represents the same kind of retainer as Guthrie's Caudill and Jim Deakins, the local experts in the employ of Peabody the advance man. Maybe the allegory pitting wilderness against development, knowledge inspired by love against money or legal ownership (absentee or otherwise), never changes, though the irony, over time, grows louder and more painful. If local expertise has gained ground, it is only after witnessing, for generations, the baleful consequences of resource overuse, if not depletion.

Historians of nature writing often credit Rachel Carson's *Silent Spring* (1962) with initiating a sea change; after Carson, environmental degradation and crises increasingly mark the genre. Between the complacency of "The Valley" and the angry fatalism of "Days of Heaven" exists Bass's *The Book of Yaak,* in which Bass often acts the part of an angry Jeremiah. The triumph of nature over development in the second Swan Valley closing Bass's big novel, *Where The Sea Used To Be,* is unavailable in the unprotected Yaak. The railroad barons who exist beyond Elisha Peabody only one generation after Part V (1843) of *The Big Sky* have turned into timber barons equally distant from the resource and landscape. Bass favors local logging and smaller finishing industries, as he makes clear; he reserves his anger for the multinational pulp and paper corporations who, as if recapitulating the historical tendency of Montana as resource colony, make decisions from afar about resource use with little or no local consultation or understanding. One wonders if we have learned anything between the time of the mountain men's beaver and the Yaak Valley's remaining old-growth larch stands, for example.

The political activism of a Bass, who ends *The Book of Yaak* and *Fiber* with a call to arms—letter-writing campaigns, with names and addresses supplied—shows him resisting the comfortable gloom-and-doom history embraced by Uncle Zeb Calloway and, later, Caudill. As our century of environmental crises lurched to its end, the literary defiance of such writers as Bass proclaims that "the whole shitaree" might be going but is not yet gone, and will not be if their own careers and influence make any difference. Through such writers as Fromm and Bass, we recognize the extent to which Guthrie's mid-century portraits of early nineteenth-century mountain men, for all their groundbreaking energy, are fabulously anachronistic, as if they constitute some childhood episode from the long ago. The fur-trapping solitaire has been rewritten just as the injunction in the Book of Genesis concerning man's dominion has been replaced, in many circles, with the discipline of ecology. I believe Bass speaks for many at the closing of "The Value of a Place," *The Book of Yaak's* second essay and one of its best, when he advocates a credo based upon giving back, rather than continually taking from, the land:

> I see more and more the human stories in the West becoming those not of passing through and drifting on, but of settling in and making a stand; and I think that there is a hunger for this kind of rhythm in towns, neighborhoods, and cities throughout the country—not just in rural areas, and not just in the West, but all over: that the blood-rhythms of wilderness which remain in us (as the old seas and oceans remain in us) are declaring, in response to the increasing instability of the outside forces that are working against us, the need for reconnection to rhythms that are stable and natural . . . and I can feel it, the notion that settling-in and stand-making is the way to achieve or rediscover these rhythms.[11]

With his "blood-rhythms of wilderness" connected to stability, Bass proposes a new definition of settlement in what remains of the Montana garden: one that Guthrie might not understand or accept but that would enable Caudill, with a lot of maturing, to remain home.

Notes

1. A. B. Guthrie, Jr., *The Big Sky* (New York: William Sloane Associates, 1947; Boston: Houghton Mifflin, 1974), 160.

2. Ibid., 117.

3. Pete Fromm, *Indian Creek Chronicles: A Winter Alone in the Wilderness* (New York: St. Martin's Press, 1994), 5.

4. Ibid., 184.

5. Ibid., 99–107.

6. Ibid., 144.

7. Rick Bass, *In the Loyal Mountains* (Boston: Houghton Mifflin, 1995), 53.

8. Ibid., 61.

9. Ibid., 131.

10. Ibid., 147.

11. Rick Bass, *The Book of Yaak* (Boston: Houghton Mifflin, 1996), 13.

Lee Rostad

The Rise of Environmentalism and Its Relation to Western Myths

I think we can all accept the definition of the word "myth"—a traditional or legendary story, one that is made up—but "environmentalism" is a little more nebulous. My dictionary is old and does not even include environmentalism, but it does have environment, and that is defined as "the aggregate of surrounding things, conditions or influences, especially as affecting the existence or development of someone or something." Is an environmentalist, then, one who lives in an environment merely, and accepts that as it is, or one who is trying to change that condition in some fashion? The modern acceptance seems to be "one who is trying to save the current environment and return it to its primal state"—whatever that may be. Unfortunately, in pursuit of this dream, many have made it their religion to worship wildness.

I would speak for the many farmers and ranchers and others who live on the land in Montana and the West and consider themselves environmentalists in a different sense. They have made their living from the land and try to live with the environment in harmony and respect. They—we—have learned from the mistakes of an earlier generation of a hundred years ago, and so we care for the land and do not plan to move on when it is depleted as that generation did.

The "new" environmentalists have used the western myth of the mountain man and the "scene primordial" to strengthen their proposals for preserving the earth as it was before man approached. Also, many of us sense that their agenda is to create a totally new political and social scene that returns to land a common use and destroys private property rights.

It is important to deal with the rise of environmentalism and its relation to western myths with an honest look at the sources and validity of those myths. I would hope to take us through a look at the conflict between the myth of the "wild" man and the actual reality of how the West was experienced and settled, but more importantly show the folly of basing environmental policies on myths and not realities.

There are many environmental myths about the beginnings and before white settlement in Montana and the West, but the idea that man can preserve the environment and still live on the land creates the most controversy. Wallace Stegner says of Guthrie's Boone Caudill, ". . . [He] is an avatar of the oldest of all the American myths—the civilized man re-created in savagery, rebaptized into innocence on a wilderness continent."

It is only natural that man should yearn for places where no man has trod in this highly developed world. A. B. Guthrie's wonderful myth in his series of books about the mountain man and Indian living on the land without spoiling it, maintaining the wildlife along with the wilderness and eating off the land, naturally has been carried into this era by a multitude of environmental movements. The idea that man could return to those days of *The Big Sky* suggests a retrogression in time to begin with, and even the original myth needs some revisiting.

Along with the "Mountain Man Myth," others surfaced during the settlement period of the West. There was the idea that the Indians were the original environmentalists, and there were myths about the West itself. William Gilpin and others saw another myth in the homestead "quarter section." In Bernard DeVoto's facetious definition,

> . . . the idea [was] that 160 acres [was] the ideal family-sized farm, the basis of a yeoman democracy, the buttress of our liberties, and the cornerstone of our economy. It was certainly true, however, that if you owned 160 acres of flat Iowa farmland or rolling Wisconsin prairie, you had, on the average, a farm which would support your family and would require all its exertions to work. So the quarter section, thought of as the proper homestead unit, became the mystical one.

Railroads and land developers promoted the myth of owning your own land in the West. In *Bad Land,* Jonathan Raban tells many stories that reveal the unhappy consequences of following that dream in eastern Montana.

Even as the agrarian myths were promulgated, voices of reason and conservation were speaking up, only to be discredited by those who wished to find that grand and glorious new life and by those who stood to profit by development.

Elliott West, in his *The Way to the West*, said of those looking for another myth, the myth of the wild,

> . . . [They] found that the vastness and the seeming emptiness encouraged the feeling that one was no longer in a world where living was a matter of dealing with other people, coping with rules and institutions, and moving within a web of human actions, past and present. Here on the plains, a man could believe

> he had put society and history behind him. Now he stood in confrontation with elemental forces, nose-to-nose with nature—and nobody else . . . perhaps the most seductive allure of the plains and the West generally—its offer of simplicity.

And then there were those who thought the Indians had the ideal world. Lewis Garrard, visiting a Cheyenne camp in 1846, wrote in his journal:

> I thought with envy, of the free and happy life they were leading on the untamed plains, with fat buffalo for food, fine horses to ride, living and dying in a state of blissful ignorance. To them, who know no other joys than those of the untaught savage, such a life must be the acme of happiness; for what more invigorating, enlivening pleasure is there than traversing the grand prairies, admiring the beauties of unkempt, wild, and lovely nature, and chasing the fleet-footed buffalo. . . .

Secretary of the Interior Stewart Udall said the Indians were the pioneer ecologists of this country, and Herb Hammond of the Sierra Club declared that "most of the indigenous nations on this continent practiced a philosophy of protection first and use second of the forest."

However, neither the view of a carefree and undisciplined life nor the idea of the American Indians as the "original environmentalists"—"people so intimately bound with the land that they left no trace upon it" (Richard White and William Cronon, *Ecological Change and Indian-White Relations,* 1988)—is correct.

As Terry Anderson of the Political Economic Research Center (PERC) at Bozeman, Montana, points out in his paper, "Conservation—Native American Style" (1996), American Indians transformed the North American landscape. He notes, "Sometimes these changes were beneficial, at other times harmful. But they were a rational response to abundance or scarcity in the context of institutions that governed resource use."

The American Indians were guided more by laws and customs among societies than by a unique environmental ethic. These territorial rights were developed from use and occupancy, and although outsiders were allowed in from time to time, the ownership rights were strictly enforced.

One can still see the border of stones near Martinsdale, Montana, that divides the Crow and Blackfoot hunting grounds. This rock line "fence" purportedly ran for a length of fifty miles east-west diagonally in the Musselshell Valley.

To the south, according to Terry Anderson, each of the Apache bands ". . . had its own hunting grounds and, except when pressed by starvation, was reluctant to encroach upon those of a neighbor. . . . Each local group had exclusive rights to certain farm sites and hunting localities, and each was headed by a chief who directed collective enterprises. . . ."

For the Plains Indians, clothes, weapons, horses, tepees, and personal items were privately owned, showing that property rights were an integral part of the Indian life. Natural resources were used communally, but also carried some property rights. On a buffalo hunt, the successful hunter was entitled to keep the skin and some choice portion of the meat for his family. The Omaha used an elaborate system whereby the killer had ownership of the hide and a side of meat and the brains. To the first helper to arrive went a side of meat and a hindquarter, and to the second the system allowed the stomach and the best of the tallow and intestines. The third helper was left with the ribs. The Indians understood the importance of incentives and built their societies around institutions that encouraged good human and natural resource stewardship.

On the other hand, Louis Warren said, "To claim that Indians lived without affecting nature is akin to saying that they lived without touching anything, that they were a people without history." They set fires in old-growth forests to improve the range land for elk, and they set prairie fires to drive the game. Animals were sometimes left to rot when the Indians had taken all they could use. As to the land itself, the buffalo had far more voracious eating habits than the sheep and cattle of today. One early settler, quoted in Alston Chase's *Playing God in Yellowstone,* complained of the bison, "Grass was eaten to the earth, as if by locusts." Buffalo also "changed the grasslands as no other beast: they made trails down hillsides into deep, eroded trenches, they bared the ridges. . . . they smashed down the alder and quaking aspen."

There is also no question that the early settlers were hard on the fragile landscapes of the West, adding to the impact of an Indian population that doubled in the first half of the nineteenth century.

Environmentalists—and this is a broad epitaph, ranging from the users of the land to those who would lock up the land to any use—were not the product of this century, but have been with us always. It is only in the last few decades that environmentalists have polarized their agendas. Wendell Berry said of these "camps":

> The defenders of nature and wilderness—like their enemies the defenders of the industrial economy—sometimes sound as if the natural and the human were two separate estates, radically different and radically divided. The defenders of nature and wilderness sometimes seem to feel that they must oppose any human encroachment whatsoever, just as the industrialists often apparently feel that they must make the human encroachment absolute or, as they say, "complete the conquest of nature." But there is danger in this opposition, and it can be best dealt with

> by realizing that these pure and separate categories are pure ideas and do not otherwise exist.
>
> . . . Obviously, the more artificial a human environment becomes, the more the word "natural" becomes a term of value. It can be argued, indeed, that the conservation movement, as we know it today, is largely a product of the industrial revolution. The people who want clean air, clear streams, and wild forests, prairies, and deserts are the people who no longer have them.

John Wesley Powell was one of the first to suggest some planning in the Great Plains to protect the environment. Powell was the director of the United States Geological Survey, and in 1878 he proposed legislation to establish a society that would recognize its responsibility to each other and to the land. It was sixty years later that some of Powell's ideas were enacted into law, including his notion that cattle should be grazed based on a commons. His fundamental principle was that large acreages are essential to support human life on the plains—a fact borne out by the manner of Indian life. Powell also advocated homestead plots figured so that each would have water, instead of plotting them along a grid. Had this been done, the homestead era might have had a different outcome.

Powell's realism, however, did not prevail. Wallace Stegner, in his book on Powell, speaks of one great mythmaker of the time, William Gilpin. He was the first territorial governor of Colorado and believed that Manifest Destiny was not just a creed or policy, but a passionate vision. Stegner said of Gilpin:

> He saw the West through a blaze of mystical fervor, as part of a grand geopolitical design, the overture to global harmony; and his conception of its resources and its future as a home for millions was as grandiose as his rhetoric, as unlimited as his faith,

> as splendid as his capacity for inaccuracy. . . . He had distinguished corroboration for his belief that artesian waters would unlock the fertility of the whole subhumid region east of the Rockies, and if he had chosen to he could have quoted everything from frontier folklore to government geologists in support of the theory that settlement improved the climate, that in the very truth "rain follows the plow."

This particular myth still existed as the homesteaders streamed west to that wonderful "land of Gilpin" where the climate changed for the better as settlement turned the sod and planted crops and trees. Powell, through his experiences in the West, recognized that adequate water needed to come with the land or the homesteaders would not succeed.

The winter of 1886 that ended the big bonanza for the cattle industry also heralded the years of drought that destroyed the grain growers. However, with the advent of the railroads, the homesteaders were once again trying their luck. Jonathan Raban speaks of the "fictions" that lured the would-be farmers. The railroad and land developer pamphlets did not deny that the land was dry or at least "dryish." But, they were careful to explain, the rain that came fell during the growing season when it was most needed and the ". . . large number of bright days, is more fitted to bring rapid and satisfactory plant growth. . . . This is one of the reasons why crop returns in Montana are greater than in areas of more rainfall."

My son has been trying for years to make this myth come true as he plants his wheat, and the simple fact is that some years there is too much bright sun, and what rain that falls does not always come when it should. Another myth is that too much rain is a curse: ". . . it washes the goodness out of the soil." And the old myth was still repeated that rain increases with settlement, cultivation, and tree planting—this moisture occurring from the disturbance of electrical currents caused by the building of railroads and settlement of the country.

The dry years of 1887, 1888, and 1889 were repeated in 1917, 1918, and 1919, and the exodus of the homesteaders began.

Something was being done, however. In 1891, the first law was passed to establish federal forest reserves. In 1886, the Audubon Society was founded. Yellowstone was established as the first national park in 1872, and John Muir founded the Sierra Club in 1892. The first wilderness area set aside in a national forest was the Gila Wilderness area in the Southwest, largely the result of the efforts of Aldo Leopold. However, during the first six decades of this century, the United States was preoccupied with two world wars, a rapid technological industrialization, and creation of a standard of living higher than any other on the planet. The environmentalists of the 1960s brought the movement to a new, more focused effort, and politics became a most important factor.

Social reform, implicit in the Powell proposal that the government control settlement and limit personal rights for the common interest, suddenly became not only the vehicle but the primary goal of the new environmentalists. After Earth Day in 1970, environmentalist organizations added full-time activists to their paid staffs, and politically oriented environmental groups such as the Natural Resources Defense Council and Environmental Defense Fund mushroomed. The first major legislation was the National Environmental Policy Act, which initiated the now-familiar environmental impact statement. Following were the Endangered Species Act, the Clean Air Act, the Clean Water Act, and the Resource Conservation and Recovery Act. Farm legislation became a landmark, setting mandatory conservation requirements for eligibility in commodity price-support programs. Guthrie's "Big Sky" was one of the major targets of this new legislation, and the farmers and ranchers in Montana found themselves beleaguered by both the environmental activists and the government. Legislation passed by Congress was interpreted and enforced by a bureaucracy apparently responsible to no one. Property and individual rights seemed to many of us to become secondary to preservation and wilderness.

A second wave of settlers hit Montana, many of them seeking the life of the mountain man away from the population and pollution of their former homes, and suddenly Montana agriculturists faced another adversary in those who sought and could afford to displace them.

This, then, is the fear of the modern rancher and farmer—that those who advocate extreme environmental measures would do so by disrupting the existing social and political structure and doing away with private property rights through legislation that can dictate use of land. Some environmentalists believe that only government has the knowledge and concern to steward the land. I would suggest that those who feel that communal property rights or the government can best preserve the natural resources look to the disastrous environment of communist countries.

In "Conservation—Native American Style," Terry Anderson added:

> Non-Indians will do well to stop promulgating myths as a solution to modern environmental problems. Especially in a multicultural society where world-views vary widely, devolution of authority and responsibility offers the best hope for resource conservation. Rather than shunning property rights solutions, we should embrace them, as did our predecessors on this continent.

Another myth of the old West concerns living off the land without polluting it and the users of the land. To many, all modern technology is bad because it is not in keeping with the natural state. Contrary to the myth that agriculture is destroying the wilderness, high-yield agriculture is saving millions of acres. In Africa, instead of buying expensive fertilizer, farmers simply moved to a new plot of land every two or three years, leaving miles of desolate wasteland. With the growing population, more ground is being farmed without leaving land fallow long enough to rejuvenate its fertility. To keep wilderness in a growing world, we must have more yield per acre.

Today, high-yield agriculture and the potential for high-yield forestry have changed the equation between population growth and destruction of wildlife habitat. The world today is feeding twice as many people as it did in the 1950s, on virtually the same amount of cultivated land. Dennis Avery, of the Hudson Institute, says,

> If people hadn't developed and begun to use high-yield agriculture, I estimate that we would already have had to plow down another ten million square miles of wildlife habitat—equal to the entire land area of North America! We could insist on using organic farming worldwide by the year 2050, but we might have to farm thirty to forty million square miles, because we would be pushing low-yield farming onto fairly marginal farmland. Plowing down the entire land area of North America, Europe, Asia, and Australia seems a strange way to save wildlife.

Mistakes were made, and the science is still evolving, but today's agricultural pesticides are highly specific, low volume, and short lived, unlike some of the earlier pesticides. They are applied carefully, so that they are virtually confined to the fields being used. Where significant patterns of harm to wildlife are documented, specific chemicals or uses are eliminated. Environmental writers who lump PCBs and DDT with modern pesticides are in error. DDT was banned because of what it might do to wildlife and ecosystems, and PCBs were never used as farm chemicals.

Chemicals make fruits and vegetables, our strongest weapon against cancer, cheaper and available for more of the year. According to the experts, five servings per day will cut a person's cancer risk by 50 percent, dwarfing any theoretical cancer risk from pesticide residues, according to some theorists. The world does not have enough organic fertilizer to meet current needs, much less the triple amount for the future as the population grows. Plants absorb all nitrogen fertilizers in an inorganic form regardless of whether the nitrogen comes from organic or inorganic sources, which means that organic nitrogen fertilizers have no advantage over synthetic nitrogen from the plant's perspective.

As to field runoff that affects the water supply, pesticides as well as plant nutrients such as nitrogen and phosphorus are a manageable problem; indeed, chemicals that run off are losses to the farmer. Moreover, organic farming and alternative systems can be just as guilty as conventional systems in poorly managing runoff.

While these trends have not had the test of time, technologists are noting that enhancement can be made with animals as well as crops. Beef producers, with the use of growth-promoting implants, can produce 108 pounds of meat with the same feed required for 100 pounds in non-implanted animals. There have been no studies to date showing an increased incidence of any adverse health condition due to eating meat from implanted animals.

The stimulation of milk cattle to produce more milk is also a biotechnological enhancement of a food source.

The latest settlers to come to Montana to find their own version of Boone Caudill's life must be willing to settle for less freedom than Caudill enjoyed. What makes Montana the "Last Best Place" is a sparse population that has learned to live in a wild land.

Unless these "newcomers" understand the development of the stewardship among agriculturists, they will destroy the open land they seek.

Wendell Berry summed it up well when he wrote:

> There does exist a possibility that we can live more or less in harmony with our native wilderness; I am betting my life that such a harmony is possible. But I do not believe that it can be achieved simply or easily or that it can ever be perfect, and I am certain that it can never be made, once and for all, but is the forever unfinished lifework of our species.

William W. Bevis

Nature and Other Nonsense: *The Big Sky* at Fifty

For twenty years I have taught *The Big Sky* in the Montana Writers course at The University of Montana, and while A. B. Guthrie's novel is never voted the best book (that award usually goes to Welch or McNickle), it is always voted, by nearly every student, the one book that cannot be dropped from the course. Why? Because serious consideration of *The Big Sky* takes us to the heart of western mythologies.

During those same twenty years, western revisionists have been saying we must "rewrite our narrative," tell a different story, change our values. *The Big Sky* provides an excellent occasion to discuss just what our story has been, and how it might be revised.

The discussion always comes down to Boone's dream. Boone himself was a boring, lonely, violent western male (although given his Pap we might have some sympathy with his fate), and Guthrie intended both the unappealing character and some sympathy. But what of Boone's dream of escape to a wild and free happiness out west? Neither Guthrie, nor the book, undercuts that dream.

This conference has been kind to Guthrie by calling his book prescient and by pointing out the tragedy of killing what we love. But we obscure the underlying narrative if we pretend that the book is politically correct because it criticizes Boone. What gives the book power is that Guthrie participates in Boone's dream of escape, and unfortunately, so do we. As H. G. Merriam said, "There's love in *The Big Sky*. I get the feeling that Guthrie was having a good time when he wrote that book."

Part I: Boone's Dream

I'll give a brief outline of my basic argument, which is more fully developed in chapters one and two of my *Ten Tough Trips: Montana Writers and the West.*

"Bigness, distance, wildness, freedom are the dream that pulls Boone Caudill westward," Wallace Stegner said in his 1965 introduction to Guthrie's book. That dream is one of escape to a natural paradise; the dream is grounded, literally, in land. "It's slick, ain't it," Boone says, looking out for the first time over what would become Charlie Russell country. It's about his only spiritual or aesthetic remark in the book, and Guthrie heartily approves.

But Boone's love of the land has a flip side: distrust of civilization. The natural world saves; civilization is damned. As one old westerner said to me, "You can't judge a man by what he does in town."

Guthrie, in this book, agrees with Boone. Civilization is not a place where a real man would want to be. "Louisville was busy as an anthill and bigger than all the places, put together, that Boone had ever seen." Boone shakes his head: "I don't hanker to live in no anthill." Boone's judgment stands. Throughout the book, Guthrie offers nothing to contradict Boone's impression of towns.

Let's consider the importance of this issue. Boone's love of nature, and Guthrie's, and ours, are mom and apple pie—but does this dream of natural paradise have to come with a rejection of cities and civilization? What are the consequences? I think the reasons for Boone's double-edged dream are profound, and the consequences plague environmentalism right to the present day. At this conference, my friend, rancher Lee Rostad, assumed that environmentalists don't like agrarians, chemicals, or other trappings of the anthill of civilization. To the extent that we're still Boone, she's right, and that's why we'd better understand Boone's dream.

Boone's dream of escape from evil civilization to a big, wild, free West is presented by Guthrie as typical of the mountain man, and therefore as central to our shared mythic western heritage. Boone is a "real mountain man," Guthrie reveals in a series of incidents, because he has certain prerequisites: He is violent and insensitive, he kills without regret, and he never wants to sleep with a woman of his own race or eat his own food or go back East.

However, William H. Goetzmann's research on mountain men—conducted during the 1960s—reveals a different pattern. Of eight hundred mountain men, half died in the field. Of the four hundred left, he could find the names and follow the careers of two hundred. Of those, only five elected to stay out west. Most made money as fast as they could and returned to St. Louis to buy a big house and marry a white woman. Like the miners and the first ranchers of the 1880s in Montana, most mountain men were entrepreneurs. The exceptions have become legends. Which means that, for some reason, we have chosen to admire those few who escaped to nature, not those more typical mountain men who used nature as an instrument of human commerce and individual advancement. Just about everyone can love mountains and sunsets and clear streams, but to foreground landscape as the only, or even the primary, attraction of the West to most trappers or pioneers, is naive history.

A second consideration is so obvious it hurts. Indians were the opposites of Boone. They preferred their own villages with their own families, killed animals with a regret often formalized in prayer, and unlike Boone, saw the beaver as their sister rather than as an object divorced from humankind (although they killed each other with gusto).

This is crucial, for at times Guthrie and some readers want to understand Boone's character, and excuse it, as a necessary adaptation to life in the harsh, wild world of the West. Stegner in his introduction of 1965 suggested this "survival of the fittest" interpretation: He called Boone a "killing machine," and "what the logic of his ferocious adaptation demands, the action of the novel fulfills." But are we really reading about the logic of adaptation? Is anyone going to stand up and claim that the Sioux and Crow and Blackfeet were not adapted to life on the plains? That their extraordinary sensitivity and tenderness (Chief Plenty-coups, tough as they come, took his advice from chickadees), their willingness to do all that Boone wouldn't do—such as honor parents, stay at home, work with others, pray, and weep—left them less able to survive in the harsh, wild West? The Indians could be vicious and brutal to other men, but they hunted, killed, and survived without reducing themselves to "a piece of a man," as McNickle put it, and without hating their own society.

So the mountain man, the prototypical westerner as represented by Guthrie and Boone, cannot be understood as either a fact of history or as the product of Darwinian natural law. Whatever Boone dragged with him from the East, made him what he was. And whatever we dragged with us from the East made us accept his book as our mythic past. *The Big Sky* was Boone's dream, and ours: a shared cultural creation, not a natural reality, not an adaptive necessity, and not an Indian paradise.

We often take it for granted that our cherished dreams are universally shared; actually, our American desire for a trackless wilderness, very possibly a fearful response to the overpopulation and industrialization of Europe in the nineteenth century, was quite puzzling to the Indians. We wanted an empty space for starting over, and wanted to arrive there with an empty mind.

There's no doubt that Guthrie shared Boone's dream of escape. Jim Deakins, Guthrie's most trustworthy observer of Boone, says: "Take Boone now. . . . He was like an animal, like a young bull that traveled alone, satisfied just by earth and water and trees and the sky over him." Boone is presented by the text as simple, innocent, satisfied. "It was as if he talked to the country for company, and the country talked to him, and as if that was enough." Boone sums up this romance of escape: "Here a man lived natural." But Boone is not just tough; he's mean. And mean men aren't simple. And Indians don't run from their past or avoid their own kind. Are Indians unnatural? Are elk unnatural, because they prefer the company of elk? Something is phony.

We have taken Boone's dream to our hearts—not Boone, but his dream—because escape from evil civilization to a saving nature is an old American dream.

A national need to extol nature, and a growing international need to value what was being lost, had by 1800 become complexly interwoven with an emerging American identity that saw itself as natural, innocent, and simple, as opposed to the industry, corruption, and complexity of Europe. In his *Notes on the State of Virginia,* Thomas Jefferson inveighed against "European luxury and dissipation," and urged avoiding "the voluptuary dress and arts of the European women" (he had considerable experience in Paris), while admiring instead "the chaste affections and simplicity of those of his own country."

Having visited the oppressive new factories and squalid mill towns of the industrial revolution in England, Jefferson also directly opposed manufacturing in America: "Let our workshops remain in Europe." Jefferson's ideal of the yeoman farmer was not only a positive pull, it was also a negative push away from the evil progress of Europe. That is, Boone's escape from civilization to a natural innocence, which was also an escape from an evil future to a nostalgic past, can be traced to founding fathers as well as to Pap. Jefferson didn't hanker to live in no anthill.

Jefferson's attitudes were typical of his day and lay at the foundation of the new nation's pride. After 1776, we had to decide who we were. Compared to European capitals, our cities were country villages: pigs in the streets of Boston, no museums. . . . What did we have that Europeans didn't? Wild nature. There was considerable pressure to make wildness a virtue, and it happens that our revolution coincided with the flowering of romantic primitivism, with Rousseau's noble savage and the cult of a wild sublime. "Nothing is old in America but the trees . . . and these alone are worth as much as monuments and ancestors," said Chateaubriand, the visiting Frenchman. "A sort of delirium" seized him in upstate New York in 1792, in the absence of "roads, towns, laws and kings." "In this deserted region the soul delights to bury and lose itself amidst boundless forests . . . to mix and confound with the wild sublimities of nature."

Chateaubriand, of course, spoke in the effusive French style, padded with the "voluptuary" luxury of Europe. An American man, a western man who fancied himself natural as the trees, who himself had given up civilization and its discontents (including reflection and language), might put it differently: "Slick, ain't it."

Like Chateaubriand, Boone longed to be "natural," which means to be beyond the law as well as the town: "It wasn't fair, bringing in the sheriff, just because a body did what he had to do." So our heritage is complex, and we should not whitewash that heritage by calling it simply a love of nature. That acculturated construction of nature came hand in hand with a distrust of civilization that remains American. All of this, of course, had to be most puzzling to the Indians, who wanted only their own law, their own society, their own civilization which to them was inseparable from a natural order, while among them settled these strange escapees—exiled from their own kind—fancying themselves "primitive," "natural," "Indian," "free."

Guthrie, writing in the 1940s, on the one hand corrected Hollywood notions of western pioneers by means of a "realist" or "naturalist" novel, gutty as the hard-hitting turn-of-the-century realism of Dreiser, Norris, or Sinclair, focusing on documentary accuracy and on strong, even stupid characters following "natural law." That was Guthrie's anti-romantic intent. Yet we can see on the other hand that Guthrie, so loving the West, could easily fall prey to a different romanticism, a primitivist dream. That dream offered the awesome beauty of the West as an antidote to a rapidly expanding industrial civilization that Boone, and Guthrie, and we too, distrust. Boone might be a son of a bitch, but Guthrie shared his dissenting dream.

Why does this dream hamper us? Primitivism, for all its ecstatic worship of western expanse, is largely a negative model; it demands that we reject our own past, our own people, and the most advanced aspects of our species: abstract thought, language, complex societies. That is why my rancher friend is quick to suspect that many environmentalists are anti-civilization and are impatient with complex analyses of the cost-benefit ratios for, say, a certain agricultural fertilizer. She thinks environmentalists want to escape to purity—and "no crampin and crowdin, christsake." Any American environmentalism runs the risk of being part of that negative heritage, and is easily associated with escape to a bogus "pristine."

The primitivist model is also regressive; the primitivist is always looking back to a golden age, a paradise that was lost, an earlier point in a curve of sure decline: "We seen a sight of rivers, clear and purty rivers. We had us a whole world to play around in . . . and no one to say it was his property and get the hell off." In this case, the golden age is childhood. For all its appeal, this is the voice of a child, the gospel according to Dennis the Menace: "Let me do what I want."

Yet all species live within boundaries, within territorial, ecological, and social realities. Doing whatever you want is not natural. It is a perversion possible only with the concentration of wealth and power in human civilizations.

The primitivist model—call it a story or narrative, the one we must rewrite—posits a paradise of doomed virginity. The primitivist then predicts the fall—a sure decline with increasing civilization—refuses to do anything about it (even Jefferson washed his hands of industry), and advocates hiding out or playing around until the end comes.

The story Guthrie tells is profound: It is the western story of killing what we love, the story we must rewrite. But the specific problems generated by our specific culture—even if insurmountable—do not make society innately evil, nor do they make civilization the opposite of nature.

Part II: Going Global

That *Paradise Lost* and its nineteenth-century primitivist versions are specific narratives from our specific culture is easily grasped and yet easily overlooked. As a matter of fact, the point is being obscured at this conference whenever we pretend that Boone's tragedy, Guthrie's tragedy, is a universal tale. Guthrie made that claim in a 1954 article in *Montana The Magazine of*

Western History, writing about *The Big Sky*: "It occurred to me . . . that another universal entered here. . . . Each man kills the thing he loves. No man ever did it more thoroughly or in a shorter time than the fur hunters."

Now if I had owned a fur company in 1830 that was making an enormous profit while wiping out the beaver, I would be delighted for everyone to believe that we must kill what we love. "Our business is your fate" would be my motto. After all, when the beaver are gone, my company could move on to some other resource, and devour that also as if there were no tomorrow.

If we imagine a God of free-enterprise capitalism, his first commandment might be, "Thou shalt kill what thou lovest." That divine command (or "natural law" in social Darwinism) would remove any need for long-range responsibility, and turn all attention to immediate profit. Get those beaver out now.

Guthrie's claim is echoed in our conference flyer, which quotes Summers—"We ain't seen the end of it yet, Boone, not to what the mountain man does against hisself."—and adds the comment: "Montana author A. B. Guthrie laid bare our human tendency to destroy what we love." I helped write the brochure, so don't say a western male is incapable of self-criticism.

Our comment was meant as standard praise in the humanist tradition ("His themes are universal. . . ."), but if Boone's dream-and-bust cycle is specifically related to Euro-American culture, and if we want to revise that narrative of decline, then by muttering "universal" we shoot ourselves in the foot. The fiction of universality suggests that a tragic decline is inevitable, indeed fated, and it kills our will for social, political, and environmental reform.

It is not universal to kill what you love. Even within Guthrie's book, the Blackfeet are left out of that formula: Guthrie does not hold the Blackfeet responsible for the buffalo's decline; Indians are not destroying their resources and changing the land. Some recent researchers such as Dan Flores think Guthrie went overboard in imagining a sustainable primitivist "other," and that of course is what he consciously and inaccurately envisioned. However, Guthrie may also have been essentially, or poetically, right about our industrial culture. While Indians of course lived in a changing world, and altered their environment, "killing what you love" may be a defining tragedy only in first world cultures.

Let's listen a minute to the quintessential "primitivist," the original "man of nature," the "Wild Man of Borneo" who for 150 years was confused by Europeans with the orangutan. In 1990–1991, I had the privilege of living with some of these uncivilized, tattooed, stretched-ear, hunter-gatherer blowpipe savages, the Penan, up the Baram river in Borneo, beyond the logging. Quoting from my book *Borneo Log: The Struggle for Sarawak's Forests:*

> Wade Davis, who has studied twenty tribes of the Amazon and South America, says, "The knowledge of the forest by the Penan surpasses all of them. It's unbelievable . . . they recognize more than a hundred fruiting trees and at least fifty medicinal plants."
>
> Sago palms grow in clumps, several trunks springing from one mass of roots (sago, a starch, is pounded from the trunks). "If there are many trunks," says a Penan, "we will get one or two. We thin it out so it will thrive. If there is a lot of sago, we will harvest some, and will leave some. We don't like to kill it all off, in case one day there is nothing for us to eat. This is really our way of life. . . . If we harvest the sago at Ula Jek first and finish the nangah [mature sago] there, we molong [put a mark and preserve for future use] the uvud [young sago]. . . . After two or three years, mature sago will grow out of the young sago that we have preserved." Scattered across the steep, intricate ridges and valleys of their district, many wild sago clumps will be

> known and claimed (marked) by a single group. They know when it is time, in two or three years, to return to a certain clump. And so with many other types of edible plants; in all their fruit and vegetable harvesting, they are careful to preserve a sustained yield. . . .
>
> An old Penan from the Magoh River said: "We know that [dipterocarp] seeds are [wild] pig food, we do not cut this tree anyhow. The river bank roots are what pigs eat, we don't pollute the rivers. Sago fruits, 'tevanga' are what pigs eat, we make sure the pigs have their share. There is a fruit tree called 'tekalet' [acorn]. That is pig food, we don't disturb the tree. But in Layun, Apho and Patah [districts] those trees are fast disappearing because they have been cut down by timber companies. If the companies come here and cut all the trees in the Magoh, there will be nothing for pigs to eat. The pigs will not come here . . . and we Penan will not have any food. That is what I fear if the companies come here. But as long as the Penan are left alone here, we will have enough food because we care for the forest, we look after it well to provide us our food, our life."

My goodness, they are not killing what they love. What they love—the rainforest habitat—is being killed by international companies cutting trees for the international timber trade.

Wait a minute. Wasn't Boone trapping beaver to sell to international companies exporting pelts to Europe for the international hat trade? Wasn't that market the reason the beaver were trapped out? Why should the mountain man be blaming himself ("Gosh darnit, I've killed what I loved"), rather than the system of which he is part? Are we sure that killing what you love is a universal human fate, or is it a pattern that our first world culture is perfecting? That is why the God of unbridled free enterprise without stewardship asks us to believe that we kill what we love: Then mature, realistic adults, feeling no responsibility to the future and feeling fated to exhaust their resources, can get down to the business of worshipping the quarterly bottom line.

We don't know exactly what caused the primitivist model of a lost virgin paradise violated by an evil civilization, but we know the idea grew quickly from 1600 to 1800 with the rise of empirical science, new instruments of manipulation and change, industrialization, and a population explosion in the major European cities. It is possible that just as nature, subdued by guns, boats, and steam engines, was becoming more manageable and hence loveable, so also civilization was becoming more frightening. Like Boone, we were all pushed west by the nasty Pap of society, and pulled west by a dream of escape. Ironically, then, while Boone fancied his escape to the West a kind of dissent, his naive blindness was mainstream and continues in our conference brochure.

That is why, especially in America, our love of nature can still be tinged with a primitivist rejection of civilization and can properly be suspect to agriculturalists and industry trying to make progress work.

Note, however, that a revolution has occurred in the last fifty years, which renders primitivism obsolete. Ecology is not escapist; it is the first use of empirical method and technology to question the limits of progress—itself based on empiricism and technology. The ecologist need not separate man and nature, need not value one over the other, need not venerate "the wild" rather than a healthy ecosystem, which may or may not include humans. The ecologist's ecosystem is where the Penan live, and the Indians lived, and in an ecosystem the question is not one of escape from society, but of species diversity and sustainability. To dramatize the difference: a primitivist environmentalist must maximize wilderness; an ecologist, on the other hand, might vote to abolish the

Selway-Bitterroot wilderness if the towns of the Bitterroot Valley and Missoula could live in a healthy and sustainable relation to the natural world. The "if," of course, is nowhere in sight; hence most ecologists are forced to support "protection and preservation" environmentalism.

Still, the shift from a primitivist love of the wild to an ecological appreciation of functioning ecosystems is huge, and ecology has already won the day. Hardly a single industry executive questions the validity of ecological approaches to our problems of earth, water, and air; no one doubts anymore that acid rain exists and can be mitigated, that our chemicals can kill the water, that resources we thought inexhaustible—trees, aquifers, fisheries—can be depleted. An environmentalism based on ecology does not need to escape civilization, technology, or man.

These issues may be globally important in the next century. If we cannot convince our rancher neighbors that we are no longer primitivists, we cannot expect to have much effect in Asia as China comes on line. Intensely proud of their five thousand years of civilization, and with no history of the European romance of the wild, the Chinese are unaffected by primitivist evocations of the pristine. They respect data on siltation behind dams (though not laments for the wild rapids of the Three Gorges), or data on the panda as part of a healthy biodiversity in a bamboo forest with other uses or even as part of a tourist economy. But the panda is not so likely to be seen as an end in itself, as a symbol of wildness, as we regard the grizzly bear.

To summarize: just how and why is this primitivist story of killing what we love the special story of our special civilization? The argument might run something like this:

1. The Renaissance was an expanding trade for expanding markets. Increased resource extraction and resource consumption were

indivisible from the expanding middle class, the new freedom of movement, the new individualism.

2. "The Frontier" has always been the edge of that capitalist and colonialist expansion. By the 1600s, the Spice Islands were a frontier, which is a place where cheap resources are extracted for expanding (often created) markets, and where people are settled to exploit or colonize or rule claimed land for Portugal, or France, or England, or Thomas Jefferson.

3. "We kill what we love" is the story of that frontier, because the narrative of expanding capitalist production and consumption is the opposite of a sustainable narrative.

That sad truth was brought home to me in Borneo when, after some months of living with native resistance to the logging, I wound up in the Tebanyi timber camp that was cutting the native land. All the major Japanese importers go to the same forests at the same time, and compete there for the timber. The Tebanyi camp had taken out 3.6 million dollars of timber from that one district in the previous month. The honest and interesting Japanese manager of that camp, Fujino, welcomed my conversation from the outside world. One night I asked him, why take the land from the natives? Why not sell or rent cheap chainsaws, and let them cut the timber themselves on their ancestral native lands? Then they could sell the logs directly to the Japanese timber ships lying at the mouth of the river. The government could get its cut by taxing the logs. The tribes would use wise cutting practices on their own lands, I said.

Fujino agreed, but shook his head. Ah Bevis-san, he said, I'm afraid the volume produced would not interest Japan. We would go somewhere else, with enough volume to keep the price down and the mills in Yokohama supplied.

That means, I observed, that Japan is not interested in sustained yield. No, he said, it is not nearly enough.

Now let's outline the rewrite of Boone's story in its historical context, no longer privileging the free individual in his fantasy of romantic escape to a wild West.

Part III: "Follow the Money"

That's our story line, our rescripting of Boone's escapist narrative. Here's what we need to know:

1. How and why did the fashion of hats in Europe shift from beaver to silk in the 1840s? Since "the West" does not exist without "the East," our history books should tell us why the price of beaver declined even as they were trapped out (contradicting supply-and-demand pricing). What was driving the fashion shift? Was it market manipulation for someone's benefit, or free consumer choice? How did the hat market work?

2. What was happening to the towns of southeast China in the 1840s as silk exports to Europe soared, in place of the beaver? What were the conditions of the workers in the new silk-weaving factories? Who was getting rich?

Boone was a worker on the western beaver plantation, while fancying himself a free man and an Indian. What about the bucket at the other end of the well rope, the Chinese worker harvesting the silkworms? And what about balancing the environmental effects: removal of the beaver, whose dams created vast wetlands in the Rockies, compared to the effects of the new mulberry plantations in China? Were fields changed, rivers, forests, towns, climate? And in general, how do boom-and-bust export fads, in their destabilizing of natural and social resources, affect frontiers? In the 1980s a slight change in market prices and tax supports caused thousands of acres of Montana pasture to be plowed up for the first time, for wheat. The economic benefit lasted only a few years. Now many of those acres are knapweed. Is that the way to treat topsoil—which we love?

Even in 1825, when the first mountain man rendezvous was covered in the Paris papers, the narrative of which Boone was a tiny part included social history, economic history, and environmental history on a global scale. Telling the old story of a "trapper" foregrounds the lone individual versus nature, yet some of Boone's anxiety surely came from having no control over his life, in a world that was slipping away. Much more common than frontier violence is frontier impotence. Telling the story of "Follow the Money" places characters in relation to the master narrative, the global movement of power and its effects.

Now is the time to rewrite this story. With the fall of the Berlin Wall, critics of capitalism need no longer be feared as "communists." *The New Yorker* recently carried a piece on the resurgence of Marxism on Wall Street, as a fashion, I presume. Perhaps, Cold War divisions suspended, capitalism can get down to the very serious business of criticizing itself.

As western historians and critics, we have gladly participated in Boone's romance of the local and discrete. We too, as scholars, are isolationist. Ironically, some cherished notions—"universal tragedy" and love of the land as the opposite of civilization—can encourage the "mythology of failure," that narrative of sure decline that we must rewrite. "She's all gone now" is not our fate; depletion of resources was, is, and shall be our responsibility. We should not allow romances of escape to nature, and of the universal, to obscure the particular ways in which our particular civilization is dysfunctional.

We need, I believe, a new telling of our story that acknowledges global realities as integral to our "frontier" experience, that compares our assumptions about nature and civilization to other assumptions from other cultures, a new story that resists the Hollywood and academic shrinking of our horizons to one small town of Lago (in *High Plains Drifter*) and one unnamed stranger (Clint Eastwood) coming from nowhere and going nowhere, killing along the way. There is no nowhere, that western utopia of escape and irresponsibility. The Big Sky is bigger than Lago, bigger than Boone's Montana, and bigger than the United States. The Big Sky arches over global interdependence, and it is called a biosphere.

A. B. Guthrie, Jr., n.d. Photograph by Stuart White.
COURTESY OF STUART WHITE

Fifty Years Later: Guthrie and Montana's Changing Politics

~

Mark A. Sherouse

The Big Sky, Humanities, and Public Policy

Public policy may seem an unlikely topic on the occasion of *The Big Sky's* fiftieth anniversary, and the humanities and public policy will strike some as an even more unlikely combination. But the three are all related, in interesting, even important ways, and it will be the purpose of this paper to draw out and explore these relations. What we will learn buttresses the case for the importance of Guthrie's work, not merely as literature, but as a socially and politically important statement of western issues and perspectives.

In the following ruminations, I take up various combinations and permutations of Guthrie, *The Big Sky*, the humanities, literature, public policy, and other matters. I will begin with the other matters which, despite the seeming impertinence, do shed some light on the issues under discussion.

The Humanities, Public Policy, and License Plates

Yes, license plates. It is sort of a public policy issue, and in Montana it has clear humanities and literary origins and implications.

It seems that Montana is the only state that advertises its literature on its license plates. I have traveled in all of the fifty states and can attest to this. Georgians, for example, do not proclaim that they are the *Gone with the Wind* state. Neither Okies nor Californians claim to be the *Grapes of Wrath* state; nor is Massachusetts the *Scarlet Letter* state. And so on. So, why Montana? And why *The Big Sky?*

In part, the answer may lie in Montana's prodigious literary output. I have heard it attributed to Bill Kittredge that Montana has more gifted writers than grizzly bears—not a comforting thought if you're a bear but, from a literary perspective, something in which Montanans should take great pride.

But license plates? How and when did this happen, I have wondered, and what is the meaning of it?

My curiosity drove me to place calls to the governor's office, to the legislative research office, to the Department of Commerce, Travel Montana, and even the Department of Transportation, which employs its own historian. In every case I received the same unhelpful response: "Gee, that's an interesting question." In each case I also received the same helpful lead: "Have you called Dave Walter at the Historical Society?" At length, I did, and as those of you who know Dave will expect, he indeed has a thick file on the matter, not only on license plates but also on all kinds of state mottoes, monikers, and promotional fantasies.

According to Dave's research, we have been referring to ourselves since at least 1895, in official state literature, as the "Treasure State." From nearly the beginning, there have been other contenders and pretenders: "the land of the shining mountains," "the Switzerland of America," "the bonanza state," "the stub toe state" (my personal favorite), the "out where the west lives on" state, "high, wide and handsome" (in 1941, which, considering Joseph Kinsey Howard's influential 1943 history, *High, Wide, and Handsome*, raises some other literary questions), the "alluring and soul-satisfying state" (I *swear* I am not making this up—it is from the 1942 Department of Highways state map), "the nation's playground," "magnificent Montana," "majestic Montana," and so on.

"The Big Sky Country" first appeared on the 1962 state highway map. In 1967, the Montana Registrar of Motor Vehicles first replaced "The Treasure State" with "Big Sky Country" (for those of us who do not indulge in affinity or vanity plates). And so it has been for thirty years now: "the Big Sky." I suppose Bud Guthrie and his heirs might have wished for some form of royalty, but as is well known, despite the occurrence of the expression "big sky" once or twice in the text, Guthrie credited the expression to his father, and for its choice as title, to publisher William Sloane. Guthrie was receptive to the idea of "Big Sky Country," which was presented to him in 1961 by Jack Hallowell of the state advertising department. According to a letter from Hallowell in Dave Walter's file, Guthrie gave his "permission" to use the "Big Sky" in state promotions enthusiastically and without hesitation. In the later 1960s, Texas promotional literature appeared to be usurping the "Big Sky" moniker, and this drew a sharp objection from Guthrie in the Helena *Independent Record,* as well as the observation from another individual, in the letters to the editor of the *Washington Post,* that Texas has only a "medium sky."

And so, we are the "Big Sky" state, and in my experience, that is generally how we are thought of, both within and without our borders. The name fits and has a ring, and we like it. Now there are hundreds of "Big Sky" businesses of all sorts: a ski resort; motels; laundromats; garages; saloons; "Big Sky" mud flaps—another important cultural icon; "Big Sky" schools; and a Big Sky Athletic Conference.

So what to make of all this? There are a number of observations one might offer. Perhaps the most interesting is that the license plate switch, in 1967, from "The Treasure State" to the "Big Sky" marked, or presaged, a change, not only in the state's economic realities, but also a change in consciousness and self-image among Montanans: a change of focus from resources to be exploited to a focus upon a place to be valued and cared for. If he thought of it in those terms, and I suspect he did, Bud Guthrie certainly would have approved.

Guthrie, the Humanities, and *The Big Sky*

As I said, the title—*The Big Sky*—was not entirely of Guthrie's own invention; he credits the titling of the novel to publisher William Sloane, who was at the Bread Loaf Writers' Conference, which Guthrie attended in 1945, in the midst of writing his novel. And that brings me to another set of observations.

The Big Sky is a great work of the imagination, to be sure, but it is also a work of scholarship. In *The Blue Hen's Chick,* his 1965 autobiography, Guthrie tells of having amassed during his journalistic career a "small but select" library of the fur trade era and, in writing the novel, of having immersed himself in it and in the world of the free trapper. Wallace Stegner once observed that *The Big Sky* was a "historian's novel." Much of the novel was written during Guthrie's year of research as a Nieman Fellow at Harvard University, and it might be said that, in addition to his research, it was there that he found his voice for the novel, under the tutelage of literature professor Theodore Morrison.

Later that summer, at the Bread Loaf conference, Guthrie found further beneficial influence and encouragement. At Bread Loaf that year were no less than Louis Untermeyer, John Ciardi, Wallace Stegner, Robert Frost (the leader of the conference), and of course, the redoubtable Bernard DeVoto. As several speakers at this conference already have observed, 1947 saw not one, but two great books of the West. The other was DeVoto's *Across the Wide Missouri,* which won the 1947 Pulitzer Prize for history. DeVoto was already a highly regarded scholar and writer, a professor at Harvard and author of several books. Stegner referred to *Across the Wide Missouri* as a "novelist's history" of the era, lauding its passion and language. What is not so well known, despite the attention Stegner gives it in *The Uneasy Chair,* his biography of DeVoto, is that *The Big Sky* was that great novel of the opening of the West that DeVoto himself had dreamed of writing. He went on to write *his* novel of the era, *Mountain Time,* serialized pseudonymously in *The Saturday Evening Post,* and later published under his own name. It is, alas, a work the world has forgotten. Nevertheless, DeVoto, to his great credit, was, until his death in 1955, a close friend of Guthrie's and an unreserved admirer and promoter of Guthrie's work.

All this is to say: If there is greatness in *The Big Sky,* and in Guthrie's later work, part of it is due to its scholarly origins and its nurturing in the humanities, and also to the stellar intellectual company Guthrie was privileged to keep during its writing, as well as in his later years in Montana.

The Humanities and Public Policy

Let me turn now to the humanities' contribution to public policy discussion. The points I wish to make are fairly straightforward and, hopefully, will simply remind us of and reaffirm much of what has gone on during "*The Big Sky* at Fifty" conference, which has resulted in this anthology. In focusing on public policy, I will not address the undoubted benefits the humanities have for us all in more personal dimensions—the ability of the humanities to touch us as individuals, to give our lives meaning, and to transform us. It is a worthy and important topic, but here, we should consider the humanities and the ways they enrich discussion of public affairs. At one level, the National Endowment for the Humanities and the state humanities councils, such as ours here in Montana, contribute greatly to public policy discussion by supporting conferences and the publications that result from them. Members of any civic or public organization can obtain our funding and support for such forums, providing only that they meet the requirement of matching funds, that their discussions draw in part from the humanities, and that their discussions, even of controversial issues, provide balance and promote reflection. We provide an opportunity for sound, civil, and informed discussion that is at the heart of a free society. We need more of such discussion.

There is a more conceptual level at which the humanities contribute to public policy. In any public policy issue, there are at least two different dimensions: the "facts" that are needed to understand and predict, and the values upon which right action will depend. The humanities are essential to both.

Economists, political scientists, statisticians, and others of the more "factual" realm can tell us what might happen if we undertake this policy or that. (Enact a tax on this or that, and demand will fall, as will prices, as will employment in the industry, and so on. . . .) They have their data and their models and their predictions, and more often than they are given credit for, they have their explanatory and predictive successes. But even in the realm of facts, there is need of interpretation and, thus, of humanistic skills and perspectives. For "facts" are often more elusive, murky, and complex than we like to admit. The factual dimension of any policy issue demands that we have the right facts, that their volume and relevance actually support some conclusion, that we are not missing other relevant facts, that the supposed facts are based on proper assumptions, that we are interpreting the supposed facts aright, that those who have presented us with the supposed facts have no interest that would alter their own perception or presentation of the facts, and so on. As you can see, even with the "facts," you have *interpretation*, and interpretation is the stuff of the humanities . . . the skills and perspectives one learns and learns best in history and literature and languages and philosophy and the other humanities disciplines. We need more of that, too.

Apart from the "facts," however, in any policy decision, there always remain questions of whether the proposed policy is fair, whether it is morally permissible, whether it or its consequences may be injurious or immoral. Policy issues have moral components: that, in part, is what makes them so interesting, and also so controversial. And this is the other way in which the humanities enter into and enrich policy discussion. For it is in the humanities—in philosophy, literature, history, religion, legal theory, and other such disciplines—that moral questions are most directly and earnestly considered and illuminated. That is not to say that there are easy answers and that all you have to do is call your local philosophy department for help. Questions of value and morality are enduringly difficult and deep and evolving. But we have learned in the past few millennia that some answers are better than others, some types of moral reasoning are better than others, some evidence more germane and powerful. . . . The moral *wisdom* we have accumulated over the ages resides in the great works of philosophy and the religions, in the literatures, and in the histories that constitute the humanities. That wisdom needs to be consulted and applied, over and over, again.

The Big Sky, Literature, and Public Policy

Where is *The Big Sky* in all this? How could a novel—a work of fiction—written 50 years ago, about an era that closed 150 years ago, possibly help us to deal with the issues we confront today?

One of the functions of literature is to fire our imaginations and, in particular, to enable us see the world through the eyes of other, if imagined, persons. The perspectives conveyed in *The Big Sky*—of Uncle Zeb, of Dick Summers, of Boone, and others—are important examples, and others in this anthology have discussed them in some detail. In these perspectives we see what may well have been some of the attitudes of the early nineteenth-century "frontier," toward the land, its resources, toward its inhabitants. Some of us would argue that many of the perspectives and attitudes persist, and need examination.

The importance of imagination and empathy in our civic life, and in discourse about public policy, should not be underestimated. It is through the imagination that we are able to see the perspectives of others, indeed, even, the perspective of the common good. A dogmatist is, among other things, a person who is unable or unwilling to imagine perspectives other than his or her own—and it is difficult, if not impossible, to engage in reasoned and civil discourse with such a person. Civic discourse could hardly exist without these imagined perspectives, and it is important to note that literature, fiction, and important novels like *The Big Sky* indeed fire our imaginations, enable us to see beyond our own narrow perspectives, and provide us with perspectives that we must address and come to understand.

As a moral treatise, I admit, *The Big Sky* has its defects. Its protagonist, if it has one, is a racist, a sexist, a speciesist, and an uncommunicative, faithless, cruel, brutal, and nearly altogether repulsive human being. He is a liar, a horse thief, a rapist, a murderer, and a plunderer of nearly everything he encounters. *The Big Sky* is not your *Book of Virtues.*

It is a provocative book, nonetheless, and an intellectual book, one that compels its readers to reflect on a great variety of moral issues and problems, as urgent today as in 1830: child abuse, alcohol abuse, sexually transmitted diseases, the plight of the poor and the disadvantaged, man's place in and relation to the environment, the limitedness and fragility of the environment and posterity's interests in it, nature and culture, our relations and obligations to other species, relations among different peoples, among men and women, and so on. It compels us to consider the myths of Eden and the Fall, of Cain and Abel, of Oedipus, of human freedom, and a variety of social and psychological archetypes and images that still exercise great power over us.

And repeatedly, of the West, this somehow special place, it asks: Whose land is this? Who has the right to it? Who shall decide? These questions are still before us, just as in Guthrie's time and in the time of his novel. *The Big Sky* provides no easy answers to these questions—that is part of its greatness—but it compels us now, as it did in 1947, to grapple with its issues from our own perspectives, to reflect, to discern, and, as we did during the two days of the "*The Big Sky*—After Fifty Years" conference, to reason with one another.

Pat Williams

A Fifty-Year Montana Political Profile

Fifty years ago the novelist A. B. Guthrie wrote *The Big Sky,* and with it he opened our minds to a truer consideration of the West. Guthrie's novel began a debate about the West and the relationship of place to people and to their politics. It is that latter subject—politics—which I want to address.

However, because this conference is about the novel, its author, and the changes of this past half century, let me first acknowledge A. B. Guthrie. I never met him, although we exchanged letters. The subject of our correspondence was the efforts of the Reagan administration in the early 1980s to explore for oil along the Rocky Mountain Front as well as in the land to its west—the Bob Marshall Wilderness. As Montana's congressman, I was as determined to prevent that exploratory drilling and blasting as Secretary of Interior Jim Watt was to see it through.

Guthrie, in his letters, encouraged me to continue the fight to spare the Front and the Bob from development. I did—to Guthrie's delight. But . . . we never met. I only had his words and the mental images I had developed from listening to others who knew him.

Although born in Bedford, Indiana, Guthrie was brought to Choteau, Montana, when he was six months old. He graduated from The University of Montana in 1923 and, soon after, was working for the *Lexington Leader* in Kentucky, where he eventually became the executive editor. He studied at Harvard during which time he revised and completed *The Big Sky* before its publication in 1947.

Guthrie's six historical novels painted the settling of the West starting in 1830. Although *The Big Sky* is the popular favorite, he received a Pulitzer Prize for *The Way West* in 1950.

It seemed to me that Guthrie's political passion was best stated in his words about the environment. He was glad he grew up where he did. "I fished the streams, hunted the thickets, swam in Spring Creek. In June I gathered serviceberries, in September chokecherries. I would save these riches for the youngsters who come along in all the years ahead. I want them to enjoy what I did. I want the places to remain rewarding for them. That's one of the reasons I am an environmentalist."

During his final years, Guthrie wondered about Montana's environment and how it would fare in the years ahead. As he measured economic progress—so-called progress—against his own desire to see the land remain as it is, he wrote, "Am I an antiquarian, an atavistic yearner that I'd like to see old things return? I'm delighted that pronghorns are beginning to roam the plains of Montana. I'm happy we have deer in numbers. I have hopes for the wild turkeys and for the peregrine falcon. I want wilderness and more wilderness, remnants and reminders of a time that was. And, yet, I know very well that we can't turn back and would probably gripe if we did. But leave me my illusions."

Well, that was the Bud Guthrie I came to know through his letters and other writings. But my purpose here this afternoon is to discuss, not Guthrie, but rather us and our politics during this half century since the writing of *The Big Sky*.

A. B. Guthrie's book was, I suppose, first read by a generation of Montanans and Americans born during World War I and raised during the Depression. Many of them served in World War II. In large measure, Guthrie's audience of Montanans and Americans believed they were, and were in fact, participants with their federal government. They knew that together they had brought us through a national economic collapse and had beat the Nazis and the Japanese, preserving America against domestic calamity and foreign entanglement. Thus, at the time of A. B. Guthrie's *The Big Sky,* those—or at least the majority of those—living under that Big Sky harbored and sustained a belief in the national government. They held that the federal government embodied a great idea which was, and remains today, that an elected national government can be the instrument of the common purpose of a free people. That government can embrace great causes and make a positive difference in the lives of individual Montanans and Americans.

Perhaps the surest way in our democracy to determine political preference, that is, to identify people's attitudes—in this instance, toward the federal government—is to examine the Montana results at the ballot box. Yes, there are political polls that purport to measure opinion and mood. There are other barometers of this state's political persuasions: the throb of its daily activities, the talk over morning coffee, the letters to the editor, the radio talk shows. But the surest way to identify a people's political preferences, and their wishes concerning the federal relationship, is to simply go to that second Tuesday every other November and tally the votes. So part of what I want to share with you are those results. They aren't foolproof in reflecting Montana's support of, or concern with, our national government. However, if anyone wants to argue that election results don't count, I'll leave that to them.

Fifty years ago, in 1948, Montanans gave a majority to Harry Truman. It had become a habit. Montanans had voted for Roosevelt as well. However, those two were the only two Democrat presidential candidates that Montanans had ever supported. And by the way, in the fifty years since Guthrie's novel, we have only supported two others: Lyndon Johnson and Bill Clinton.

But back to 1948. Montanans elected Mike Mansfield in the western district, a Democrat, and Wesley Dewart, a Republican, in the eastern district, and they chose a Democrat, Jim Murray, to go to the United States Senate. As they had throughout the Depression and war, Montanans in 1948 signaled their support for an activist national government by casting 57 percent of their total votes that year for those candidates who had campaigned for having a relatively aggressive federal partner. Those were the political results fifty years ago. Like people everywhere, the political opinions and demands of Montanans have ebbed and flowed in each of these past five decades, but the essential question for me is this: What have Montanans come to expect from their national government as a partner?

Upon even cursory examination, the first thing one notices is this: Montana is terribly schizophrenic politically, particularly east to west. In Montana's two congressional districts, one is struck by the differences: in landform, in the economy, in the culture. And reflecting each of those, of course, is the politics. Since 1948 we've had twenty-five elections concerning candidates for federal office. During those years, the eastern congressional district has elected a Republican to the U.S. House seventeen times, and a Democrat eight times. In the west, Montanans have more than reversed that trend, sending a Democrat to Congress twenty-two times and a Republican three times. During those same years, we have had twelve U.S. Senate elections. We chose a Democrat ten times, and a Republican twice. And since Montana began to be represented by an at-large House member in 1992, you have elected a Democrat twice and a Republican twice.

My point is not partisan. It is not Democrat versus Republican, but rather it is an attempt to dissect the policy preferences of all of us in regard to the federal relationship during these past fifty years. With notable and obvious exceptions, Montanans have, according to their election-day decisions, voted in the majority for those federal candidates who were most supportive of an active federal government. And we clearly expect that even our most conservative federal officials practice that activist habit of bringing home the federal bacon. Bacon, not pork, is the preferred term of incumbents—be they Democrats or Republicans.

But it's true: We expect all of our officials to bring it home, and to keep the federal government as an active partner on our behalf. And I believe that if we are to understand Montana's historic partnership with the federal government, we have to look at the legislative performance of our elected members of the U.S. House and Senate. There clearly have been major differences between them on what is commonly referred to as social policy. Even among members of the same party elected federally from Montana, there have been differences—differences on Social Security, on Medicare and Medicaid and welfare and Head Start and the arts, on tax policy, and to some degree, even on defense and foreign policy.

However, on those issues that have defined the western federal partnership, there has been continually remarkable agreement. When is the last time you can remember two senators differing on interstate highway funding for Montana, regardless of their party affiliation? There has been no difference in how members both Republican and Democrat, eastern and western, have encouraged an active federal partnership when it comes to Montana's airline service and airport construction. On energy, they are clones, all supporting hydroelectric development, all supporting energy research such as MHD in Butte and Billings, all supporting the energy needs of people living in rural areas who get their power from the co-ops, all supporting federal money necessary for environmental clean up. On agriculture, there has been virtually no difference: All have supported an active federal position on farm payments and agriculture research. I cannot find one time in half a century that any member of the Montana congressional delegation voted against impact aid for Montana's schools. On funding of our national parks, alike. On funding of our federal forest and grazing land, alike. There has been a quiet, sometimes almost camouflaged, but nonetheless remarkable unanimity among all the members of the Montana delegation for fifty years—agreement that there are critical elements that absolutely cement the Montana partnership with the federal government.

It seems to me that our state's more than half-century tradition of partnership with the federal government is now waning. Although change is impossible to autopsy because it is always alive, it does seem clear that Montanans, westerners, like all Americans, are examining—as we all should from time to time—how government at all levels can better serve us. The age of preeminently powerful presidencies may be over. Congressional power and leadership has been dispersed by self-imposed congressional reforms during the past twenty-five years.

It may not be coincidental that the diffusion of leadership arises at a time when persons of the baby-boom generation sit in positions of leadership. It is a baby boomer who now occupies the Oval Office; a baby boomer, Newt Gingrich, who was speaker of the House; a baby boomer is the House minority leader. A baby boomer runs the Senate, and a baby boomer is the minority leader of that body. In a sense—not referring directly to any of those good people—baby boomers generally never learned leadership. And it is no wonder: They came along at a time of political suspicion and corruption. That generation came of age during the lies of Vietnam and Watergate. They watched as their leaders were gunned down: Kennedy and King and Kennedy again and Wallace. They were moved from asking not what they could do for their country, but rather, am I better off than I was four years ago? The leaders at the time that Guthrie wrote *The Big Sky* were expected to have vision and wisdom, and above all they were to move out front and lead. For the moment at least, a new expectation seems to have emerged. As a people, we want to sort through the inundation of information and opinion and find our own solutions as Montanans here at the local level.

There is no doubt that the federal/state relationship has been marked as a very tense fellowship in this state. But for the most part, I submit it has been incredibly productive. If, in fact, America and Montana are programmed to reinvent the federal relationship, we should do so with a factual understanding of the social and economic benefits that have accrued this past half century and more to the West, and most notably to Montana. I believe we should recognize both the new vitality inherent in today's political devolution as well as the vital energy and creativity that the federal/state partnership has played out in Montana and throughout the West. We citizens must seek this new order not out of artificially conjured political anger or indignity, but rather with a determination toward what is the best way to accommodate the continuing—and in fact now growing—needs of the West.

For fifty years and more, the Iwo Jima generation, and the several since, have purposely in this state chosen a partnership between their governments: local (including school boards), county, state, and national. Each entity, for all these decades, has been a cautious, tense, watchful, but willing partner. Montanans have been wise enough to recognize that the federal partner was necessary to help balance our economy, assist with access and equity in our locally run schools, assure the cleanliness of our air and water, and restrain corporate greed, particularly here in this state.

Montanans are now rethinking that partnership. There is no question about it. I think we can all urge each other to rethink it carefully.

Daniel Kemmis

Of Poets, Place, and Politics

This celebration of the fiftieth anniversary of A. B. Guthrie's *The Big Sky* has put me in mind of that stage of my life when I was first claimed by Guthrie's work, particularly *The Big Sky.* I have since concluded that what affected me so deeply was not only the book itself, but that it seemed to proclaim an epoch in the West's history. Now this fiftieth anniversary of the book's publication gives us an opportunity to triangulate a bit, to reflect on how things stand in this region today, to compare the present to that time roughly fifty years ago, when the West was beginning to see itself in a new light.

This anniversary celebration, then, encourages us to examine not only A. B. Guthrie, but those of his colleagues who, at approximately the same time, had been engaged in similar kinds of work. I'm thinking of people like Joseph Kinsey Howard, Wallace Stegner, and Bernard DeVoto. In DeVoto's case in particular, since this year is also the centennial of his birth, we have an opportunity to consider him at age fifty, to consider his work and life, both of which, like Guthrie's, have contributed so much to our own understanding of ourselves as westerners.

So this conference is for me not only about A. B. Guthrie, but about that whole cluster of remarkable people, and how their work has helped us understand ourselves. What happened in that period, roughly fifty years ago, is that in some important way the West found its voice. This is not to say that there weren't many earlier writers of great depth who made tremendous contributions to our culture; there certainly were. But there are moments in history when a culture quite suddenly moves to a different plateau. Something like that happened in this region with or around Guthrie's publication of *The Big Sky.*

"No place is a place," Wallace Stegner wrote in one of his last books of essays, "until it has had a poet."[1] The essay was titled "A Sense of Place," and the place in question was of course the American West. If the West had been needing a poet—needing someone who had learned to speak in an authentic western voice—many of us might settle on Stegner himself as the single best candidate. But in fact we don't have to name one, and no one writer could have accomplished alone what was accomplished in that time. Right around 1947, a number of people, most of whom had been working with Robert Frost at the Bread Loaf writer's program in Vermont for a number of years, people who had been born in the West, or lived in the West, began to apply their steadily expanding literary talents to speaking of that region in a new way. The real significance of *The Big Sky* may be that it speaks in that voice, a voice the West had not heard before, but which it instantly recognized as its own. From that point on, we began to have confidence about the West as a real place both deserving and capable of a real and quite distinctive voice. It is certainly appropriate for westerners to celebrate the remarkable people who developed that voice.

But the question remains: How does such a thing happen? Here again, Stegner is helpful. In the essay I quoted earlier, Stegner goes on to say that "a place is not a place until people have been born in it, have grown up in it, lived in it, known it, died in it—have both experienced and shaped it, as individuals, families, neighborhoods and communities over more than one generation."[2] So perhaps we can understand the years right around 1947 as a point when the white settlers in the West had finally been here long enough to begin to actually know the place. In one sense, the writers of that time may have been working out something that their mentor Robert Frost had said in one of his poems, that "the land was ours before we were the land's."[3] By the late 1940s, Stegner and Guthrie and DeVoto had all come to understand this about the West—to understand that we had claimed the land before we knew how to allow it to claim us; that we had laid title to it long before we had learned how to let it speak through us. But they also understood that, after a few generations of living on the land and paying attention to it, it might actually be possible to let that power of the land speak up through us. That's what I hear above all else in *The Big Sky*—that hard, straight, honest voice of this place speaking up through its people. It takes time for that to happen, generations of hard country beating its lessons into us, but once it does happen, it's real; it's decisive; it dwells among us. It becomes part of our lives together; it reaches us as a great gift to accompany us on the next stage of inhabiting this place. And we have, I think, received that gift wholeheartedly. We have not let go of that voice, and we have tried our best to use it to work out the challenges of life in this land. Sometimes at least, we have done it with a degree of success of which we can fairly be proud.

Let me illustrate the point by engaging in a little Missoula chauvinism. For many years I was professionally bound to be proud of Missoula; I was in fact paid to be proud of Missoula. That is no longer exactly the case, but I am going to re-assume that mantle for just a minute. Here's something from a different essay in that same last book of Stegner's I cited before. Here he speaks of what the West "growing up" might mean, and suggests where you might look for that more mature West:

> If I were advising a documentary film maker where he might get the most quintessential West in a 56-minute can, I would steer him away from the broken-down rodeo riders, away from the towns of the energy boom, away from the cities, and send him to just such a little city as Missoula or Corvallis, some settlement that has managed against difficulty to make itself into a place and is likely to remain one. It wouldn't hurt at all if this little city had a university in it to keep it in touch with its cultural origins and conscious of its changing cultural present. It would do no harm if an occasional Leslie Fiedler came through to stir things up, to stir up its provincialism and set it to some self-questioning. It wouldn't hurt if some native born writer, some Doig or Hugo or Maclean or Welch or Kittredge or Raymond Carver was around to serve as culture hero, the individual who transcends his culture without abandoning it, who leaves it for awhile in search of opportunity and enlargement but never forgets where he left his heart.[4]

As a Missoulian, I have benefited along with my neighbors from having so many excellent writers living and working in our community. The result is a deepened understanding of what this place is all about, an understanding drawn from life and literature in the same breath.

As an occasional writer about the West, I have also been blessed by having so many excellent western writers so near at hand. But though I do write occasionally, I'm not really a writer. What I am, fundamentally, for good or ill, is a politician. And so my interest here is finally not about what 1947 and *The Big Sky* might tell us about our literary life, but what it might tell us about that aspect of our life together which is our politics. The question I would frame in Stegner's terms, then, is whether, in the end, a place can be a place without its own politics. Listen now to how Stegner describes the politics of the West: "I have . . . pretty consistently despised its most powerful politicians," he says, "and the general trend of their politics."[5] We can certainly understand what led Stegner to say that. There are multitudes among us who have generally despised the politics of the West. But we have to ask ourselves whether it is possible to be a mature people, or indeed to be a place in Stegner's terms, while continuing to loathe the politics of that place. In the literary realm, we recognize readily enough the impossibility of being a place we are proud of if we "pretty consistently despise" the work of our writers. We know that America itself did, in effect, despise the work of its writers for many years, before a recognizable and credible American voice began to emerge. In its turn the West went through the same self-effacing phase, and it was the great gift of those writers I've referred to that led us beyond that. But if we are still despising our politics as thoroughly as ever, then we have to ask ourselves if we have, quite yet, become "a place." What might we learn if we asked ourselves, fifty years after the publication of *The Big Sky,* how our politics now compare to those of 1947? The question brings into focus what Bernard DeVoto was up to in his fiftieth year.

DeVoto spent most of 1947 using his regular "Easy Chair" column in *Harper's* magazine to defeat an effort by western Republicans to devolve authority over the public lands to the states. This immediately raises the question: How far have we come in our politics? Are we getting anywhere? Has anything changed? Since 1947 Republican senators have, several times, reverted to that same theme, while later incarnations of Bernard DeVoto have come back repeatedly to exactly the same means of resisting that effort. Our politics, then, may seem simply to be going in circles; the case could be made that nothing has changed, and that our politics are as hopeless as ever. But on the ground in those places Stegner spoke most hopefully about—in Missoula and dozens of other communities, watersheds, and ecosystems throughout the West—something has indeed begun to change.

This is a story almost totally unknown outside the West, but urgently discussed every day now in the western press: the story of the steadily growing number of local agreements among western environmentalists, ranchers, loggers, miners, and recreationists about how the public land should be managed in their particular river drainage or their ecosystem. The list of such local collaborative efforts is growing too fast now to be catalogued, but names like the Henry's Fork Watershed Council, the Quincy Library Group, the Willapa Alliance, the Malpai Borderlands Group, or the Applegate Partnership are beginning to add up to a matter of genuinely historical proportions. A steadily growing number of westerners on both sides of the political fence are coming to believe they can do better by their communities, their economies, and their ecosystems by working together outside the established, centralized governing framework (which had only taught them how to be enemies) than by continuing to rely on the cumbersome, uncertain, underfunded, and increasingly irrelevant mechanisms of that old structure.

Having observed this phenomenon for many years, I am convinced it is of a piece with the great literary revival of fifty years ago. Westerners who have absorbed the lessons of generations in a place have learned that, if they let that place speak through them, they can not only produce a genuine regional literary voice, but they can also, by talking to one another in that voice, very often work out otherwise intractable issues among themselves. This is not always easy by any means, nor is it always successful, but repeatedly and with increasing frequency, westerners are learning to do this kind of work and do it successfully across the old ideological dividing lines. This is a tremendously hopeful sign of change. But this phenomenon is still always localized; it takes place in very specific western localities, and it leaves open the question: "What about the West in general?" Yes, we have developed our own poets, but have we even begun to develop our own genuinely western politics?

Such authentically western politics might begin to emerge from a recognition of the vicious cycle our old politics has fallen into. There is a definition of idiocy as a matter of trying the same thing over and over again and never getting anywhere with it. In those terms, we might characterize the continued efforts of Republicans to turn over control of the federal lands to the states as a kind of idiocy. But if Republicans have been idiotic in the West, it is a very clever and successful form of idiocy. This region has become fundamentally a one-party region; the presidential and gubernatorial elections, senate and house delegations, state legislatures throughout the public lands states present now a picture of a West that has become, far and away, the most Republican section of this entire country. So if we're going to speak about idiocy, we might ask Democrats how successful they've been at doing the same thing over and over. Are they succeeding? Are they doing by this landscape what they would hope to do? They make often small, sometimes larger, gains. They fight hard and well. But are they doing as well by this place and by the lives lived on it as they could or should?

In 1947, Bernard DeVoto had no choice but to turn to the federal government to resist the effort to denationalize the public lands. Wallace Stegner, when he wrote his famous "Wilderness Letter" twenty-five years later, had no choice but to invoke the power of the federal government to combat the next recurrence of those same efforts. But finally, we have to ask whether you can really have a politics of place when you're consistently invoking an outside power to protect that place against its own people. If there is one reason that Democrats are such a distinct minority in the West, it is because westerners clearly understand that the Democratic Party is the undemocratic party in the West. Westerners know that Democrats do not trust them, finally, to govern their own landscape. And when you say to people repeatedly that you do not trust them to govern their own place, you might not be altogether surprised to become a minority party in that region.

The question of whether a place can be a place without its own politics might be reframed then, especially for the West, as whether a place can call itself a democracy without having real control over its own landscape? In those terms those who have worked to give westerners more control over their places are actually the democrats, though they have too often confused democracy with demagoguery. There is little for the West to be proud of in their politics. It seems clear that growing up politically might mean figuring out how we could govern our own beloved landscape in a way that we could all take pride in. To do that though, leaders on both sides would need to challenge their basic assumptions, bringing to bear that level of intellectual honesty that so distinguishes *The Big Sky* and all the other great western writings of that era. Challenging ourselves in that honest western way would mean that Democrats must ask themselves how democratic they have really been in the West, and that conservatives would ask themselves what a truly conservative agenda would mean in the West. Is their conservatism merely a vehicle to enrich corporations? If so, it protects and preserves nothing but moneyed privilege, and there is nothing fundamentally conservative about that.

But there certainly is something to be conserved in this place. The power of western landscapes to inspire us leads invariably to a desire to live well in such places, which in turn leads to a fundamentally conservative agenda which can never be captured in the tired terms of "growth" and "economic development," but must express its conservative thought in language like that of "sustainable prosperity." In order to achieve that sustainable, good life in good but hard country, liberals and conservatives, Democrats and Republicans, environmentalists and businesses, are going to have to keep working at coming together. I am convinced that part of that work lies in figuring out how, together, we might persuade Washington that the West should be given greater control over this place. That in turn would require everyone changing how they operate; Democrats would have to challenge their reliance upon Washington, while conservatives challenged their reliance on the profits of exploitation.

In order to establish the level of trust required to build a real politics of place, we will at a minimum have to learn to speak more respectfully to one another. Liberals need to learn to say that there is something of fundamental value in conservatism, a value without which this landscape cannot be preserved. For their part, thoughtful conservatives might begin to question the cheap trick of trashing liberalism. Reading *The Big Sky* or *The Blue Hen's Chick* might lead to an understanding of how it is that a deep strain of liberalism is of the essence of this place. That great sense of expansiveness in the first pages of *The Blue Hen's Chick* is not simply an expansiveness of landscape, but an invitation to and invocation of a fundamentally liberal expansiveness of mind.

This place invites people to be open, which is the fundamental attitude of liberalism. Liberalism has no apologies to make to this place. Mike Mansfield and Pat Williams are not accidental products of this place. For western conservatives to continue to trash liberalism for the demagogic value they can wring from it is finally to demean this place and its humanizing power. The University of Montana, for example, is called a liberal arts university, which means simply that it is dedicated to openness, intellectual honesty, and the willingness to challenge all unquestioned presumptions. In those terms, Montanans' dedication to their liberal arts university is a dedication to the best they have ever known in themselves. It is a dedication to the truth speaking for which A. B. Guthrie stands in our memory.

Fifty years after the establishment of that powerful western voice, the time has arrived when Montanans, and all westerners, both liberal and conservative westerners, can start to look each other in the eye and ask each other honestly, "What are we capable of in this great good place?"

Notes

1. Wallace Stegner, *Where the Bluebird Sings to the Lemonade Springs* (New York: Penguin Books, 1992), 205.

2. Ibid., 201.

3. Robert Frost, "The Gift Outright," in *Selected Poems of Robert Frost* (New York: Holt, Rinehart and Winston, 1966), 299.

4. Stegner, *Where the Bluebird Sings,* 115-16.

5. Ibid., 58.

Works by A. B. Guthrie, Jr.

Books ~

Murders at Moon Dance. Introduction to the Bison Book edition by William Kittredge. New York: E. P. Dutton, 1943; Lincoln: University of Nebraska Press (Bison Book), 1993.

The Big Sky. Foreword to the Houghton Mifflin edition by Wallace Stegner. New York: William Sloane Associates, 1947; Boston: Houghton Mifflin, 1992.

The Way West. New York: William Sloane Associates, 1949; Boston: Houghton Mifflin, 1993.

The Big Sky: An Edition for Young Readers. New York: William Sloane Associates, 1950.

These Thousand Hills. Boston: Houghton Mifflin, 1956, 1995.

The Big It, and Other Stories. Introduction to the Gregg Press edition by Richard Etulain. Boston: Houghton Mifflin, 1960; Boston: Gregg Press, 1980.

Mountain Medicine. New York: Pocket Books (Pocket Cardinal Edition), 1961; Sausalito, CA: Comstock Editions, 1991.

The Blue Hen's Chick: A Life in Context (Bison Book edition subtitled: *An Autobiography*). Afterword to the Bison Book edition by David L. Petersen. New York: McGraw-Hill, 1965; Lincoln: University of Nebraska Press (Bison Book), 1993.

Arfive. Boston: Houghton Mifflin, 1971.

Once Upon a Pond. Illustrated by Carol B. Guthrie. Missoula, MT: Mountain Press, 1973.

Wild Pitch. Boston: Houghton Mifflin, 1973.

The Last Valley. Boston: Houghton Mifflin, 1975.

The Genuine Article: A Novel of Suspense. Boston: Houghton Mifflin, 1977.

No Second Wind. Boston: Houghton Mifflin, 1980.

Fair Land, Fair Land. Boston: Houghton Mifflin, 1982.

Playing Catch-Up. Boston: Houghton Mifflin, 1985.

Four Miles from Ear Mountain. Missoula, MT: Kutenai Press, 1987.

Big Sky, Fair Land: The Environmental Essays of A. B. Guthrie, Jr. Flagstaff, AZ: Northland Press, 1988.

Murder in the Cotswolds. Boston: Houghton Mifflin, 1989.

A Field Guide to Writing Fiction. New York: HarperCollins, 1991.

Films *(compiled by James V. D'Arc)*

The Big Sky (Winchester Productions/RKO Radio Pictures, 1952). Producer: Howard Hawks. Director: Howard Hawks. Associate Producer: Edward Lasker. Screenplay: Dudley Nichols, from the novel by A. B. Guthrie, Jr. Photography: Russell Harlan. Music: Dimitri Tiomkin. Running time: 2 hrs. 40 minutes; reedited to 2 hrs. 2 mins. Release: August 1952. Cast: Kirk Douglas (Jim Deakins), Dewey Martin (Boone Caudill), Elizabeth Coyotte Threatt (Teal Eye), Arthur Hunnicut (Zeb), Buddy Baer (Romaine), Steven Geray (Jourdonnais), Hank Worden (Poordevil).

Shane (George Stevens Productions/Paramount, 1953). Producer: George Stevens. Director: George Stevens. Associate Producer: Ivan Moffat. Screenplay: A. B. Guthrie, Jr., from the novel by Jack Schaefer. Additional dialog: Jack Sher. Photography: Loyal Griggs, in Technicolor. Music: Victor Young. Running time: 1 hr. 58 mins. Release: April 1953. Cast: Alan Ladd (Shane), Jean Arthur (Mrs. Starrett), Van Heflin (Mr. Starrett), Brandon de Wilde (Joey Starrett), Jack Palance (Wilson), Ben Johnson (Chris), Emile Meyer (Ryker), Elisha Cook, Jr. (Torrey).

The Kentuckian (Hecht-Lancaster/United Artists, 1955). Producer: Harold Hecht. Director: Burt Lancaster. Screenplay: A. B. Guthrie, Jr., based on the novel *The Gabriel Horn* by Felix Holt. Photography: Ernest Lazlo in CinemaScope and Technicolor. Music: Bernard Herrmann. Running time: 1 hr. 43 mins. Release: September 1955. Cast: Burt Lancaster (Big Eli), Dianne Foster (Hannah), Diana Lynn (Susie), John McIntire (Zack), Una Merkel (Sophie), Walter Matthau (Bodine), John Carradine (Fletcher), Donald MacDonald (Little Eli).

These Thousand Hills (Twentieth Century–Fox, 1959). Producer: David Weisbart. Director: Richard Fleischer. Screenplay: Alfred Hayes, based on the novel by A. B. Guthrie, Jr. Photography: Charles G. Clarke in CinemaScope and DeLuxe color. Music: Leigh Harline. Song: "These Thousand Hills" by

Ned Washington and Harry Warren (sung by Randy Sparks). Running time: 1 hr. 36 mins. Release: May 1959. Cast: Don Murray (Lat Evans), Richard Egan (Jehu), Lee Remick (Callie), Patricia Owens (Joyce), Stuart Whitman (Tom Ping), Albert Dekker (Conrad), Harold J. Stone (Ram Butler), Royal Dano (Carmichael), Fuzzy Knight (Sally, the Cook).

This Rebel Breed (a.k.a. *Three Shades of Love*; *Lola's Mistake*) (William Rowland/Warner Bros., 1960). Producer: William Rowland. Director: Richard L. Bare. Screenplay: Morris Lee Green, from the story "All God's Children," by William Rowland and Irma Berk. Story editor and consultant: A. B. Guthrie, Jr. Photography: Monroe Askins. Music: David Rose. Running time: 1 hr. 30 mins. Release: March 1960. Cast: Rita Moreno (Lola), Mark Damon (Frank), Gerald Mohr (Lt. Brooks), Jay Novello (Papa), Eugene Martin (Rudy), Tom Gibson (Muscles), Diane [Dyan] Cannon (Wiggles).

The Way West (Harold Hecht/United Artists, 1967). Producer: Harold Hecht. Director: Andrew V. McLaglen. Screenplay: Ben Maddow and Mitch Lindemann, from the novel by A. B. Guthrie, Jr. Photography: William H. Clothier in Technicolor and Panavision. Music: Bronislaw Kaper. Song: "The Way West" by Bronislaw Kaper and Mack David (sung by the Serendipity Singers). Running time: 2 hrs. 2 mins. Release: May 1967. Cast: Kirk Douglas (Senator William J. Tadlock), Robert Mitchum (Dick Summers), Richard Widmark (Lije Evans), Lola Albright (Rebecca Evans), Michael Whitney (Johnnie Mack), Stubby Kaye (Sam Fairman), Sally Field (Mercy McBee), Katherine Justice (Amanda Mack).

About the Contributors

Louie W. Attebery ~

Louie W. Attebery earned his M.A. degree at The University of Montana–Missoula in 1951, taught for eleven years in the public schools, finished his Ph.D. at the University of Denver in 1961, and retired in 1998 after thirty-seven years of teaching and administering at his undergraduate alma mater, Albertson College of Idaho. The former editor of *Northwest Folklore,* he has written or edited six books. His most recent, *J. R. Simplot: A Billion the Hard Way,* was published by Caxton Press (2000).

William W. Bevis ~

William W. Bevis has taught English at The University of Montana–Missoula since 1974. He served on the editorial board of *The Last Best Place: A Montana Anthology* and has published *Ten Tough Trips: Montana Writers and the West,* as well as books on the poetry of Wallace Stevens, on native resistance to the logging in Borneo, and most recently a novel on Shorty Harris, a Death Valley prospector.

Mary Clearman Blew ~

Mary Clearman Blew teaches creative writing at the University of Idaho, Moscow. She is the author of six books, most recently *Bone Deep in Landscape: Essays on Reading, Writing and Place* and the fiction collection, *Sister Coyote.* She co-edited *Circle of Women* with Kim Barnes as well as *Written on Water: Idaho Writers on Idaho Rivers.*

James V. D'Arc ~

James D'Arc is Curator of the Arts and Communications Archives and the Motion Picture Archives at Brigham Young University, Provo, Utah. He also teaches courses in film and in American Studies at BYU.

Ken Egan, Jr. ~

Ken Egan, Jr.'s essay in this volume is an excerpt from his forthcoming book on Montana literature (University of Nevada, 2002). His first book, *The Riven Home: Narrative Rivalry in the American Renaissance,* appeared in 1997. He teaches Western American and American literature at Rocky Mountain College in Billings, Montana.

Fred Erisman ~

Fred Erisman is Lorraine Sherley Professor of Literature Emeritus at Texas Christian University. A specialist in American culture, he is the author of numerous studies of the Western, science fiction, and children's literature. His books include the Boise Western Writers studies of Tony Hillerman and Laura Ingalls Wilder, and a reading of A. B. Guthrie's *The Big Sky.*

Dan Flores ~

Dan Flores is the A. B. Hammond Professor of Western History at The University of Montana–Missoula. An environmental historian and writer, he has produced a body of award-winning work on the West, including most recently, *Horizontal Yellow* (1999) and *The Natural West* (2001).

Dee Garceau ~

Dee Garceau is Associate Professor of History at Rhodes College in Memphis, Tennessee, where she teaches courses on gender and the American West. She holds a Ph.D. in American Civilization from Brown University. Garceau is author of *The Important Things of Life: Women, Work and Family in Sweetwater County, Wyoming, 1880–1929* (1997), a contributor to *Sifters: Native American Women's Lives* (Oxford, 2001), and co-editor of *Across the Great Divide: Cultures of Manhood in the American West* (Routledge, 2000).

Sue Hart ~

Born and raised in Detroit and educated in Michigan, New York, and Montana, Sue Hart has lived well over half her life in Billings, Montana. She claims Montana citizenship by virtue of teaching at Montana State University–Billings for thirty-eight years and introducing hundreds (maybe thousands) of Montanans to their literary heritage through classes, talks, a television program on "Montana Books and Authors," and a book review column with the same name.

Richard Hutson ~

Richard Hutson teaches English and American Studies at the University of California, Berkeley. His Ph.D. in English is from the University of Illinois, Champaign–Urbana. He is working on a project analyzing writings from the open range cattle industry after the Civil War. His essay on Andy Adams' novel, *The Outlet* (1905), appeared in *Heritage of the Great Plains* (Fall/Winter 2000).

Daniel Kemmis ~

Daniel Kemmis, Director of the O'Connor Center for the Rocky Mountain West, is the former mayor of Missoula, a former speaker and minority leader of the Montana House of Representatives, and a four-term Montana legislator. He is the author of three books, *Community and the Politics of Place; The Good City and the Good Life;* and *This Sovereign Land: A New Vision for Governing the West,* as well as numerous articles published in national and regional magazines and journals on bioregionalism and the economy and politics of the West. In 1998, the Center of the American West awarded him the Wallace Stegner Prize for sustained contribution to the cultural identity of the West, and in February 2000, he was honored as the Pinchot Distinguished Lecturer in Washington, D.C.

Celeste River ~

Celeste River received a master of interdisciplinary studies degree in journalism, religious studies, and Native American studies from The University of Montana–Missoula in 1989. Her essay, "The Great Stillness: Visions and Native Wisdom in the Writings of Frank Bird Linderman," appeared in *New Voices in Native American Literary Criticism* (Washington: Smithsonian Institution Press, 1993). She wrote the introduction to the Bison Books reprint of Frank Bird Linderman's *Kootenai Why Stories* (1926, 1997) and recently wrote the introductions to Bison Books' second reprints of *Indian Why Stories* (1915) and *Indian Old-man Stories* (1920), both due in 2001. River is currently working on a book and multi-media series entitled *Spirit of the Land in the Big Sky—An Inside View of Montana Territory as Seen through the Writings of Frank Bird Linderman and the Photography of Celeste River,* funded in part by the Montana Committee for the Humanities, the Montana Arts Council, and the Matthew Hansen Endowment from the Wilderness Institute at The University of Montana.

Lee Rostad ~

Lee Rostad is a native Montanan. She ranches with her husband in central Montana. She is the author of several books and articles on history and biography and continues to be active as a landowner environmentalist. A graduate of The University of Montana–Missoula, Rostad spent a year at the University of London as a Fulbright Scholar. She received an Honorary Doctor of Letters from Rocky Mountain College in 1994, and in 2001, she was honored with the Governor's Humanities Award.

Mark A. Sherouse ~

Mark A. Sherouse is Executive Director of the Montana Committee for the Humanities, Montana's affiliate of the National Endowment for the Humanities. Prior to coming to Montana, he served as Vice Provost and Special Assistant to the President at Southern Methodist University in Dallas, Texas, and as Assistant to the Chancellor of the Ohio Board of Regents. He holds a Ph.D. in philosophy from Ohio State University. A native of Miami, Florida, he and his wife, Vicki, reside in Missoula and have two daughters.

Jo-Ann Swanson ~

Born in northern Saskatchewan, Canada, Swanson is an associate professor of English at the University of Great Falls. Named a 1986 Artist in the Schools, she received an MFA in Creative Writing from The University of Montana–Missoula in 1987. A previous staff writer for the *Great Falls Tribune,* she has contributed numerous stories to *Southwest Art* magazine and is a current member of the Montana Committee for the Humanities..

James Welch ~

James Welch was born in Browning, Montana. He attended The University of Montana–Missoula. His latest novel is *The Heartsong of Charging Elk.*

Alan Weltzien ~

Alan Weltzien is Professor of English at Western Montana College of The University of Montana, where he has taught *The Big Sky* and other Montanan authors for years. Weltzien has completed *Rick Bass: Mapping the Landscape of Art and Activism* (University of Utah Press, forthcoming) and is at work on a book on John McPhee, *John McPhee and the Art of Literary Nonfiction* (with Susan Maher, also forthcoming from University of Utah Press), as well as a memoir, *At Home on Camano,* about Camano Island in Puget Sound.

Pat Williams ~

Pat Williams is a teacher and former member of the U.S. Congress and the Montana legislature. Williams, a Montana native, served two terms in the Montana Legislative Assembly in 1967 and 1969. His career in the U.S. House of Representatives spanned nine terms from 1979 until 1997. Williams is now Senior Fellow at the O'Connor Center for the Rocky Mountain West of The University of Montana–Missoula.

Index